BURGUNDY

BURGUNDY

Ian Dunlop

HAMISH HAMILTON

LONDON

HAMISH HAMILTON LTD

Published by the Penguin Group
27 Wrights Lane, London W8 5TZ, England
Viking Penguin Inc., 40 West 23rd Street, New York, New York 10010, USA
Penguin Books Australia Ltd, Ringwood, Victoria, Australia
Penguin Books Canada Ltd, 2801 John Street, Markham, Ontario,
Canada L3R 1B4
Penguin Books (NZ) Ltd, 182–190 Wairau Road, Auckland 10, New Zealand

Penguin Books Ltd, Registered Offices: Harmondsworth, Middlesex, England

First published in Great Britain by Hamish Hamilton Ltd 1990

Copyright © Ian Dunlop, 1990

1 3 5 7 9 10 8 6 4 2

Filmset in 11/13pt Baskerville at The Spartan Press Ltd, Lymington, Hants
Printed in Great Britain by Butler and Tanner Ltd, Frome, Somerset

A CIP catalogue record for this book is available from the British Library

ISBN 0–241–121884

ACKNOWLEDGEMENTS

I would like to thank the following for their help and hospitality: M. and Mme Aubert de Villaine, of the Domaine de la Romanée-Conti; the marquis de Breteuil, Président de la Demeure Historique; the comtesse Caumont La Force of the Château de Fontaine-Française; the Chanoine Denis Grivot of Autun Cathedral; Mr and Mrs Hawkes of the Château de Missery, who gave me the idea of writing this book; M. and Mme Bernard de Loisy and M. Antoine de Loisy of the Château d'Arcelot; the duc de Magenta of the Château de Sully; the comtesse Léonce de Mazin of the Château de Brandon; the marquise d'Ormesson of the Château de Saint-Fargeau; M. and Mme Pierre Poupon of Meursault; the comte and comtesse Bénigne de Saint-Seine of the Château de Vantoux; the comte and comtesse Tony de Vibraye of the Château de Bazoches; Mlle Françoise Vignier, Archiviste en Chef of the Département de la Côte d'Or; the marquis de Virieu of the Château d'Antilly; the comtesse Louis de Vogüé of the Château de Commarin. I would also like to thank the marquise de Brissac and the princesse Pia d'Orléans-Bragance, comtesse de Nicolay, for their charming hospitality at Brissac and Le Lude. Finally I would like to thank Angus Mayhew and Alexander McDowall for their help with printing from my word processor.

Ian Dunlop
The Close
Salisbury

CONTENTS

LIST OF ILLUSTRATIONS

LIST OF ILLUSTRATIONS

Pagny-le-Château (*London Library*)

Dijon. Église St Michel (*The British Library*)

Dijon. Rue des Forges (*Cabinet des Estampes*)

Auxerre (*The British Library*)

Château de Vallery (*The British Library*)

Château de Monthelon (*The British Library*)

Château de Bussy-Rabutin (*Archives Photographiques Paris*)

Château de Bussy-Rabutin (*Archives Photographiques Paris*)

Mlle de Montpensier (*La Réunion des Musées Nationaux*)

Vauban (*Archives Photographiques Paris*)

The Grand Condé (*Archives Photographiques Paris*)

Château de St Fargeau (*Cabinet des Estampes*)

Dijon. Hôtel Legouz de Gerland (*Cabinet des Estampes*)

Dijon. Place Royale (*The British Library*)

Buffon (*Archives Photographiques Paris*)

Château de Vantoux

Dijon. Château de Montmusard (*Musée des Beaux-Arts de Dijon*)

Château d'Arcelot (*Rosso Duthu*)

Line drawings (pp 156–157) by Ian Dunlop

The Château of Ancy-le-Franc as built

The Columbia design

The Munich design

The Albertina design

Courtyard, Albertina design

Courtyard as built

TO
DEIRDRE
WITH ALL MY LOVE

INTRODUCTION

'Burgundy', wrote Pierre Huguenin, 'is one vast museum'. In a sense it is true, but Burgundy is far more than that, for a museum is a mausoleum. Its exhibits, whatever their excellence, are seen divorced from their context. They no longer serve the purpose for which they were created. We can admire them, we can study them but we cannot understand them nearly so well as when they are still in the place for which they were designed. Also there is something a little dull and daunting about the prospect of visiting a museum, whereas a visit to Burgundy is an enchantment. Its beautiful buildings, whether little Romanesque churches in which holiness and homeliness have met together, or the comfortable houses of the Age of Enlightenment, all are set in a countryside as lovely as any in France.

There are about 150 *demeures seigneuriales* still standing in Burgundy: great castles of the age of feudalism, such as Posanges, guarding the road from Dijon to Montbard, or Châteauneuf, partly rebuilt in the fifteenth century for more luxurious living but still retaining its militant disposition; great houses of the Renaissance – Ancy-le-Franc, Pailly, Sully and Tanlay; great palaces of the age of Versailles, like Grancey, perched on the site of an older castle and raising its balustraded front high above the containing curtain wall. Then there are the smaller châteaux of the parliamentary aristocracy of Dijon – Vantoux, Talmay, Arcelot, Beaumont-sur-Vingeanne, each a period piece.

But alongside these are châteaux which offer a medley of styles, buildings that have grown slowly with the centuries, where features which were no longer useful have been discarded and replaced by others, more adapted to the new life style of the age. Such modernization, however, was usually carried out with a respect for the past which produced harmonious integration.

Just such a building is the Château de Commarin, not far from Châteauneuf. Commarin is anything but a museum, although it is filled with furniture, paintings and tapestries that would grace the

Victoria and Albert; it is the home of a family and families have memories. The pictures that hang upon the walls hang here because they belong here; they belong to the memories. They would not look the same on the walls of some museum. Commarin particularly illustrates this point because it is a domain with the rare distinction of having always been occupied and never been sold. It has often passed through the female line and by their marriages has become associated with many of the noble names of Burgundy.

It emerges from the mists of history in 1346, its name coupled with those of Jean and Jacques de Cortiamble. Jacques was chamberlain to Duke Philippe le Hardi. Between them, father and son created Commarin as a *place forte* and thus established the size and disposition of all the future buildings. Their dynasty dwindled to a single heiress, Agnès de Cortiamble who brought Commarin with her to the distinguished house of Dinteville. Three generations later another sole heiress, Bénigne, daughter of Jacques de Dinteville and Alix de Pontailler, united the destinies of the château with one of the greatest names in Burgundy, that of de Vienne. Her marriage took place at Commarin and they hung the walls with tapestries which proudly emblazoned their arms – Pontailler-Dinteville and Dinteville-Vienne.

The château was to remain with the family of Vienne until 1744 when, with the death of Anne de Chastellux, widow of Charles de Vienne, the estate passed to their daughter Marie-Judith. She married Joseph-François de Damas, marquis d'Antigny; their granddaughter Zéphirine inherited the château. She married the comte Charles de Vogüé, whose descendants are the present owners.

Commarin owes much to its châtelaines, those devoted ladies who have, often at great self-sacrifice, maintained the fabric, held the household together and kept the lamp of hospitality burning brightly in the hall.

At the beginning of this century Marie de Contades, wife of the comte Arthur de Vogüé, was châtelaine; she had the instincts of an historian and discovered beneath the dust of the archives the living people of the past.

One day I mounted with my husband into the attics of the château. My attention had been attracted by an old, worm-eaten coffer, from which a few papers were projecting. At the bottom of it I discovered a multitude of letters in which the personalities, connected with us by family ties which were direct if sometimes remote, discoursed on every matter which occupied their thoughts. My husband and I gave ourselves up to the long work of patience to classify these pages. I treasure the most moving memories of those long winter evenings during which we were bent over those papers by the soft light of the old lamps. These letters revealed before our eyes the characters of individuals and the relationships between them. Thus I began to penetrate the privacy of Anne de Chastellux and her husband, of Marie-Judith their daughter. They had once lived in this old house of ours; our eyes met their portraits; we used the same vessels that had belonged to them. Their Household Books lay next to the Terriers and Inventories.

Marie-Judith, last of the Viennes, and châtelaine for much of the eighteenth century, devoted herself to restoring the fortunes of the family. 'My mother', wrote Jacques-François, 'employed herself solely in building up the finances, denying herself everything in order to be able to make an honourable and advantageous marriage for my sister.' Alexandrine married Charles-Daniel de Talleyrand and was to be the mother of the famous prince Charles-Maurice de Talleyrand, diplomat and bishop of Autun.

The memory of Marie-Judith is easily evoked today by the suite of rooms which she occupied in the east wing. Near one of the windows in her bedroom stands a charming little secretaire in the style known as *en pente* or *à dos d'âne*, at which she wrote her Household Book, or *Livre de Raison*, noting her alterations and improvements to the house. 'I had the window embrasure panelled', she writes, 'in the bedroom of the Tour de l'Horloge. I had put in false windows of looking-glass to make the room lighter . . . I placed there a mirror which came from my mother's coach in 1759.' Thanks to her meticulous records, we can be confident that these rooms are still as she knew them. The porcelain peacock on the console has been there since 1756.

Marie-Judith had ideas of conservation that were unusual for her time. In 1744 the roof of the stables fell in. She had the building restored 'comme elle était en 1622'. She particularly treasured the heraldic hangings in the ante-room. 'I have had the tapestries repaired with the arms of Dinteville-Choiseul-Vienne', she wrote, 'in which the crimsons are more lovely than those which we produce today. I set more store by these tapestries than by the best from Brussels.'

Marie-Judith lived in the apartment which had been her mother's before her. Mother and daughter both appear in the same portrait in the Grande Salle. Like her daughter, Anne de Chastellux recorded in her *Livre de Raison* the annals of Commarin. One day in 1701, 'à l'heure de midi pendant notre dîner', the south-east tower collapsed. 'This tower adjoined the wing in which was my daughter's room, which caused me the greatest fear. I ran out into the court. The nurse held up my daughter in the window. We did not know how to get up to the room, the staircase having fallen with the tower. This accident determined us to rebuild.'

The southern and western ranges of the court, all that remained of the medieval house, were pulled down and replaced by the architect Philippe Paris with the simple but dignified façades which we see today.

The eastern range of the courtyard, together with the stable block, had been part of the reconstruction by the first Charles de Vienne of the whole forecourt. Two tall pavilions, 'les Pavillons Louis XIII', which mark the north-east and north-west angles, were built and united by a new wall to the fine ornamental arch, which has now been moved to form an outer entrance. With its broken pediment and its Tuscan columns it suggests the studios of du Cerceau and Gentilhâtre.

Commarin shows, perhaps more clearly than any other building in Burgundy, the close connection between a house and its owners, between architecture and human life. For what is Commarin without Marie-Judith? And what is Marie-Judith without Commarin? It is this connection between buildings and people that makes the 'museum' of Burgundy something human, fascinating and alive.

Burgundy is an area difficult to define. It has no precise frontiers, save for the Loire on its western side. It contains the départements of the Côte d'Or and the Saône-et-Loire in their entirety, a large slice of the Yonne and a small slice of the Nièvre. It has its own subdivisions: l'Auxerrois, le Châtillonnais, l'Auxois, le Morvan, le Charollais and le Maconnais. Perhaps it is best, with the historian Pierre Poupon, to divide it into *la Bourgogne des Vignes* – Chablis, Maconnais and the Côte d'Or; *la Bourgogne des Prés* – Auxois and Charollais; *la Bourgogne des Forêts* – Châtillonnais and le Morvan. But if geography cannot provide a clear definition, history at least has given it a personality.

Among the first creators of Burgundy were the monks, driven here
by the necessity of retreat from the Norman invader. The two greatest
Orders of the early Middle Ages, those of Cluny and of Cîteaux, were
both centred on Burgundy. They transformed the landscape. 'Silent
men', wrote Cardinal Newman, 'were observed about the country or
discovered in the forest, digging, clearing, building.'

They also gave to Burgundy its richest architectural inheritance,
the Romanesque churches. These range from the great abbey of
Cluny, the largest ecclesiastical building in medieval Christendom, to
the little churches of Chapaize and Brancion; they include such
masterpieces as the cathedral of Autun and the churches of Paray-le-
Monial and Sainte-Madeleine de Vézelay.

Described by Sacheverell Sitwell as 'one of the major architectural
sensations of the western world', Vézelay is probably the most
appreciated of all today. It was Viollet-le-Duc who rediscovered,
rescued and restored the church of Vézelay. He did the same for
medieval architecture as a whole. When he was a student, he tells us,
'masters of architecture scarcely recognized the existence of these
monuments which covered the ground of Europe and above all of
France. The study of a few buildings of the French or Italian
Renaissance was just permitted, but as for those which had been built
before the fifteenth century, they were hardly mentioned except to be
cited as instances of barbarous ignorance.'

It was the special vocation of Viollet-le-Duc to open the eyes of
Frenchmen to the incredible richness of their medieval heritage. He
saw more clearly than anyone the interpenetration of architectural
style and human history. 'The study of costume is not admissible
apart from the study of the man who wears it.' He saw the need for a
nation to keep alive its contact with its past. Just as a fully mature man
is one who has not lost contact with his childhood, so a country must
not lose touch with the childhood of its race. 'The civilizations which
have marked their furrow most deeply on the field of history are those
in which the traditions of the past are most respected, and in which
their maturity has preserved the characteristics of childhood.' It was
in Burgundy that he found some of his most typical examples and it
was at Vézelay that he accomplished one of his earliest restorations.

There is always a danger in restoration. It was at Vézelay that
André Hallays pronounced his solemn warning: 'to disaffect this
basilica is to take from it what little soul remains to it. When once the
little lamp that burns at the end of the choir is extinguished, Vézelay

will be no more than an archaeological curiosity. It will have the sepulchral smell of a museum.'

Anyone who doubts this may compare the abbey of Fontenay in Burgundy with that of Saint-Benoît-sur-Loire. Fontenay is a museum, albeit a delightful one: Saint-Benoît is a living monastery. The church of Fontenay stands empty; it requires a great effort to refurnish it in the imagination with altar, stalls and choir screen and the simple paraphernalia of Cistercian worship; to hear the monks chanting their Gregorian plainsong and to see the candles guttering in the draught. One has only to slip into the back of the nave at Saint-Benoît during Mass or one of the Offices to experience the real thing. One sees the architecture as it was meant to be seen.

For if a château or an *hôtel particulier* requires the presence of the family to preserve that loved and lived-in look, a church requires the presence of a worshipping community. It needs to be in use for the purpose for which it was built. What makes Commarin so impressive to visit is the sense of continuity with the past. It is alive because it has grown, each generation adapting it to new needs. Of course this process entails loss, loss in this case of most of the medieval buildings. No doubt the antiquarian will mourn their disappearance and the conservationist will determine to prevent any further growth. But conservationism kills. It extinguishes the little light at the end of the choir.

ROMANESQUE BURGUNDY

It was the year 1000. The Christian world expected that the world would end, for was it not stated in the Apocalypse that Satan must be bound 'until the thousand years should be fulfilled'? There were, however, a significant number of dissentients.

'The dread of the year 1000,' wrote Jean Virey, 'which would explain the lack of solidarity in the construction of churches, since the ending of the world would obliterate all things at one blow, was not as universal as has been thought. Bishops and monks attacked this belief in the end of the world and explained to their people the true sense of the passage in the Apocalypse.' Abbon, the famous abbot of Saint-Benoît-sur-Loire, went all over France refuting the error and restoring confidence among the faithful.

It can be presumed, however, that if the clergy had to take such steps to combat them, the fears of the people must have been real. Such a climate of opinion would provide no encouragement for the erection of durable buildings. What is certain is that the start of the new millennium was the occasion for a campaign of church building which was without precedent. The number of eleventh-century churches which survive is witness enough to this campaign, but if we add the number of those known to have been destroyed we are faced with a truly remarkable phenomenon. It found its chronicler in the Burgundian monk, Raoul Glaber.

'As the third year after the year 1000 was about to begin', he wrote, 'there arose throughout the world, and particularly in Gaul and Italy, a movement to renew the vessels of the churches, although the greater part of these were sufficiently sumptuous to render such an operation unnecessary. But Christian countries rivalled one another as to who possessed the most remarkable temples. One would have said that the world shook itself to discard its old age and to put on a white robe of churches.' With these words he ushered in the style known in France as *Roman* – Romanesque.

It was a style which owed its immediate origin to Lombardy and perhaps especially to Ravenna. When Rome had ceased to be the seat of the emperor, Ravenna became the capital of Italy and it looked eastward for its artistic inspiration. The ultimate roots of the Lombard style are in Persia and Mesopotamia. By the eleventh century the art of Ravenna was ready for export. The *magistri comancini* – craftsmen from Como – were organized into a sort of college.

Their first appearance in Burgundy was the result of the arrival, in the year 985, of William of Volpiano at Cluny. A few years later he was sent by the Abbot Mayeul to Saint-Bénigne de Dijon to reform the monastery and to rebuild its sixth-century basilica. He summoned a colony of monks from Lombardy 'well versed in all the sciences' to assist him with his task.

William of Volpiano was extremely well connected, both in France and in Italy; he was typical of that not uncommon medieval figure, the nobleman turned monk. His many contacts with persons in high places enabled him to exercise an influence not only in Burgundy, but in Lorraine, Normandy and western Germany.

Saint-Bénigne de Dijon

The church of Saint-Bénigne de Dijon retains in its crypt one of the oldest Christian sanctuaries still to be seen in France. The rebuilding by William of Volpiano began on 14 February 1001 and his church was consecrated fifteen years later.

The most outstanding part of his building was the great rotunda to the east of the apse – described by Raoul Glaber as 'the most marvellous in the whole of Gaul'. It was destroyed by the Revolution and much of the rubble was used to fill in the lowest storey, which was the crypt. In 1843 this crypt was 'rediscovered' and reinstated. Fortunately the two upper storeys had been described and engraved in 1739 by the historian of Burgundy, Dom Plancher. The building can be reconstructed in the imagination.

The crypt preserves its original lay-out – an inner circle ringed round by an arcade of eight columns and surrounded by another ring of sixteen columns, with a circular ambulatory outside this. To the east the ambulatory opens into a small rectangular chapel in which the relics of St Bénigne, the apostle of Burgundy, were venerated. The rotunda was clearly designed to enable pilgrims to circulate more easily in the vicinity of the sepulchre. The ambulatories were repeated at ground-floor and first-floor levels, but the inner ring formed an open well which rose through all three storeys into the cupola from which the building was largely lit. The present vaulting of the centre of the crypt is therefore not original.

In this concentric plan, William of Volpiano follows the type of mausoleum of which the finest examples were in Italy – the churches of St Peter and St Marcellinus and that of St Constance, both in Rome, and the tomb of Theodoric in Ravenna. In the eleventh century William's rotunda provided the model for a similar building in Canterbury Cathedral.

To this sophisticated and Italianate structure was given a decoration which is almost barbaric. 'I know of nothing in sculpture', wrote Violet Markham, 'comparable with the monstrous decoration of these capitals. The workmanship is rude and primitive. The chisel is only learning its work, but to what hag-ridden imagination does it not seek to give expression! The interlaced beasts of the twelfth century are tame domestic animals side by side with their forerunners at Dijon. Horrible suggestions of the human figure appear with suggestions, no less horrible, of the animal world . . . If this is sculpture in its youth, it is dreaming very evil dreams.'

Saint-Bénigne de Dijon has been rebuilt in the Gothic style and has nothing today to teach us of the architecture of the eleventh century. The distinctive marks of the Lombard style are quickly recognized. The first is the use of small stones – *le petit appareil* – shaped almost like bricks, which are used as ashlar to contain an infilling of rubble. The second is the use of vertical bands, like broad, flat buttresses, which stand a few inches proud of the wall surface. These bands are joined at their summits by little attached arcades, which may follow a horizontal line, forming a cornice, or climb the sides of a gable, lending a welcome touch of ornament to an otherwise severe façade. One of the first and finest examples of this style is the church of Saint-Philibert de Tournus, a building roughly contemporary with Saint-Bénigne de Dijon. Closely connected with it is the church of Saint-Martin at Chapaize.

Saint-Philibert de Tournus and Saint-Martin de Chapaize

One of the reasons why Burgundy became the nursery of French monasticism is that it was thought to be safe from the Norman invaders. Monks and nuns, driven from their monasteries, sought refuge here and often put down roots which were to endure.

In the year 836 the monks of Saint-Philibert de Noirmoutiers fled before the Normans and carried with them the relics of their saint. They tried to establish themselves at Cunault on the Loire, near Angers, but the tidal wave of the invasion swept on. From Cunault they were forced to retreat to Messay and from Messay they moved, in 871, to the abbey of Saint-Pourçain in Auvergne. Four years later Charles the Bald offered them asylum in the abbey of Saint-Valérien at Tournus. Here they deposited their relics and established their monastery. 'In the fortieth year after their exodus', wrote Dom Chifflet in 1669, 'this new people of Israel found in Tournus their Palestine and a promised land which distilled for them both milk and honey.'

But if they were safe here from the invader from the north, they were exposed to the invader from the east. In 937 the Hungarians sacked the town and their monastery was destroyed. In 1006 the buildings were again destroyed, this time by fire. The monks must have set about the rebuilding without delay, for by 1019 the new church was consecrated by the bishop of Chalon. It is today one of the earliest and the most important examples of the Lombard style in Burgundy.

The first sight of Saint-Philibert, set back behind the twin towers of the abbey gateway, gives an impression of massive strength, even of fortification. Before the building of the steeple on the north tower – it was a later addition – the west front must have looked more like a castle than a church. Its window apertures are as thin as arrow slits and over the central door is a machicolated projection which was certainly not intended for ornament. The attacks of the Hungarians had not been forgotten.

Charles Oursel insists upon the defensive role of the narthex as accounting for its sturdy, two-storeyed construction. The elephantine piers and solid groined vaulting convey an overwhelming impression of strength. It must be remembered, however, that the way these piers seem to grow out of the ground with not so much as a ring of stone to do duty for a base, is due to the raising of the floor level. The excavations carried out by Jean Martin in 1900 revealed the foundations, nearly 2 metres down, showing the concentric rings of the bases as they originally appeared.

By contrast with the heavy solidity of the narthex, the nave and aisles convey an immediate sense of lofty spaciousness. The impression is created by the extreme height of the side aisles which carry their vaults almost to the same level as those of the nave.

The nave vaults are of particular interest. Each vaulting arch supports a partition wall above – no doubt a device for isolating any outbreak of fire in the timbers. Between these partitions each bay carries a transverse barrel vault, running from north to south.

Charles Oursel offers a convincing explanation of this unusual disposition. He argues that the original roof was of timber and so placed as to admit of the tall clerestory windows which provide so abundant an illumination to the nave. After the fire it was decided to replace the timber ceiling with a stone vault, but the height of the windows posed a problem. A longitudinal barrel vault – the most common solution – would have required arches springing from a point slightly higher than the tops of the windows. The keystone of the vault would have been several feet above the present roof ridge. So high a vault would have been a very daring structure for that date. The only way to avoid this excessive height was the solution adopted.

One of the great attractions of Tournus, seen from the inside, is the beautiful salmon-pink colour of the stone from the local quarry of Préty. But this rough-hewn, naked grandeur is a modern innovation. Prosper Mérimée, writing in 1834, was hampered in his attempts to date the different parts of the interior by 'the thick plaster with which they are covered'. We know, in fact, that in 1719 the whole church was whitewashed. It was probably so originally.

Another church which has had its plaster removed as recently as 1974 is Saint-Martin de Chapaize, some 16 kilometres west of Tournus. Their common nudity brings out certain resemblances. The proportions of the nave at Chapaize are very similar to those of the upper storey of the narthex at Tournus. In both, the rather squat drums of the main piers support tall, attached half-columns. At Tournus these are flat pilasters; at Chapaize they are half-cylinders. At Tournus the drums have two little rings of stone for a capital; at Chapaize a crude transition is made from round to square by four triangular projections. At Tournus the pilasters rise without inter-ruption to become the vaulting arches; at Chapaize there is a large impost projecting towards the interior. At Tournus the vaulting arch is semicircular; at Chapaize it is slightly pointed. On stylistic grounds Chapaize would appear to be the later of the two.

But here we come up against the problem of rebuildings. In the last bay of the nave before the crossing, above the vaulting arch, can be seen the remains of an earlier vault of slightly lower pitch and of semicircular form. From this it must be inferred that the original vaults fell in, or were deemed in danger of falling in, and were replaced by what we see today. The semicircular arch has a tendency to flatten, as can be seen in the south aisle. Since the upper walls of the nave are out of true, especially on the north side, it is probable that the vaults did become thus deformed and may even have collapsed.

There is clear evidence, also, of rebuilding in the north aisle; the vaulting arches, where they spring from the drums of the main arcade, are in the same small stonework known as *petit appareil*, but just before the keystone this changes to large blocks of whitish stone.

The other obvious alteration is the blocking-in of the clerestory windows, which are plainly visible from inside. From the outside the tops of the aisle roofs cut across the windows just below the spring of the arch. The height of the original roof must have been below the bases of the windows. But the angle of the present roof is 30 per cent, which is the minimum gradient for a slope bearing the stone tiles with which it is now roofed. The only explanation possible is that the original roof had a gradient of 10 per cent, in which case it must have been roofed with pantiles.

The roof of the nave sits directly on top of the vaults; there is no timber. This obviously reduces greatly the risk of fire. There are evidences of a fire in certain parts of the building, which suggests that the original vaults were covered with a *charpente*. The presence of a little half-obscured window above the remains of the original vault in the nave confirms this conclusion, for it must have opened into the roof tent.

The apse and its two side chapels are clearly of a later date than the rest of the building. They offer the closest similarity with the remains of Lancharre, not 2 kilometres distant. Both are built of the same excellent freestone from the quarries of Venière; both are lit by large windows with precision-cut keystones; both have the same arrangement of an arcaded cornice to the main apse and modillions for the chapels; both may be dated from the beginning of the thirteenth century.

But the great glory of Chapaize is the tower, which is exceptionally tall and probably built for look-out purposes. It is a lovely example of Lombard architecture, with its narrow, vertical 'bands' and shallow horizontal arcading. So lofty a structure needed solid support and its huge buttresses enclose the transepts on either side.

Saint-Bénigne de Dijon; Saint-Philibert de Tournus; Saint-Martin de Chapaize; these three great churches can be said to have established Romanesque architecture in Burgundy. But by far the greatest influence, both in the impetus which it gave to the monastic movement and in the perfecting and popularizing of the style, came from the abbey of Cluny. It is difficult to overstate its importance. The destruction of Cluny by the French Revolution was the most devastating loss not only to Burgundy, but to France and, indeed, to Christendom.

Cluny

'I remember playing, as a small child,' wrote Prosper Lorain, the first historian of Cluny,

among the ruins of an ancient abbey. We climbed audaciously up broken stairs and under crumbling roofs; we craned our necks with a shiver of fear beneath the arches of the great vault, now open and tottering above our heads. We were told that, in the high niches, where now the swallows fed their young, there used to be figures of the Twelve Apostles in solid silver. We were told the names of the great towers and the biggest of the bells . . . and when we were allowed to enter the choir and circle round the marble columns which we embraced with our little arms, our wondering gaze was always attracted to the great staring eyes of the immense figure of Christ painted in the deep recesses of the apse, which seemed to direct its steady stare down at us out of the golden mosaic.

It was not twenty years since the monks had departed and already their history and their traditions had sunk into oblivion, 'but from time to time we would notice a few old priests walking sadly in the abbey gardens, passing and repassing at the foot of the great towers, and the syllable "Dom" which preceded their names was all that told us that they once were monks'.

It was on 25 October 1791, the 600th anniversary of the consecration of Cluny, that the last Mass had been said in the great abbey church. Only twelve monks were present and their presence can only have emphasized the vast emptiness of the building.

A list drawn up during the previous August showed forty-two monks still living in a monastery designed for ten times that number. By the law of 13 February 1790, their Order had been abolished and they were given the choice between a pensioned 'liberty' or some regrouping of monastic life. At Cluny only two ultimately opted for continuing. From that moment they pass out of history.

The church was now the parish church of Cluny. All the objects of value had been sold, but none of the proceeds were made available for the upkeep of the building. In January 1792 the municipality appointed two entrepreneurs, Louis Colas and Claude Giraud, to survey the fabric. It was found to be in need of urgent repair.

Little had been done so far in the way of deliberate destruction. The coat of arms of Richelieu, who had held the position of abbot, had been defaced and some of the mausoleums, which spoke too plainly of a noble past, had been demolished. It was not until the following year that any serious pillage was reported. The General Headquarters of the Revolutionary Army was set up at Chalon and in October a detachment of troops was sent to Cluny. They started by smashing statues, altars, pulpits and what remained of the tombs and ended by having a gigantic *auto-da-fé* of all the paintings, wooden statues and archives. The bonfire lasted a whole week.

This act of vandalism illustrates the deep-set hatred of the Church which motivated even some of the more moderate among the revolutionaries. Madame Roland, who went to the guillotine saying 'Oh Liberty! Liberty! What crimes are committed in your name!', made a passionate attack on the wealthy abbeys of France. 'Make certain', she said, 'that the Church lands are sold, for we can never be freed from these wild beasts until their lairs are destroyed and they have been smoked out.'

It is doubtful if any of the remaining monks at Cluny merited the term 'wild beast', but the spectacle of a powerful and opulent Church in close alliance with an aristocratic and repressive regime was enough. Perhaps a hint as to the true source of revolutionary anger is given by Gibbon, who 'had somewhere heard or read the frank confession of a Benedictine Abbot: "my vow of poverty has given me a hundred thousand crowns a year; my vow of obedience has raised me to the rank of a sovereign prince". I forget what were the consequences of his vow of chastity.' It is perhaps not surprising that most of the abbeys of France were singled out for demolition.

The destruction at Cluny of the works of art and of the archives, however, contented the *enragés*. The great church remained, architecturally, intact.

Since it was, officially, the parish church it came under the Conseil Municipal and on 24 June 1795, they set forth their reasons for wishing to retain it, because 'this vast and curious monument, which has so great a claim to our respect, could contain more than six times the whole population, and that this would perhaps be the best means of preserving it and of avoiding the agony of seeing this immense edifice, which excites the greatest interest of the community, fall more and more into ruins'. But at the same time they recoiled before 'the excessive cost which would be necessitated to remedy even to a feeble and partial degree, the atrocious and deplorable degradations perpetuated by the brigands and by the army of the Revolution'.

In July of that year the church of Notre-Dame became the parish church of Cluny. Some other use was needed for the now redundant abbey. None of the suggested uses was found to be practicable and on 28 February 1798 the decisive move was made which sealed its death warrant. A decree of the department ruled that it should be divided into four lots and put up for sale. The division was to be marked by the piercing of a new road which was to cut through the nave at the fourth bay from the west and to link the main street of the town with the Porte des Près. It became known as 'la rue Scélérate' – 'Scoundrel Street'. As Violet Markham states, 'it is very difficult to write in temperate language about the ignoble beings masquerading as sons of liberty who tore the Abbey to pieces during the Revolution and, since the twelfth-century masonry resisted their efforts, finally blew the building up with seventy-five charges of gunpowder'.

The whole ensemble was valued at 2,014,000 francs. It was knocked down to a merchant from Macon named Batonnard. It was later discovered that he had expended 7,000 francs' worth of wine in bribes to ensure that no one outbid him. In April the demolition of the west end of the church was begun and the materials sold.

The larger half of the church – that lying to the east of the rue Scélérate – remained for a time in a condition which was still not beyond hope of repair. On 7 August 1800, Alexandre Lenoir, a man who did more than anyone to try and save the architectural heritage of France from the devastating effects of the Revolution, was sent by the government to Cluny. His report to Chaptal, Minister of the Interior, deserves to be quoted at length.

Citizen Minister, the House of Cluny, so famous in France, merits your particular attention. The church is the most beautiful nave in existence, its aspect is imposing, the style of architecture is a mixture of the art of Greece with the taste of Arabia. Citizen Minister, this monument, famous for its antiquity, for its extraordinary size, is going to be destroyed from top to bottom; a greedy purchaser is having it demolished to sell its materials. The inhabitants deplore this and have promised to recover it at their own cost if you will be pleased to prevent the destruction of so remarkable a building, which was sold contrary to the laws . . . Citizen Minister, I demand in the name of Art the conservation of this beautiful monument.

In case his appeal was unsuccessful, he begged as a last resort that proper plans and elevations should at least be drawn 'to leave posterity with a record of a monument as great as those of Greece, which was built by a Frenchman'.

It was not until the end of November that Chaptal intervened, and then only after several representations had been made by the mayor of Cluny. 'Je vous autorise à suspendre toute démolition jusqu'à nouvel ordre.' For the time being the destruction was halted, but what the government never did was to vote the subsidies necessary for a restoration of the building. In August 1801, Chaptal wrote to the prefect declining to offer any help.

In February 1809, the central tower fell. Its falling was recorded by the Abbé Louis Caumont.

One witness, still quite young at the time, happened to be on the Fouëtin at the moment when the great square Clocher du Choeur fell in. He retained until the end of his life the imprint of that terrible experience; first he saw the cross, which dominated the building, topple sideways; then great cracks appeared in the walls of the tower which collapsed upon itself with a terrifying roar. At the same instant there rose a thick cloud of dust which lay for a long time on the horizon.

From this moment there could be no question of the preservation intact of the east end. A water-colour in the Collection Rambuteau shows the apse and ambulatory as they were at the end of 1818. Had even this portion survived it would have constituted not only an imposing and picturesque ruin, but also a priceless visual aid on which to base a reconstruction in the imagination of the whole edifice. It was not to be. The following year the apse also was demolished to facilitate the erection of a stud for horses. In the space of twenty years – the same time which it had taken to build it – Cluny was unbuilt.

By 1823 the remains of the abbey church had been reduced to the fragments which can be seen today – the Clocher de l'Eau Bénite surmounting the south transept, with the Tour de l'Horloge attaching to it, and the first apsidal chapel of the second, or eastern, transept with the Chapelle Bourbon appended to its southern wall.

It might be thought that so tiny a portion of so vast a complex would be insignificant, but a visit to Cluny is still a strangely evocative experience. Even such vestigial remains have much to tell us of the rise, decline and fall of this great house.

The surviving fragment of the second transept includes a chapel in the simplest Romanesque style; it is little more than a niche such as might have been the apse of one of the numerous parish churches of this period which still abound in this part of Burgundy.

People today often express a preference for the Romanesque, perhaps because they find the Gothic overpowering. The Romanesque architects usually built small and strong, which is probably why so much of their work has survived. Their churches are therefore à l'échelle – built to human scale. It is easy to feel at home in such buildings. Their evident strength has something protective and permanent about it, which is what many people value in their religion. The architecture is straightforward and uncluttered – a simple style to match a simple faith; but the decoration is mysterious – fantastic figures leering down from the capitals and painted pictures dimly seen upon the walls. They sometimes speak of dark, subconscious fears that haunt the human soul; sometimes of the terrifying realities of Heaven and Hell; sometimes they invite us to recoil in horror from some Judas sin, or, inspired by some local worthy's tale, take ghostly comfort from a martyr's death. But all are placed in submission to the overarching figure of Christ in Majesty, looming high above the altar on which his real presence was assured. Such was the primitive architecture of Cluny in the days of its spiritual humility.

To pass from this chapel into the great transept is to pass from one religious climate to another. Here is a building designed to convey a breath-taking sensation of the greatness of God. It is the architecture itself which creates this impression. Ninety-two feet in height – an amazing figure for a Romanesque church – it anticipated by about a hundred years the vertiginous vaults of the great Gothic cathedrals.

It has become the fashion in recent years to label such architecture 'triumphalist'. It is true that only a wealthy, and therefore a powerful, Church could have built such an edifice, but that does not necessarily imply that the building was consciously intended to proclaim the wealth and power of the Church as, for instance, a palace proclaims the power and wealth of a prince. It was Joseph Addison who wisely said that the great cathedrals, 'by opening the mind to vast conceptions, fit it for the conception of the Deity'.

Another building which conveys an overwhelming impression of the wealth of Cluny is the one designed to provide a cellar below and a granary above. It was considerably reduced in length, from 54 metres to 36, to make room for the spacious claustral buildings of the eighteenth century, but it can easily be restored in the imagination to its original proportions.

The granary communicates at its southern extremity with the Tour du Moulin by means of an inclined plane which provided a gravity feed for the corn. The room is chiefly remarkable for its roof, a timber barrel vault of ingenious design and impeccable workmanship which has survived intact from the thirteenth century. It is constructed in chestnut, a wood largely repellent to insects.

The lower storey, half sunk below ground level as befits a cellar, forms a magnificent double nave. The central arcade supports a system of ribbed vaults which has all the strength and beauty of simplicity. At the far end there used to run a little stream which provided the double advantage of maintaining the necessary humidity of the cellar and of enabling the washing-out of the *cuves* without their having to be removed from the building. Only one window of the original fenestration survives; the rest were enlarged and have flooded the cellar with a light which was never intended.

The magnificence of the cellar reflects the prestige of the position of the cellarer in the hierarchy of the abbey. He ranked fourth after the abbot and exercised a function similar to that of steward in a great house in England. He had a keeper of the wine and a keeper of the granary under him as well as a gardener and keeper of the fishpools. But the cellar had pride of place among his charges and he slept here with the keeper of the wine.

Next in chronological order, and more indicative of historical change, is the Chapel of Jean de Bourbon, built in 1456. The

18

decorative theme of the chapel is a statement of theology. The Apostles were erroneously supposed to have been responsible each for one article of the Creed. Each article was then matched with the teaching of one of the Prophets, who thus became regarded as precursors of the Apostles. This was expressed by placing the statues of the Apostles on plinths upheld by the Prophets. It was an intriguing piece of intellectual dexterity, but of no theological validity. In the sterility of its thinking the Church of the fifteenth century had declined a long way from the great works of the twelfth-century scholars.

But the most significant feature of the Chapelle Bourbon is the little room opening to the south of it equipped with a large fireplace and a small squint where the abbot could sit in warm and comfortable insulation from those in the chapel proper and could observe without inconvenience the elevation of the Host, a ritual which had become the main requisite of medieval worship.

Jean de Bourbon was the first of a long line of abbots appointed by the king, or *abbés commandataires*. While Henry VIII was suppressing the monasteries in England, François I had made a concordat with the Pope and was undermining monasticism in France by appointing men whom he wished to reimburse for often secular services with the well-endowed abbacies throughout the land. The Benedictine system depended to an almost dangerous degree upon the character and integrity of the abbot. A wealthy absentee, whether clerical or lay, spelt spiritual disaster to the community. In the sixteenth century the religious life of France was at a low ebb.

To pass from the Chapelle Bourbon to the claustral buildings erected in 1750 by the Abbot Dom Dathose is to understand the last chapter in the decline and fall. Imposing only by its size and palatial only in its proportions, it must be accounted one of the more banal achievements of eighteenth-century architecture. In order to make room for it the original monastic buildings, including important remains of the earlier church, were simply swept aside. The loss to posterity entailed in this rebuilding is almost as tragic as the loss of the great basilica already described. The style of the new buildings, however, sorted well with the style of the last abbots; the names of Bourbon-Conti, de La Tour d'Auvergne and La Rochefoucauld set the tone for the seventeenth and eighteenth centuries. The monastery of Cluny had travelled a long way from the intentions of its original founders. It is not possible to understand Cluny without going back to the days of its foundation.

On 11 September in the year 910 Duke William of Aquitaine was holding an assize at Bourges. He was old; he had no direct heir; he had a murder on his conscience. He was for this reason disposed to feel generous towards the Church. He had summoned Berno, abbot of Gigny, to discuss with him the foundation of a new monastery. Berno had suggested the lands of Cluny, near Macon. The site was one which lent itself to the purpose; 'It was a valley shut off, far from all human contact,' wrote Raoul Glaber, 'which breathed such a perfume of aloofness, repose and peace that it seemed like a heavenly solitude.' Perhaps for that very reason it formed a natural sanctuary for game and was recognized by Duke William as his best hunting forest. But Berno insisted: 'Drive your hounds hence', he said, 'and put monks in their place; for you know which will serve you better before God – the baying of hounds or the praying of monks.' His reasoning prevailed and Duke William signed the charter. Some of its clauses shed an interesting light on the mentality of the times.

'That this benefaction may endure, not only for a time, but may last for ever,' it runs, 'I will provide at my expense for men living together under monastic vows, with this hope and faith, that if I cannot myself despise all the things of this world, at least by sustaining those who do despise the world, those whom I believe to be righteous in the eyes of God, I may myself receive the rewards of righteousness.' Seldom can there have been a more explicit statement of the double standard of medieval Christianity, nor of the vicarious nature of the monastic vocation. Seldom can there have been a more frank admission that there could be one divine law for the rich and another for the poor.

The donation included not only land but 'all the property that depends thereon, cottages, chapels, serfs both men and women, revenues . . . with no reservations'. It was important that this land was free from the domination of any overlord. Cluny was made directly dependent on the Pope and thus eluded the authority of the diocesan bishop. The monks were unencumbered by any of the obligations of feudalism and unrestricted by any of the limitations of being a local institution.

Cluny was, on the whole, fortunate in its succession of abbots. Between 927 and 1157, there were only seven, one of whom lasted for only three months. Of these St Odon, St Mayeul, St Odilon and St Hugues were known as the 'quatre grands Abbés de Cluny', and there was a special set of Offices to commemorate them. The greatest of these, Hugues de Semur, occupied the chair for sixty years.

Under their influence the number of monks rose to 300, and Cluny became the greatest monastic establishment in the west. In the words of Pope Gregory VII: 'Among all the abbeys beyond the Alps there shines first and foremost that of Cluny, which is under the protection of the Holy See. Under its sainted abbots it has reached so high a stage of honour and religion that, because of the zeal wherewith God is there served, without doubt it surpasses all other monasteries, even the most ancient.'

Unlike other monasteries of the Benedictine Order, Cluny became the centre of an empire. Other houses which attached themselves to Cluny, and new houses founded under its influence, had the status only of priories and were ruled direct from the mother house. Joan Evans has accounted for 1,450 priories attached to Cluny in its heyday; just over 1,300 were in France.

But nothing fails like success. There seems to have been a rhythm of decadence and reform built into the monastic system. A monastery was founded for the strict observance of the Benedictine rule; it became famous for its sanctity; rich men, anxious for their salvation, made bequests of land; the monks became involved in the secular affairs of their estates: worldliness and wealth invaded the cloister; rules were relaxed and spirituality declined; a new Order was founded for the strict observance of the Benedictine rule; it became famous for its sanctity . . .

This downward process is described by Abelard in the early twelfth century.

We, who ought to live by the labour of our own hands (which alone, as St Benedict saith, maketh us true monks) do now follow after idleness, that enemy of the soul, and seek our livelihood from the labours of other men. So that, entangling ourselves in worldly business, and striving, under the sway of earthly covetousness, to be richer in the cloister than we were in the world, we have subjected ourselves to earthly lords rather than to God. We take from the great men of this world, in the guise of alms, manors and tenants and bondsmen and bondswomen . . . and to defend these possessions we are compelled to appear in outside courts and before earthly judges, before whom we contend so shamelessly that we compel our own men not only to swear for us, but even to fight for us in single combat to the extreme peril of their lives. Who doth not know that we exercise heavier exactions upon those subject to us and oppress them with more grievous tyranny than worldly potentates?

Abelard

Cluny was to be the scene of the last days of Abelard, that 'orthodox rebel' who called his autobiography the *Historia Calamitatum*; whose greatest crime was that, in Gordon Leff's words, 'he prised theology away from Authority and exposed it to the scrutiny of human reason'. This brought down upon him the outraged opposition of Bernard of Clairvaux. At the Council of Sens, in June 1140, Bernard obtained the condemnation of fourteen of his doctrines as 'pernicious, manifestly damnable, opposed to the Faith, contrary to truth and openly heretical'.

Abelard extricated himself from the Council of Sens by appealing to Rome and set off in person to answer his charges there. The road from Sens to Rome passes by Cluny. Roger Lloyd, perhaps Abelard's most sympathetic biographer, describes his reception by Peter the Venerable, who was then the abbot. 'He gave Abelard a warm welcome and pressed him to stay for several days, for he saw in him not so much a condemned heretic . . . as a weary and unhappy man, whose world had crumbled about his feet.'

Peter the Venerable achieved what most men would have deemed impossible – a reconciliation between Bernard and Abelard. 'His long persecution was over', continues Lloyd, 'and now he wanted refuge. He gladly agreed to remain at Cluny at the side of the peacemaker, Peter. Permission from Rome, since Peter asked for it, was readily forthcoming, and Abelard settled down to spend the evening of his days amid the peace, the love and the beauty of Cluny.' Here, or at the little daughter house of Saint-Marcel near Chalon, Abelard lived, and here on 21 April 1142, he died.

It was Peter the Venerable who wrote his epitaph in a letter to Heloïse.

I do not remember to have known a man whose appearance and bearing manifested such humility. I sent him to Chalon for the mildness of the climate, which is the best in our part of Burgundy, and to a home well fitted for him, near the town, but yet with the Saône flowing between. There, as much as his infirmities permitted, returning to his former studies, he was ever bent over his books . . . nor did he ever allow a moment to pass in which he was not either praying or reading or writing. In the midst of such labours Death, the bearer of good tidings, found him.

All the monks of Saint-Marcel can tell you with what saintly devotion he made his profession of faith and confessed his sins; with what fervent love he received the holy viaticum, the pledge of eternal life, the body of our Redeemer; and with what trust he commended his body and soul to him.

Then, turning his mind to Heloïse, he ends on a touchingly human note.

Venerable and beloved sister in Christ, he to whom you were first united in the bonds of the flesh and then by the stronger and more sacred bonds of divine love, he with whom and under whose guidance you have served the Lord, is now cherished in his bosom . . . God keeps him for you, and when the day comes that he shall descend from Heaven to the voice of an Archangel and the sound of a trumpet, he will restore him to you for ever.

It is not difficult to guess the spiritual atmosphere of an abbey ruled over by the author of those lines.

Peter the Venerable may be accounted the last of the great abbots of Cluny, for, as Joan Evans puts it, 'its dynamic force was exhausted and its potential growth was at an end'. In 1162 Pope Alexander III released Vézelay from its subjection to Cluny, saying that it had 'fallen away from its earlier holiness and saintliness of life'.

The Abbot

Peter's immediate predecessor, Pons de Melgeuil, had been a disaster. Deposed by the Pope for personal extravangance and wasting the abbey's wealth, he had returned with an army of ruffians, attacked the monastery and carried off most of its treasures. Pons de Melgeuil was clearly exceptional, but even without his contribution, the monastery was set on a downwards course. Even the more saintly abbots became infected by the same disease which was undermining the spiritual strength of the movement. Men of piety and erudition were in high demand at the courts of kings and emperors and an abbot such as Hugues de Semur (1049–1109), who reigned for sixty years at Cluny, was as often in Rome or Paris or in the Imperial Palace at Cologne as he was with his monks.

The close association with the papacy conferred upon the abbots a prestige which had never been dreamed of by Berno. In 1095 Urban II, who had first entered the gates of Cluny as a novice, was received back with great splendour to consecrate the high altar of the new basilica. He conferred upon Abbot Hugues the right to wear pontifical vestments at Mass – purple gloves, a jewelled mitre and gold-embroidered shoes.

Gone were the days when the abbot had slept in the dormitory, eaten in the refectory and shared the self-imposed privations of his monks. Gone was the sense of family life when the numbers were small enough to make that a reality.

A further dimension to this image of the family had been provided by the presence of boys. It was the custom for parents to dedicate their sons at an early age to the monastic life. The boys were trained to sing, but were excused some of the severities of the rule until they were fifteen, when they were considered old enough to be received as novices. The monk Bernard wrote of these: 'It hardly seems to me that any king's son is brought up in the palace with more diligence than one of the little boys at Cluny.' It was not unknown, even, for young princes to be brought up at Cluny. The English king Stephen sent his son William of Blois here in 1140 and in later years his generous benefactions to his Alma Mater suggest that his memories of the place were not unhappy.

There is a delightful picture of Abbot Odilo (994–1049) painted by his biographer Jotsaldus.

With what joy did he advance among his brethren! With what an air of festival did he take his seat in the sacred choir, casting his eyes from left to right over the plantation of youth that was around him, remembering that verse of David 'thy children like olive plants around thy table . . .' He knew how to unite them all into one community by the strength given by moderation and prudence, by the love of a mother and the care of a father, so that all seemed to have but one heart and soul.

The title 'Abbot' derives, of course, from the Aramaic word *Abba*, 'father'. St Benedict, in drawing up his rule for the monks at Monte Cassino, devoted one of his finest passages to the position of the abbot.

An Abbot who is worthy of his position will always be mindful of the title he bears, and will not belie, by what he does, a name that belongs to a greater than himself . . . seeing that he is called by God's title in the words of the Apostle: 'Ye received the spirit of adoption whereby we cry, Abba, Father.'

Let the Abbot's affection be equal for all, and to all alike let him give what is due for their teaching. For in his teaching the Abbot must have regard ever to that saying of the Apostle when he says: 'reprove, rebuke, exhort'.

Let him show both the stern affection of a master and the dear love of a father . . . Those whose goodness is to be trusted he will more than once chastise, if chastisement is needed, with his tongue; but the insolent, the obstinate, the arrogant and the disobedient he will keep in check with the lash of bodily punishment at the very outset of their sin, remembering how it is written: 'the fool is not ruled by words', and again: 'beat thy son with a rod and thou shalt free his soul from death'.

The vows of chastity, poverty and obedience; the strenuous alternation between manual labour and worship, frugal fare and discipline enforced by corporal punishment were the main features of the Rule, but Benedict infused a spirit of reasonableness and moderation into it which probably accounts for its survival.

The church of St Peter and St Paul

At the centre of this communal existence, and providing the focal point of the architectural ensemble, was the abbey church of St Peter and St Paul. There were three successive churches built at Cluny. The first has left no traces. The second was begun by Abbot Mayeul soon after 950. It was the earliest example of what was to become the 'Benedictine plan': a long choir set between narrow side aisles each ending in an apse; deep transepts with apsidal chapels at their extremities; and a nave centered between two western towers. By the end of the tenth century this church, which was only 55 metres long, became far too small for the ever increasing numbers attracted by the great occasions of the abbey. It was imperative to rebuild on a much larger scale, but the old church, known to historians as Cluny II, was retained as part of the whole complex.

The new church, Cluny III, probably owed its origin to a visit by Hugues de Semur in 1083 to Monte Cassino where the Abbot Didier was busy enlarging and redecorating his church. But at a very early date it was believed that the real author of Cluny III was St Peter, who conveyed the plans by means of a vision to Gunzo, abbot of Beaune, who was paralysed and had come to Cluny to be nursed.

It was certainly an inspired plan, an affair of the greatest audacity and elegance, and it had, in Professor Conant's words, 'a truly imperial majesty of conception and scale'. At 187 metres in length and 28 metres to the keystone of the vault, it was by far the largest church in Christendom, only to be surpassed in the Renaissance by the building of St Peter's, Rome.

On 10 September 1088, the first stone was laid. In November 1095 Pope Urban II consecrated the main altars. The *Book of Miracles* of St Hugues claims that the building of Cluny was one of them, and states that it was carried out within twenty years. Gilon's *Life of St Hugues* gives the same figure. 'In twenty years he constructed such a basilica that if an emperor had built it in so short a space it would have been considered as a marvel.'

It is probable, however, that when St Hugues died in April 1109 the nave was still unfinished. It is generally agreed that Pons de Melgeuil was responsible for completing this and that Peter the Venerable added the narthex.

One of the finest views of Cluny was that obtained from the east. It was captured in a water-colour by Lallemand in its last days as a monastery, just before the coming of the Revolution. He has taken his viewpoint slightly from the south, thus avoiding the exact symmetry of an elevation. He shows a most impressive build-up of radiating chapels, ambulatory and apse, backed by the roofs and gables of the double transepts and crowned with the cluster of towers that soars to its climax in the great Clocher du Choeur which marked the central crossing. The scene was presumably drawn 'from the life', but Lallemand has taken the liberty of imagining a sunlight almost directly from the north which provides a shadow projection of high pictorial quality. Behind the vast complex of the east end the nave stretches uneventfully towards the twin towers of the west front, all partly concealed by the classical buildings of Dom Dathose, which were added in the eighteenth century.

Seen from the north or south, with the façade in elevation, the nave of Cluny was a little dull – a three-tiered, monotonous repetition of buttresses and windows extended to the west by the narthex, a two-tiered version of the same façade on a smaller scale. But, as Ruskin wrote of the Gothic style, 'the outside of a French Cathedral is to be thought of as the wrong side of the stuff, in which you find how the threads go that produce the inside'. Certainly to pass into the nave at Cluny after an inspection of its façades was to have one of the greatest architectural experiences afforded by the Middle Ages.

The overture was provided by the narthex. The appearance of this is known from another water-colour by Lallemand and from Professor Conant's reconstruction. It was a building not unlike the nave of

Autun Cathedral and on about the same scale, but already tending towards the Gothic by reason of the tall clerestory windows and cross-ribbed vaults.

But the glory of the narthex was the huge portal at the east end. This had been the exterior door to Abbot Hugues's building. Finished in about the year 1110 and enclosed within the narthex not later than 1130, its rich polychroming had been exposed to the elements for only twenty years and would thus have retained to a large degree its original brilliance.

Passing through this door, the visitor entered the nave. Those who entered for the first time must have been arrested in speechless admiration of its magnificence. The stately procession of the great arcade, the double avenue of piers, fifty-six of them free-standing, and the diminishing perspective of the high vaulting arches all combined to lead the eye towards the sanctuary, the culminating splendour of the apse. This was the architectural setting of the high altar, the holy of holies in a Christian church.

Nine elevated arches, supported on ten slender columns, curled in a graceful hemicycle round the sanctuary; between the columns could be seen the radiating vistas, across the ambulatory and into the five chapels which projected from the apse. At clerestory level a ring of windows corresponded with the arches of the great arcade. Above them a half-dome, or *cul de four*, provided the enormous canvas for the Christ in Majesty depicted against the rich mosaic upon its concave ceiling.

The figure of Christ, whose eyes had so mesmerized the young Lorain, was 10 feet tall. 'All this painting', he wrote later, 'stood out against a background of gold . . . in the form of a mosaic. This beautiful piece of work which decorated the cupola of Cluny had preserved right into the nineteenth century all the brilliance and all the freshness of its pristine colouring.'

The appearance of these great frescoes must be left largely to the imagination, but the imagination can at least be guided by the paintings at Berzé-la-Ville, for Berzé is a miniature of Cluny.

Berzé-la-Ville

This is one of the most delightful buildings in Burgundy. It is on the road from Cluny to Macon, near where the pass is protected by the fine fortress of Berzé-le-Châtel. A fortress almost by definition commands a wide horizon, and the views from here are dramatic.

Berzé was an outpost of Cluny, sometimes referred to as a 'priory', sometimes as a 'grange', but more often as the '*Château des Moines*', though the buildings are far too unpretentious to deserve such a title. Their real purpose seems to have been to provide a private retreat for the abbot. In the first years of the twelfth century we begin to find charters signed by Abbot Hugues *apud Berziacum* or *apud Berziacum villam*. The word is used in the literal sense of a villa; there is no town. These references suggest that the building was contemporary with the east end of the great basilica of Cluny, in which case the surviving murals of Berzé must have much to teach us about the vanished glories of the mother church.

The paintings at Berzé had a lucky escape during the Revolution. On 16 February 1791, the property was sold and became the private residence of a vigneron from Macon, Benoit Benon. He had a floor inserted to provide a granary above, and he applied a thick coat of whitewash which concealed the frescoes. Thus it remained until 1887, when the Abbé Jolivet, curé of the parish, obtained permission to remove some of the whitewash: the head of Christ was revealed. Antiquarian interest was aroused and in 1889 the building was classified as a *Monument Historique*. In due course the whitewash was all removed and the murals revealed in their entirety.

In 1947 Dr Joan Evans got up a subscription to purchase the buildings and presented them to the Académie de Macon. Her great knowledge of Cluny and of Berzé was equalled only by her love and she has left a moving, though perforce imaginary, description of what such a retreat must have meant to the ageing Abbot Hugues.

There, looking out upon the strange hills of Solutré that rise up like breaking waves, the old Abbot could meditate upon all that he had seen and known: his home in the Brionnais, his school at St Marcel, the recurring rhythm of the chanted offices at Cluny: the beggars to whom he had given alms, the peasants and farmers of the cluniac estates, the great flock of cluniac brethren, ever renewed as death depleted it, Priors and Abbots, Bishops and Popes, Kings and Emperors. He could imagine the basilica that was to be the greatest church in Christendom, and know that his masons were even then toiling to make it fair; he could view the great

Order that in all the lands of western Christendom followed the rules and customs of the mother house; and full of thankfulness he could go into the lovely Chapel of the Grange and for a space be alone with God.

It is easy to believe that those who built and decorated the chapel were aiming to create an interior conducive to meditation. This is particularly evident in the provision of windows which are so disposed as to cast an even light upon the wall surfaces. The subject-matter of the murals suggests the sort of theme on which a religious mind could dwell.

Central to the whole composition is the figure of Christ, framed between two arcs which form a mandorla within which he is enclosed and insulated from the twelve Apostles, who incline towards him from either side. The delimiting frame of the mandorla is transgressed at only two points: one where the Christ hands a scroll to St Peter, who is thus made the contact between himself and the other Apostles; the second where Christ's right hand conveys His blessing on the world. The space at the feet of the Apostles is occupied by smaller figures; those to the north have been identified as St Vincent and St Laurence.

All this is depicted within the half-dome of the apse. Beneath this, at the level of the windows, an arcade encircles the apse, providing a blind bay on either side for the use of the painter. Here the theme is martyrdom – St Blaise being decapitated by a seated executioner on one side, and St Laurence roasted on the grill on the other.

Below the arcade there is a further stratum of paintings devoted to a ring of saints – possibly those held in high regard at Cluny. They cannot be identified and they do not appear to be all from the same hand.

Such is the subject-matter of the murals. The artist's palette is confined to the earth colours, mainly Prussian blue and terra cotta, which provide a rich and sombre decoration. The rest of the wall space is taken up by very pretty borders and frames of white flowers on a blue base which are often used to underscore the main lines of the architecture. Thanks, no doubt, to Benoit's protective coat of whitewash, we have here one of the most complete examples of Romanesque mural painting that has come down to us.

Early Christian art had not looked to ancient Greece for inspiration but to Syria, Byzantium and Mesopotamia. Theirs was the art of the mosaic, of mural painting and of tapestry. They were not concerned to copy nature, but were more interested in the abstract and in the caprices of their own imaginations. These were the sources on which the artists of Cluny drew.

The carved capitals of Cluny

But if the paintings in the apse looked back to a long tradition, the sculptures of Cluny represent a leap ahead. If the two American antiquaries, Kingsley Porter and Conant, are right, Cluny should receive the credit previously accorded to Moissac as the point of departure for French Romanesque sculpture, leading to Charlieu, Vézelay, Saulieu and Autun – and, indeed, to Moissac.

The argument, to which hundreds of pages of print have been devoted, hinges on whether the capitals of Cluny were carved first in a workshop and then mounted on their columns, or whether they were mounted rough-hewn and then carved *in situ*. If they were carved before mounting, they must of necessity have been finished well before the consecration of the choir and transepts in 1095. If they were carved *in situ* it is possible to attribute to them a much later date. Professor Conant has demonstrated that the carving immediately below the impost block could not have been accomplished after that block had been mounted on the capital. If his reasoning is accepted a date previous to 1095 becomes imperative. All that is required for the acceptance of Conant's dating is the supposition that Hugues de Semur was able to call upon the services of a sculptor who was not only in full possession of his art but also a man with an original imagination and capable of real innovation. As the same supposition would be required to account for the novelty of Moissac, this should pose no extra difficulty, especially in a building which was in other respects without precedent. But even if Moissac is still given the priority, the credit still goes to the Cluniac Order, for Moissac was a priory of Cluny. In either case Emile Mâle was right in saying that 'the art of the Middle Ages began with the sublime'. Wherever it appeared first, it was something new to Christendom. 'This resurrection is one of the most curious phenomena of history: humanity recovered a lost secret and set out once more on its way.'

After the destruction of Cluny a number of the capitals from the ambulatory arcade were recovered from the debris and are now exhibited in the granary. 'These capitals,' writes Violet Markham,

'though grievously mutilated, are of superb quality and workmanship. Romanesque sculpture can show nothing finer or more
imaginative than the Eight Musical Tones, the Four Cardinal
Virtues, the Seasons and the Rivers and Trees of Paradise.' The
capitals are of an original design, most of them presenting beneath
each of the four sides of the abacus a figure framed in a mandorla.
Flowers and foliage take the place of volutes and the whole makes a
shape not unlike that of the Corinthian order.

Miss Markham has pointed out that the themes are very
unecclesiastical – the figure symbolizing Spring is a girl in the
secular costume of the day; around her, in the form of a mandorla, is
carved the inscription 'Spring brings the first flowers and the first
scents.' The First Tone of Music shows a round-faced boy playing
something like a lute, and evidently having some difficulty reading
the music. His short tunic and tousled hair proclaim him a layman;
choristers wore long robes and received the tonsure. 'These shat-
tered fragments are still the most eloquent of all witnesses to the
humanist spirit of Cluny and all that it has meant to the mind of the
civilized world. Their subject-matter is unique . . . These serene and
gracious figures are far removed from the demons and devouring
beasts who appal us in many churches of the period.'

It is certainly significant that in the most sacred place in the most
celebrated abbey of Christendom the subject-matter of the sculpture
should be so unecclesiastical. 'The Seasons and the Virtues',
continues Miss Markham, 'are not out to frighten ignorant men and
women with devil talk . . . Ruined and deserted though Cluny is
today, let us remember that here, eight hundred years ago, beat a
pulse of noble life to which Europe vibrated. The broken capitals of
the little Museum, tragic though their mutilation, give us some
measure of that life, and turn our thoughts in gratitude to the men
who relit the lamps of beauty and of truth.'

Violet Markham paints the picture of Cluny as a great centre of
culture, with its vast library, its wide repertoire of music and its high
standard of architecture, painting and sculpture. It was a
thoroughly aristocratic institution.

The abbeys of the early medieval period were, in fact, closely
linked with the aristocracy. Not only did they owe their foundation,
in many cases, to some local count or baron, but many of the monks
themselves were recruited from among the noble families of France.
One might have expected, in these circumstances, that the monastic

communities would have lived on amicable terms with their feudal neighbours. Such, however, does not appear to have been the case. The chronicles of Cluny give ample evidence to the contrary.

As early as 990, only eight years after its foundation, a confirmation of the abbey's properties was obtained from the Council of Anse; with it was included an anathema against those who plundered the abbey's churches and cellars, built castles upon its lands, carried off its cattle and ravaged its crops. It may be inferred from such a prohibition that the abbey had been constantly subjected to such treatment. This is confirmed from the annals of Brancion.

Brancion

The great lords of the early medieval period were mostly compulsive brigands. They looked down from their hilltop castles upon the fat pastures and ripening vineyards of the valley bottoms as an eagle might survey, from his lofty eyrie, the more vulnerable livestock of the cultivated glen.

Just such incorrigible raptors were the lords of Brancion. Perched on its own summit and commanding the pass between the Monts du Maconnais and the Mont Saint-Romain, Brancion is the perfect site for a fortress. From the roof of its keep and from the west front of its church one overlooks a magnificent view of the country – south towards Cluny, westward to Chapaize with its tall watchtower of a belfry, north-west towards Saint-Gengoux, backed by the high hills of the Monts du Charollais and the Mont Saint-Vincent. Here the seigneurs de Brancion kept their eyrie – a square keep with another square tower called the Tour du Préau, linked at a later date by the buildings of the Grande Salle or Salle de Beaujeu, where a fine, hooded mantelpiece still clings to the ruined masonry at first-floor level. Three curtain walls, which followed the contours at three different levels, made Brancion almost impregnable.

The name of the family was Gros. They emerge from the unrecorded mists of the first millennium with Bernard I, placed under anathema for his depredations against Cluny and sent to Rome to seek absolution. He died on the way. Of his nine sons, two became monks at Cluny, a circumstance which did not prevent their eldest brother, who succeeded in 1070, from maintaining the love–hate relationship with the abbey traditional to his family. Savage attacks on its property alternated with liberal donations to its funds, made by the seigneur 'pour le salut de son âme et de celles de son père et de ses autres parents'.

In 1147 Louis VII launched his great crusade from Vézelay. Inspired by the preaching of St Bernard and animated by a curious blend of piety, penitence and bellicosity, the cream of France's chivalry set out for the Holy Land. Among them was Bernard II of Brancion. Before departing he had cleared his conscience so far as Cluny was concerned. He renounced all claim to seigneurial rights, including the passage of armed men through their lands and the administration of justice over their tenants. He died three years later, probably in Palestine.

No sooner had he departed, however, than his son Josserand II renewed the attacks upon Cluny and was excommunicated by Eugenius III. So persistent was he in his brigandage that Pope Alexander III, Louis VII and Philippe-Auguste all had to inter- vene. But, as advancing age brought on the pangs of conscience, Josserand II in his turn signed on for a crusade in expiation of his sins. He died in 1180 before the troops departed.

Another Josserand, who succeeded in 1214, earned himself the title of Le Grand. He showed a magnanimity hitherto unrecorded in his family history and made generous donations to Cluny, including the Château de Boutavant which constituted a continual threat to their Château de Lourdon on which they relied for their protection.

Josserand le Grand found an outlet for his aggressive instincts in two expeditions to the Holy Land. Here he could live up to his motto 'Au plus fort de la mêlée' ('To the thickest part of the fray'), and here he received at Mansourah the wounds from which he died. On Good Friday, 1250, according to the chronicler Joinville, 'he knelt before the altar and begged forgiveness from God . . . for the wars between Christians where he had lived so long . . . and that he might die in His service so that he might reign with Him in Paradise'.

It is almost certain that Josserand le Grand is represented in the recumbent figure of a knight in the little church of Brancion, but it has only been here since 1959, when it was transferred from the Château d'Uxelles. This was another property of the family and in all probability the site of Josserand's sepulchre.

With the death of Josserand the long tradition of rapacity seems to have come to an end. The gifts to Cluny did not. The generosity of the family is depicted in a mural on the walls of the donjon, showing

Josserand and his knights carrying 'moult riches dons' to Hugues de Courtenai, abbot of Cluny. The picture, however, is a nineteenth-century pastiche and it contains a notable anachronism. The building shown to the right of the main gate, with its two towers *en poivrière*, known as the Maison de Beaufort, is of fifteenth-century date. By this time the château no longer belonged to the Gros family. Salvation, on the terms at which they purchased it, was an expensive commodity; the cost of pilgrimages and crusades to the Holy Land had seriously undermined the family fortunes and in 1259 Brancion was sold to the dukes of Burgundy.

It was they who built the church as we see it today. The architecture is of the late thirteenth century and the mural paintings date from the visits of Duke Eudes IV between 1325 and 1330.

It is a charming little building – a miniature in the style of Cluny. Seen from the château it forms an agreeable composition of apse and apsidal chapels – a pleasing interplay of angular and rounded shapes, triangular pediments and conic roofs, all backed and overtopped by the walls and gables of the choir and transepts, which build up to the climax in the tower with its tall pyramidal spire.

This was the great success of the Cluniac style. Its failure was, as so often, the nave and aisles. Here at Brancion their respective roofs are so nearly on the same plane as to leave no room for clerestory windows. There is thus no direct lighting to the nave and, since the aisle windows are needlessly small, the church is extremely poorly lit. The loss, however, is not great, for it is as dull as it is dark. The architecture of the nave represents the point at which simplicity borders on crudity. The only architectural effect contrived is the perspective of the vaulting arches, distinguished by a slightly pink stone, which, to anyone standing at the west end, provides a series of diminishing frames to the apse. Here was the sanctuary, the focal point of the church, enriched with paintings but usually relying upon the light of candles for the brilliance of its illumination.

The apse bears a certain resemblance to that of Berzé-la-Ville, but it lacks the natural lighting. Indeed, it almost seems as if the three windows were a later insertion, for the hemicycle is painted as an arcade which, without the windows, would offer twelve niches for the twelve Apostles.

On the north wall, behind the tomb of Josserand, is another mural painting of the Last Judgement. It is of a somewhat unusual nature. To the right are the elect in a rather large version of Abraham's bosom, to the left is another bag, held by two angels, reserved for the damned.

Next to it, in the third bay of the north aisle, is a painting showing the interment of a nun at the nearby convent of Lancharre, down in the valley west of Brancion and next to the church of Chapaize. Lancharre is another example of a typical and delightful Romanesque east end, which stands with its tower in an impressive group of farm buildings. It dates from about 1300 and served a convent of a somewhat exclusive nature. The nuns were all of noble birth. Each lived in her own dwelling and each had a servant to wait upon her.

The remains of Lancharre and the church of Brancion are fairly late examples of the extraordinary outcrop of Romanesque churches with which Burgundy is so plentifully provided. Of these the church of Sainte-Madeleine at Vézelay and the Cathedral of Autun are outstanding.

Vézelay

'Vézelay', wrote André Hallays in 1923, 'is a church with no life, no mystery, which one would have said had been built yesterday, a restoration in fact. It is one of Viollet-le-Duc's worst misdeeds.' It is nothing more, he says, than an archaeological curiosity, an interesting example of architecture, a collection of fascinating sculpture; 'on y respire l'odeur sépulchrale des musées'. He is extreme in his judgement. 'The Huguenots who sacked the church and smashed the sculptures, the churchmen of the eighteenth century who demolished the old medieval palace of the Abbots, the Revolutionaries who mutilated the tympanum of the Grand Portail – all these workers of devastation are less to be blamed than Viollet-le-Duc and his mania for restoration.'

Hallays speaks for many today in his disapproval of Viollet-le-Duc; he probably speaks for rather fewer when he says that Vézelay has no soul. Those who come as sightseers may linger as pilgrims. But neither sightseers nor pilgrims would be able to visit Vézelay at all today if it were not for Viollet-le-Duc.

He may sometimes have been guilty of over-restoration, but without what he did France would have lost some of its most precious buildings. What is beyond dispute is that Viollet-le-Duc was a very great scholar of Gothic architecture. It was a lost and a despised art, and he did more than anyone to rediscover it, to revive an interest in it and to make it possible for men to build again in that style. He was greatly aided in his task by Prosper Mérimée, the first director of the Commission des Monuments Historiques.

It is to Prosper Mérimée that the credit belongs for having rediscovered Vézelay. In August 1835, he made his first visit, arriving by way of La Marche and Clamecy – that is to say, from the west. 'The little town of Vézelay', he wrote,

is built on a rock of limestone which rises abruptly from the middle of a deep valley, enclosed by hills in the form of an amphitheatre. One can distinguish the houses from a long way off, so disposed upon a steep incline that one would take them for a flight of steps, the remains of fortified walls forming a terrace, and above them all the church, placed on the highest ground of the hill, which dominates its surroundings.

The sun was rising. Over the valley there lay a thick mist, pierced here and there by the tops of the trees. Above them the town rose like a pyramid resplendent in the sunshine. At intervals the wind had made long furrows in the vapour and created a thousand varieties of light and shade such as English landscape artists contrive with such happy effect. It was a magnificent spectacle and it was with a predisposition to admire it that I directed my steps towards the Church of La Madeleine.

My first view of the monument somewhat damped my enthusiasm. The façade presents an old restoration in Gothic style, awkwardly appended to the lower parts, which are Romanesque. The left-hand tower was knocked down by the Protestants in 1569; during the Revolution the tympanum had been destroyed and, lest the nineteenth century should yield anything in the way of vandalism, they have just built a sort of observatory on top of it.

Both without and within the church presented a sorry scene of desolation. 'The vestibule (the narthex) does not seem to be regarded by the inhabitants of Vézelay as forming part of the church. Men keep their hats on when entering it; lewd persons gather to gamble in it and in fact things are done here that would not be done in the streets.'

He recognized that the tympanum over the entrance to the nave was 'le morceau capital', but it was so mutilated that he could not guess whether a figure was of a man, a woman, or an angel.

Whoever was the creator of the tympanum was an artist of the first quality. He had a tremendous sense of composition. The Apostles who surround the figure of Christ, some turning away from him as if to pass on the message, some looking back as if to catch what he is saying, fill the half-circle with a perfect equilibrium.

The varying scale of the figures is vital to the composition. The Christ, so large that his head breaks into the arc above him, dominates the whole; the Apostles are less than half his stature; a special emphasis is given to St Peter, who is seated beneath his right hand and reflects his pose, the knees bent in the same direction. Smaller still are the figures crowded into the compartments in the inner ring which enframes the central scene, and in scale with the smallest of these are those who people the long processions which ornament the lintel and which converge upon the central figures of St Peter and St Paul. The whole is inscribed within an outer ring carved with the signs of the Zodiac. Each of these is coupled with a scene illustrative of the season, thus providing the theme for twenty-four roundels. The architect, however, had seen fit to build his arch with twenty-nine keystones. Undeterred by this numerical discrepancy, the sculptor has filled the gaps as his fancy suggested.

As a work of art, the tympanum of Vézelay has a claim to be the finest achievement of the Burgundian Romanesque. As Violet Markham writes: 'the whole composition in its nobility and strength comes to us as a breath from the childhood of the world. The iconoclasts of the Revolution inflicted considerable damage on the heads, but the figures remain to interpret the emotion of the agitated group filled by a sense of new and marvellous light.'

Sooner or later the question imposes itself: what is the scene meant to represent? Emile Mâle has made a detailed study of the matter and his interpretation is probably the best. The scene is Pentecost. The rays that streak like lightning from the fingers of the Christ represent the pentecostal fire which appeared on the heads of the Apostles. The figures in the inner ring round the head of Christ, who seem 'with passionate gesticulation to communicate to each other some astonishing news', are perhaps the 'Parthians, Medes and Elamites and the dwellers in Mesopotamia' who were witnesses of the outpouring of the Spirit. Emile Mâle has shown how frequently Pentecost was depicted in early miniatures of eastern or Byzantine origin as the gospel being preached to the whole world. Honorius of Autun, in a sermon, describes the Apostles, in the new power of the Holy Spirit, giving sight to the blind and hearing to the deaf, enabling the lame to walk and restoring the dead to life. These little figures, revealing their naked legs or arms or baring their bosoms, could have been inspired by such teaching. Alongside them are men with dogs' heads – surely the fabulous cynocephali of India.

This also could provide the key to the strange collection of characters in the running frieze which decorates the lintel. On the right the people with elephantine ears are the Scythians; the little man trying to mount a horse with a ladder is a pygmy. Both are mentioned by Honorius of Autun and Isidore of Seville as representing the unknown world. On the left-hand side of the lintel a sacrificial procession denotes the pagan peoples to whom Pentecost offered redemption. The lintel is upheld in the middle by a column bearing the statue of John the Baptist, towards whose head these strange but animated processions converge. The message is clear. It is through baptism that the peoples of the world are offered the gifts of the Holy Spirit. Both as a masterpiece of pictorial art and as a brilliant expression of twelfth-century theology, the tympanum of Vézelay was seen by Mérimée as the *pièce de résistance*.

He also admired the capitals in the nave: 'it is above all the richness and variety of the ornament which distinguish the church of Vézelay'; but while praising their workmanship he deplored their subject-matter.

The choice of subjects revealed the spirit of the times and the manner in which they interpreted religion. It was not by means of kindness or persuasion that they wished to convert people, but by terror. The message of the priests could be résuméd thus: 'Believe, or you will perish miserably in this world and you will suffer eternal torment in the next.'

'I do not find at Vézelay', he continues,

any of those subjects which sensitive souls would like to find, such as the forgiveness accorded to the penitent or the recompense of the just, but, on the contrary, I see Samuel cutting Agag's throat; devils dismembering the damned and dragging them into the abyss; horrible animals, hideous monsters, grimacing faces which express the suffering of the rejected and the glee of the denizens of Hell. If one considers the devotion of men formed in the midst of such images one is less surprised by the massacre of the Albigensians.

Mérimée was moved by the subject-matter and the spiritual implications of the sculptures; Viollet-le-Duc was more naturally interested in the technique and artistry. 'The execution of the sculpture of Vézelay', he wrote, 'is distinguished by its dramatic

38

intention, often very grossly expressed but always in evidence. The artists sought to express it by movement. The gestures are energetic, often violent, and, despite the inaccuracies of an art which was still in the cradle, one is often struck by the truth of the pantomime.' He noticed that the technique of the sculptors was to use a deep relief but little modelling – almost as if the scene were a cut-out mounted on the background. Even the most slender objects, such as the shaft of a lance, are never free-standing but project, often as much as 7 or 8 centimetres.

In 1846 Mérimée was again at Vézelay and on 9 July he wrote to Viollet-le-Duc: 'the vaults of the nave and choir were all letting in the rain. Most of the vaulting arches were broken; all of them were badly deformed. The walls were out of true on all sides. So ruinous was the condition of the church that several times, in the General Council of the Département de l'Yonne, the question was discussed whether it would not be better to demolish it in the interests of the safety of the public.' Viollet-le-Duc was only just in time. While he was working on the nave, one of the vaults in the narthex collapsed.

At Vézelay, as Mérimée makes clear, Viollet-le-Duc was dealing with a near-ruin. It is interesting to read his own professional opinion of the original building. 'The construction of the nave', he wrote,

indicates a considerable lack of experience, or rather a remarkable carelessness. The vaults, which are exceptionally thick, are inadequately buttressed by walls built of small stones, a sort of thin outer facing which encloses rubble. The stones are, on the whole, ill-chosen – the keystones of the arches, for example, are made of clayey limestone which splits in all directions and were most of them in so bad a condition that they had to be replaced.

But if the builder of the nave was somewhat lacking in knowledge and experience, he was certainly a master of decoration. He understood well the principle that in architecture one should ornament a construction and never stoop to construct an ornament. The delicate little bands of finely chiselled sculpture are used to emphasize the arches and string courses. The effect is like that of a discreet use of lace upon a rather severe costume.

The perspective down the nave is one of the most beautiful that the Romanesque style has bequeathed to posterity. The exterior façades of the nave have been radically altered, for Viollet-le-Duc was obliged to add flying buttresses. It is just the sort of improvement that builders of the thirteenth century might have made, and had they done so here no one would have accused them of over-restoration.

But if Viollet-le-Duc discovered in the nave evidence of faulty construction, he found in the narthex the work of a master-builder in the full possession of his technique. 'One recognizes here that the art of construction has been evidently perfected.' The narthex, started in about 1120, was consecrated in 1132 by Pope Innocent II. It may have been unfinished at the time but was almost certainly completed by 1138 when Pons de Montboissier became abbot. His chronicler, Hugues le Poitevin, attributes the structure of the church to his predecessors.

The narthex differs from the nave in the use of the pointed arch, and its own nave is solidly abutted by the provision of tribunes over the side aisles. The nave and aisles, both in the main church and narthex, are unusual in being roofed by a series of groined vaults – and there may be more to this than meets the eye. The churches which were directly inspired by Cluny – Beaune, Paray-le-Monial and the cathedral of Autun – were roofed with barrel vaults, whereas at Anzy-le-Duc, Saint-Martin d'Autun and its priories Gourdon and Bragny-en-Charollais, the groined vault is preferred. This grouping may have more to it than coincidence. Charles Oursel, author of the important study *L'Art Roman de Bourgogne*, sees a political significance in this variation of styles.

The monks of Vézelay and the monks of Saint-Martin d'Autun and its priories, in order the better to make manifest their independence and to prove that they could manage without the great Burgundian abbey, withdrew from its architecture in the same way that they claimed to be emancipated from its discipline and from the observance of its rules. They had their own style and they adapted the ancient, traditional formulas which owed nothing to Cluny; they worked out their own particular methods.

If so, it was a brave venture, for, as Viollet-le-Duc perceived, those who built the nave of Vézelay still had a lot to learn.

The carelessness of which Viollet-le-Duc accuses the first builders may have some relation to the great speed with which the nave was put up. It was begun in 1096, consecrated in 1104 and probably completed by 1106. Its manifest unity of style argues a single campaign of building. This in turn argues the availability of the necessary money.

The financing of Vézelay is directly connected with a somewhat discreditable story. The church is dedicated to St Mary Magdalene. Shortly after 1037, when Abbot Geoffroi was elected, it was put about that the relics of St Madeleine were here at Vézelay. A pious but improbable legend claimed that she had died in France and was buried in the church of Saint-Maximin at Aix en Provence. One story is that a monk named Badilon removed the relics from Aix and brought them to Vézelay. The other is that the claim that Vézelay possessed the relics was quite simply untrue. In 1279 Pope Boniface VIII decreed that Saint-Maximin possessed the true mortal remains of La Madeleine. With that the fortunes of Vézelay declined. For nearly two and a half centuries the abbey had profited from its supposed possession of the relics. The relics attracted the pilgrims and the pilgrims provided the money with which the church was built.

Girard de Roussillon, in his original foundation in 860, had endowed the monastery with two apparent benefactions which were to be the cause of endless hostilities. He provided it with a rich estate and he placed it under the immediate authority of the Pope – 'ad Romam nullo medio pertinentes'. It was thus excluded from the authority of the bishop of Autun. The abbey was *in* his diocese but not *of* it – 'in diocesi sed non de diocesi Augustodunensi'.

But Rome was remote. Their more immediate neighbours, the citizens of Vézelay itself, the comte de Nevers, who claimed to be their feudal overlord, the bishop of Autun, who claimed to be their spiritual overlord, and the abbot of Cluny, who claimed to rule all Benedictine monasteries, never ceased to plague them with their pretensions. The hostilities were pursued with such violence that they resulted in the murder, in 1106, of the Abbot Artaud, who had been responsible for the building of the nave, and in an uprising, in 1152, against his successor, Pons de Montboissier, who was obliged to seek refuge at the village of Montet while the insurgents seized the church and used it as a fortress from which to intimidate the monastery. The inhabitants of Vézelay had reason to resent the domination of the abbey. In 1150 an ugly incident occurred which gave the comte de Nevers a pretext to make common cause with the citizens. A monk had surprised one of these cutting wood with an axe in one of the forests which belonged to the abbey. He tried to secure the axe to use it as circumstantial evidence and was struck off his horse. The next night a group of servants from the monastery broke into the offending woodcutter's house and put his eyes out.

In the same year Pons had been to Rome to complain of the behaviour of the bishop of Autun, who replied in his defence that he would rather see the abbey of Vézelay destroyed from top to bottom than excluded from his authority. As he was brother of the duke of Burgundy he had some strength behind his arm.

It was the steadily increasing power of the king of France that ultimately gave the monks of Vézelay their protection. 'They could only free themselves from the tyranny of feudalism', wrote the historian Aimé Cherest, 'by bowing their heads to the monarchy.' In due course the monarchy was to destroy the community. In 1537 it was 'secularized' and canons substituted for monks. In 1673 Louis XIV finally placed them under the authority of the bishop of Autun.

It is difficult to say whether the cathedral of Autun was contemporary with Vézelay or slightly earlier. Both were consecrated in 1132 by Pope Innocent II, but it is unlikely that either of them was finished at the time.

The Cathedral of Autun

The name 'Autun' must be one of the briefest of abbreviations. It is a contraction of 'Augustodunum', the name of a Roman city founded by Caesar Augustus. For some reason the Eduens, who inhabited the region, formed a close alliance with Rome; Rome was not ungrateful. It built them a city – 'une ville champignon' as the Abbé Denis Grivot puts it – a town that arose out of nothing more durable than an emperor's whim and had not the *raison d'être* to endure. As so often happened, however, the Church moved in when Rome moved out and established here in about AD 300 one of the oldest bishoprics in France.

But while it lasted, Augustodunum was magnificent. It had a containing wall nearly 20,000 feet in circumference and set about with sixty-two towers. It had the largest theatre in Gaul, second only to the Colosseum, with seating space for 30,000 spectators. It was built on the usual Roman grid system and at each of the four main entrances was an imposing gatehouse. Two of these survive today, the Porte d'Arroux and the Porte Saint-André. There were probably more Roman ruins to be seen in the eleventh century and they clearly made an impression on the builders of the day, for the cathedral of Saint-Lazare, while following the general lines of a church built under the influence of Cluny, has a strongly classical flavour. If the builder had only stuck to the rounded arch one might fancy oneself in some colossal vestibule by Vanbrugh. At first sight the fluted columns on the inward surfaces of the great arcade appear to be properly proportioned to the Corinthian order. The clean-cut profiles of the piers and sharply defined angles of the groined vaults create a strong impression of architectural precision.

Above the main arcade a false triforium almost exactly reproduces the upper gallery of the Porte d'Arroux. Autun owes nearly as much to Augustodunum as it does to Cluny. The difference is in the decoration. The capitals are not Corinthian; they are not Roman but Romanesque.

These capitals, many of which rank among the most esteemed in Burgundy, have excited much interest among antiquarians. Their arguments are resumed by the Abbé Denis Grivot.

A large number of details from the capitals can be found in the tympanum. If one examines the wing of the angel in the *Sleep of the Magi*, and if one compares it with the wings in the tympanum, and with others in the cathedral, the little scales and feathers are executed in such an identical manner that it would be difficult to suppose that there were two sculptors. The general rhythm of the wing is the same throughout; it is enough to examine the other wings carved by other Burgundian artists to establish the fact that the models have an infinite variety; the little band decorating the head of the angel . . . is to be found again on the head of an angel in the tympanun (one of those upholding the *gloire* of the Christ): this little band is a signature.

In the capital of the *Adoration of the Magi* one of the Magi can be seen holding a casket; the iron clasp of this casket is very characteristic; now a clasp exactly identical to this can be found in the tympanum, in two places; on the door to Heaven and on the lid to Hell . . . the clasp is a signature.

And so he continues: the mane of the donkey in the *Flight into Egypt* is treated in the same way as the hair on the Devils of the *Last Judgement*; the feet of the infant Christ in the *Adoration of the Magi* are miniature versions of those of the Christ in the tympanum; the haloes and crowns receive identical treatment. The Abbé Grivot leaves us in little doubt that the greatest of the capitals are from the same hand as the great *Last Judgement* over the west door – and here, for once, the artist has signed his name: 'Gislebertus hoc fecit.'

Denis Grivot has drawn attention to the way in which the lines and forms of the sculpture cross the joints between the twenty-nine slabs of stone involved without the slightest interruption. It would be impossible, he argues, for these stones to have been carved individually and then assembled on the tympanum: they must have been carved *in situ*. This enables a slightly later dating than the erection of the portal – he suggests 1140.

In 1766 the *Last Judgement* was deemed to be in bad taste and plastered over and the tympanum of the side door sold to an entrepreneur. The figure of Eve has found its way into the Musée Rolin, where it has been joined by three of the statues from the shrine of Lazarus, also evicted from the cathedral by the fastidiousness of the dean and chapter.

Vézelay and Autun are buildings of the first importance, both in their architecture and in their sculpture, but Burgundy is well supplied with Romanesque churches of great interest and charm which are not of the stature of these. Some were priories of Cluny and some the parish churches of obscure hamlets. A delightful tour of some of the more outstanding ones can be made by following the right bank of the Loire a few miles inland, starting at Charlieu and working one's way up to Paray-le-Monial.

Charlieu, Saint-Julien-de-Jonzy, Montceaux-l'Etoile and Anzy-le-Duc

In the south-west corner of Burgundy is Charlieu, mostly in ruins, but with a miraculously preserved *portail* set, oddly, on the side wall of the narthex. 'Here we have a work', writes Violet Markham, 'which in power, originality and superb execution can look the work of Ancient Greece in the face without fear or misgiving.' The concentric arcs, however, which are accorded this embellishment, take up so much of the space that the tympanum is reduced to a relatively small size. It is none the worse for that. Set within a mandorla and upheld in almost heraldic fashion by two angelic side-supporters, the Christ in Majesty is surrounded by the symbols of the Evangelists. There is a tremendous movement about the composition; the bull and the lion charging outwards from the feet of

Christ; the supporting angels in dramatic attitudes, one foot on each of these beasts, are also moving away from the mandorla which they hold. But if all is movement in the tympanum, all is repose in the lintel. The Virgin takes the central place between attendant angels with the Apostles arranged symmetrically on either side; all are seated sedately; all are facing forwards.

To the right of the main doorway, a secondary entrance carries a decoration no less remarkable. The lintel is used to represent sacrifice under the law of Leviticus; above it, in the tympanum, is the Last Supper, representing the Sacrifice of the Mass. This is enframed within the semicircle and the table has been made in the shape of an arc to fit its setting. The table-cloth, with its elaborate festoons, adds greatly to the decorative effect, making the whole, in the words of Emile Mâle, 'un des plus beaux monuments de l'art clunisien'.

One of the controlling influences is, of course, the quality of the local stone. The quarries of the right bank of the Loire produce a high-quality limestone which offers the sculptor every opportunity for delicate detail, whereas the Saône valley abounds in a limestone of coarser grain which makes carving almost impossible. The builders of Tournus and Chapaize could hardly have dreamed of decorating their porches in the manner of Charlieu.

Another treatment of the Last Supper links Charlieu with Saint-Julien-de-Jonzy, some 12 kilometres to the north. Here, however, it is depicted on the lintel and the table is straight, but the same features appear on the table-cloth, with its flounced panels. Above, in the tympanum, a central Christ in the usual mandorla is upheld by angels who lunge towards him, and their draperies, caught in a split second of agitated movement, accentuate their pose.

Another delightful pair of angels supports the mandorla at Montceaux-l'Etoile, between Anzy-le-Duc and Paray-le-Monial. The scene represents the Ascension, and the figure of Christ, balanced a little precariously, appears to be borne aloft by them as they jump into the air, steadying the mandorla with one arm and with the other indicating, with an upward gesture, their heavenly destination. Beneath them on the lintel the Apostles – fourteen of them this time – form the most animated scene, pointing, waving, gesticulating, while Peter holds his enormous keys as if he were leading a procession.

There are often family likenesses about these pictorial portals, and in many cases one was clearly inspired by the other. But sometimes there is evidence of a prototype that has come from further afield.

Emile Mâle has drawn attention to the similarity between an Egyptian mural at Baouit, which follows exactly the form of a tympanum surmounting a lintel, and the original portal of Anzy-le-Duc, now in the Musée du Hiéron at Paray-le-Monial. How the mural came to be known at Anzy-le-Duc is a matter for conjecture, but the likeness is there. The sculptor, however, has made no slavish copy of the painting and has, in fact, considerably improved upon it. His central figure of the Virgin about to suckle the infant Christ is a far more lively composition and the Apostles and Saints, who stand to either side, show the typically Romanesque concern to reflect the gestures of the figures in the movement of their garments. The side-supporter angels in the tympanum, turning away from the Christ, are almost genuflecting, as if the weight of the mandorla were too much for them. As the Abbé Grivot writes of this spirited group, 'C'est une des plus belles pages de la sculpture bourgignonne.'

All these churches are distinguished chiefly by their sculptures. Their architecture is more remarkable for its similarities than for its differences, and this for a very simple reason: all were inspired by the one prototype. As Emile Mâle puts it: 'Everywhere one finds Cluny.' Only Anzy-le-Duc proclaims its independence by the groined vaulting of its nave, and is at once identifiable by its tall octagon tower of three storeys opening on all sides in a series of twin arches.

Of those which reflect Cluny more closely there are two which are outstanding: Semur-en-Brionnais and Paray-le-Monial.

Semur-en-Brionnais

Semur is more distinguished in its architecture than in its sculpture. All these other portals show the art of the Romanesque sculptor at his best, all in a recognizable tradition – the tradition of Cluny – but each with his own originality and his own vitality. But at Semur-en-Brionnais the main doorway shows the style in its decadence. The artist seems to have run out of inspiration. The symbols of the Evangelists are just crowded round the inevitable mandorla; the angels are stiff and stylized; the figure of Christ is dull and wooden and his robes are treated in an almost summary fashion. The lintel offers a little more interest, if only because its theme is unusual. The scene is the Council of Seleucia, which took place in the year 359. It shows St Hilaire of Poitiers, rejected by his fellow bishops and seated, to emphasize the fact, on a low child's stool. But he is vindicated by an angel descending from above. Meanwhile, on the extreme right, the false Pope Leon has just died and two demons take charge of his soul, represented, as always, by a small child escaping from his mouth. But if the sculpture is disappointing, the architecture is magnificent – 'the synthesis', writes the Abbé Grivot, 'of all that had been built in Brionnais and, more generally, in Burgundy'.

The east end of the church is, as one would expect, its greatest success. It has retained its very low-pitch roofs – not more than 10 per cent, which is rendered possible by the use of pantiles; but the architect, presumably for aesthetic reasons, has designed the gables of the choir and transepts with an angle of 40 per cent. The tower, octagonal as at Anzy, is of two storeys built at different times. The lower storey, with coupled arches separated by fluted pilasters, is of a simplicity consistent with that of the rest of the building. The upper storey is more elaborate; the windows are deeply recessed in frames of concentric arches springing from three columns on either side. The architect seems uncertain, however, whether to use the round or the pointed arch.

The nave is a magnificent achievement, reminiscent of Autun in its use of tall, fluted pilasters betwen the arches, but resembling Notre-Dame de Beaune in the use of half-columns on the inward faces. Beaune also should be our guide in imagining the original ceiling, for the arches were pointed and the barrel vault followed their lines, forming what is known in French as a *berceau brisé*.

But the real distinction of the nave at Semur is the triforium, a lovely arcaded gallery running right round which breaks into a great arch over the west door. In front of this arch is a semicircular projection, railed with a balustrade and supported by a series of corbels forming an inverted cone of which the point reaches the keystone of the door.

Semur also possesses the imposing ruins of its seigneurial castle. This was the birthplace, in 1024, of Hugues de Semur, abbot of Cluny from 1049 until his death sixty years later. His father, Dalmace de Semur, and his mother, Aremberge de Vergy, came from two of the most noble families of Burgundy, and like many noble families they were great builders. Hugues was not only responsible for the construction of Cluny, but also of the basilica, some 25 kilometres north of Semur, of Paray-le-Monial. Here, not unnaturally, we have the church that bears the closest resemblance to Cluny.

Paray-le-Monial and Saint-Andoche de Saulieu

The first glimpse of Paray-le-Monial from across the waters of the Bourbince is an exciting experience. The two western towers, backed and overtopped by the central octagon of the Clocher du Choeur, their richer architecture contrasting with the severe simplicity of the nave and transept, make a delightful picture, which is doubled by its reflection.

A more attentive inspection, however, reveals an odd disparity between the western towers, with a little façade just squeezed in between them, and the rest of the building. They are on a much smaller scale and their central doorway is not central to the axis of the nave. There can be only one explanation; we have here in the west end the remains of an older building which forms a sort of narthex to the new church.

A glance at a ground plan would make this clear at once. Nobody could possibly have built a narthex like that. Nobody could have *designed* a nave of only three bays in a church that was in all other respects a grandiose conception. Clearly the intention was to pull down the west end and extend the nave towards the river and to give it a narthex worthy of its proportions. The church of Paray-le-Monial is unfinished.

One further detail might be observed from across the Bourbince; on the central tower the transition from square to octagon is marked by four little red triangular roofs. Exactly the same solution to this problem can be seen at Cluny on the Clocher de l'Eau Bénite.

But it is at the east end of the church that the likeness to Cluny becomes so obviously apparent: the same impressive build-up of radiating chapels, ambulatory and apse, backed by the roofs and gables of the transepts, which soars to its climax in the great octagon tower over the central crossing. Only in one respect does Paray differ significantly from its prototype: the apsidal chapels, which at Cluny were mere semicircular projections, are elongated at Paray by one bay. This gives to each chapel a low pitched gable behind the roof of its apse. This extension of the chapels was presumably necessitated by the smaller scale of the whole building. An exact copying of Cluny would have reduced these chapels to little more than niches. One feature which, in Charles Oursel's words, has 'the character of a signature' is in the buttresses to the apsidal chapels, which take the form of an almost Corinthian pilaster with a little sloping *glacis* above the capital.'

The interior also reflects almost exactly the architecture of Cluny. To stand at the west end and to look down the perspective of the nave to the choir and apse is to see in miniature all the features of the great basilica. Nine elevated arches, supported on ten slender columns, curl in a graceful hemicycle round the sanctuary; between the columns can be seen the radiating vistas, across the ambulatory and into the three radiating chapels which project from the apse. At clerestory level a ring of windows corresponds with the arches of the great arcade. Above them, a half-dome, or *cul de four*, provides the enormous canvas for the Christ in Majesty. Here, more than anywhere, we can see the truth in the French pun: 'A Paray apparaît Cluny.'

The proportions of the nave, also, are similar. It creates the same impression of towering height. The total width of nave and aisles is 52 feet; the height to the keystone, 72 feet. We might compare it with another contemporary church built on about the same scale, Saint-Andoche de Saulieu. Here the width is much the same – 49 feet – but the height is just under 59 feet.

Saint-Andoche de Saulieu is another church of the Cluny family, but only the nave survives. In 1359 the English, under Edward III, attacked the town and set fire to the church. The choir, apse and transepts were so badly damaged that they could not be repaired. It was not until 1704 that the present east end was built.

It is therefore not so much in its architecture that we look for the inspiration of Cluny, but in the carving of its capitals. These rank among the finest in Burgundy and have strong similarities with those at Autun. This is hardly surprising, for both churches were built by Etienne de Bage who was bishop of Autun and abbot of Saulieu. Charles Oursel pictures the same team of sculptors moving on from Saulieu to Autun and possibly having come from Cluny in the first place. 'They are the same scenes treated in the same style: fighting cocks, fighting lions, the Women at the Tomb, the false prophet Balaam, the Temptation of Christ in the Wilderness, the Flight into Egypt, the hanging of Judas, the appearance of Christ to Mary Magdalene.'

A large number of these capitals are of biblical or religious subjects, but many have no obvious business in a place of worship. Attempts have been made to find some all-embracing symbolism into which these figures and scenes might fit, but these theories all run into difficulties in face of the fact that St Bernard of Clairvaux inveighed against such decorations. He must have known what the religious symbolism was, if there *was* any. Violet Markham has drawn our attention to the strongly secular and broadly humanist outlook of Cluny, which we have seen developed in a whole series of churches inspired by Cluny.

That was not, however, the intention of the original foundation. Under the abbacy of Peter the Venerable, at the turn of the eleventh century, Cluny provoked a passionate outburst from St Bernard. In 1098 the Order of Cîteaux, to which Bernard belonged, had been founded on the edge of the Forêt d'Izeure, some 23 kilometres south of Dijon and opposite the sunny slopes of the Côte d'Or. The future of monasticism lay with the Cistercians.

The Cistercians

'Give the Cistercians a desert', wrote Gerald Cambrensis, 'and in a few years you will find a dignified abbey in the midst of smiling plenty.' In an age of anarchy they set the example of order, of disciplined life and stern renunciation of the world. To achieve this they retired physically from all sight of human habitation. High up some green, forgotten valley, empty and deserted since the Roman legions left, or deep in some 'horrid wood' which no man ever planted, on lonely moors or rocky mountain wastes they built their simple huts and wooden churches. 'Silence and perpetual remoteness from all secular turmoil' were decreed by St Bernard 'that would compel the mind to meditate upon celestial things.' But the silence of these sites was a silence enhanced by the murmur of running streams, by the distant roar of the rutting deer and 'the wheeling kite's wild, solitary cry'.

At the heart of the Cistercian Order was the strict revival of the Rule of St Benedict, and with it a renewed insistence on the duty of manual work, an aspect of the Rule somewhat neglected at Cluny. As the result of their labours the huts soon became houses, the wooden churches were rebuilt in stone, the trees were felled, the marshy places drained, the barren land began to yield its increase, the wilderness became a fruitful field.

To some extent the founding of Cîteaux in 1098 was a reaction against the decadence of Cluny. St Bernard, who had been a monk at Cîteaux before becoming abbot of Clairvaux, attacked the pomp of the abbot of Cluny, the gluttony of the monks and the luxury of their architecture in terms of often intemperate abuse which were customary in medieval controversy.

'They that should have shown us the way of life', he wrote, 'have become in their pride the blind leading the blind. Where is their humility when they walk proudly in the midst of an escort of many men, surrounded by a crowd of servants awaiting their orders? A man would take them not for fathers of monasteries but for the lords of castles; not for directors of souls, but for princes of provinces.'

That was fairly restrained language for Bernard. When he came to the diet of the monks it is difficult not to suspect him of exaggeration.

Like hawks and vultures they gathered wherever they saw smoke from a chimney, wherever they smelt cooking . . . beans, cheese, eggs and fish disgusted them; they only found savoury the fleshpots of Egypt. Roast or boiled pork, a well-fatted heifer, rabbit, hare, a goose well chosen, chicken, in fact every kind of luxury of meat and fowl appears on the table of these holy monks. But soon such food ceases to be good enough; satiety brings fastidiousness; rare and royal luxuries may be provided.

Luxury in food was bad enough, but luxury in building was the most inexcusable of all. Bernard must have been thinking of Cluny in particular when he asked: 'Why this excessive height in churches, this immoderate length, this superfluous width? Why these sumptuous ornaments, these curious paintings which attract the eye and distract the attention and the meditation? But let that pass – it is for the worship of God.' It was all very well for bishops in their cathedrals to use such material means to incite the spiritual devotion of the people, but for monks – 'we who have left the ranks of the people, who have renounced the riches and the glitter of the world for the love of Christ; we, who possess Christ, have trodden under our feet as if it were dung all that charms the eye, all that flatters the ear, all that delights the nose, the taste, the touch – whose devotion do we think we are inciting with these ornaments?'

In particular the grotesque subject-matter of the Romanesque carver came in for his stinging censure: 'What business has here that ridiculous monstrosity, that misshapen shapeliness and shapely misshapenness? Those unclean monkeys, those fierce lions, those monstrous centaurs, those semi-human beings?' How could monks, he asked, spend their entire days in admiring such baubles rather than on meditating on things divine? 'For God's sake,' he ends, 'even if you do not blush at such follies, at least spare yourselves the expense of them.'

The newly formed Order of Cîteaux was to put poverty back in its place as the condition of sanctity, but, as André Michel said, 'it would be impossible to be poor with such nobility'. Many of those who sought this renunciation of the world were men of noble birth and they brought to their poverty the dignity of self-sacrifice.

Dignity of the same sort may be seen in Cistercian architecture, for, as Marcel Aubert has put it, 'the fear of luxury and the fear of wealth . . . did not stifle in the abbots their sense of beauty, of art, and the grandeur and nobility of austerity. It obliged the builder to seek solutions that were simple and logical, and often it was precisely this which led them to perfection.' The austerity of their buildings was the natural expression of the austerity of their lives.

The renewed insistence on manual labour restored a balance between physical and spiritual exercise which most men need for their stability, and it took its place in the rhythm which formed the light and shade of the devotional life – the rhythm between feast and fast, between Office and sacrament, between prayer and study. It was a way of life that had been stripped down to its essentials. Nothing superfluous to the pursuit of sanctity was allowed to rear its ugly head.

Nothing superfluous to the strict requirements of their buildings was permitted either. Balance, stability, rhythm, light and shade – these were the ingredients of their style. It was an architecture stripped down to its essentials. A Cistercian abbey was the expression in stone of the Cistercian Rule. Here God was worshipped and the self denied; here the sick were cared for and the poor were fed; even the animals came within the all-embracing charity of the Order. It was believed at Cîteaux that the storks would not embark upon the autumn migration until the prior had blessed them and invited them to return.

As with Cluny, the first years of the Cisterian revival offer a picture of religious devotion which is attractive to those who can appreciate it. As with Cluny, the later history is one of progressive deterioration. Corrupted by wealth and exploited by those who coveted their wealth, the great abbeys of the twelfth century became an easy prey to the predators of the French Revolution. Many have disappeared; some survive in ruins; a few, such as Cîteaux itself, have been rebuilt. But Burgundy possesses one Cistercian abbey which is almost complete and largely unspoilt – the Abbaye de Fontenay, in the neighbourhood of Montbard.

The Abbaye de Fontenay

The founding of Cîteaux by Robert de Molesmes in 1098 gave birth to the new Order. Eleven years later Stephen Harding from Sherborne became abbot and was soon joined by St Bernard and some thirty companions. From then on there was no looking back. Pontigny, La Ferté, also in Burgundy, Clairvaux and Morimont were colonized by Cîteaux. Soon Clairvaux was ready to colonize and founded Trois Fontaines in 1115 and Fontenay in 1118. The original site of Fontenay was further up the valley towards Touillon. It was moved to its present position in 1130. It forms a most beautiful group of buildings and offers an object lesson in the dignity of austerity.

There is a point of high ground immediately to the north-west of the abbey building from which the whole lay-out can be overlooked. It is best seen in the grip of winter, when the naked trees imbrown the slopes and leave the claustral buildings bare for our inspection. From this altitude it is possible to appreciate the façades and be conscious also of the ground plan.

To the left is the west end of the church, now denuded of its porch, which probably resembled the one which still exists at Pontigny. Before it stands the capacious drum of the *colombier* or dovecot with its conical roof, like the tower of some provincial château, and, as at any château, proclaiming the feudal rights of *colombage* – for the Cistercians were landowners and only landowners possessed the right to harbour pigeons.

Behind the pigeon house the historical imagination must remove the L-shaped block of the abbot's lodging. This is an eighteenth-century building which obscures the view which would originally have been obtained into the cloister garth. This would have shown one of the features which have been demolished, the lavabo, which projected into the garth from the south walk of the cloisters. It formed an exact square, roofed by four quadripartite vaults. The four vaulting arches met in the middle and were supported by a cylindrical pier. Around this pier two shallow circular basins, such as may be seen today in the grounds of Pontigny, were superimposed with water flowing from the one into the other. Here the monks had to wash both face and hands several times a day and their feet once a week. It is not recorded if their ablutions ever extended further.

Across the cloisters from the lavabo, and also, alas, demolished, the refectory projected southwards for some 196 feet – almost as long as the nave of the church. It was rebuilt thus in the mid thirteenth century when the Cistercians were beginning to allow themselves a little more grandeur in architecture and it must have resembled the beautiful refectory which survives today at Royaumont. The original refectory at Fontenay had been a humbler building, parallel to the south walk of the cloisters with which it shared a wall. It was thus placed between the chauffoir and the kitchens.

These two buildings would have been very easy to identify from our elevated viewpoint by the presence of the only chimneys in the whole lay-out. The chauffoir, which still exists, afforded a place where the monks could warm themselves, prepare their parchments and grease their shoes. The chimneys, together with the little belfry at the north end of the monks' dormitory, provided the only projections from the roofscape of the monastery, which is one of its most attractive features. The brown Burgundian tiles were so perfect in their manufacture and so faultless in their mounting that nearly all which we see today are original.

The buildings of Fontenay are clearly articulated, so that church, chapter house, refectory and scriptorium can each be identified, and to each is given an architecture which is subtly graded according to the status of the component part.

Obviously the church occupied the first rank; in this the art of building was taken to its highest degree. In second place came the chapter house. From here was regulated the life of the community; here the Rule of St Benedict was read each day and here offenders against that rule were punished. It was given an architectural excellence appropriate to its importance. It is a most accomplished piece of quadripartite vaulting. There is, indeed, no obtrusive ornament, but it is not denuded, for just as St Benedict allowed some slight indulgences at the discretion of the abbot, so the stonemason has been permitted a discreet touch of embellishment.

The vault ribs – not one of which has suffered the slightest deformation in over 800 years – are given a simple but elegant moulding. The eight ribs of each compartment are received on an octagonal capital beneath which their lines are continued down to the ground in the eight colonettes which together form the pier.

In line with the chapter house, and across the passageway which connects the cloisters with the garden, the scriptorium offers a slight but significant contrast. Although the architectural scheme is almost identical with that of the chapter house, the treatment is, by comparison, rough-hewn. It is a fine building, but it lacks refinement. The great vaulting arches – flat ribs of stone which hold the skeleton together – are devoid of mouldings; but the transverse arches are allowed a torus moulding of the simplest profile; the ribs spring from stout cylindrical piers which would look rude beside the clustered colonettes of the chapter house.

A third example of the same architectural procedure is in the old forge, which stands to the south of the claustral buildings in order to use the current of the stream to turn its wheels. Here even the torus moulding is suppressed; but the profiles are clean-cut and prismatic, and, as ever, the structure is faultless and conveys a great impression of strength and dignity – the dignity of manual labour which was expressed in the motto 'Laborare est orare', 'To work is to pray'.

In the centre of all these buildings the cloisters formed the unifying link, offering a covered way between one part of the monastery and another, and an area of great peace and beauty.

Cistercian cloisters vary considerably, from the simple, round-arched apertures, like railway tunnels, which pierce the massive walls of Silvacanes, or the equally simple openings of Le Thoronet, each subdivided into twin arches supported by a single pier set deep in their cavernous recesses, to the slender, complex tracery of Noirlac.

The cloisters at Fontenay stand midway between these two extremes. They follow the design of Le Thoronet but without its deep relief; the same twin arches are here, but only lightly recessed behind their retaining arch. These are divided by coupled columns whose slender shafts and delicately sculptured capitals add grace and lightness to the composition. The repetition of this feature, the double arch within the arch, creates the rhythm of the cloisters, but it is saved from monotony by the occasional openings, disposed without regard for symmetry, which give access to the cloister garth.

Repetition, and the rhythm engendered by repetition, is one of the principles of beauty in architecture. It is more in evidence in the Cistercian style than elsewhere because of the absence of ornament which might otherwise distract attention from it. A column in isolation is architecturally meaningless; a colonnade is a thing of beauty. A single arch is just a single arch; an arcade can be a joy for ever. The nave at Fontenay is a combination of arcade and colonnade and upon this the rhythm is built. But exact repetition, like exact symmetry, can become monotony. A subtle note of variety just saves the nave at Fontenay from monotony – it is in the capitals of the half-columns which line the inner arches of the main arcade. They are hardly carved at all, but the slight differences between them are enough. The whole creates a variety of light and shade which gives great spirit, beauty and effect to the perspective of the nave.

Standing at the west end of the church and looking east we must remember that there was always a choir screen in the days of the monastery. The enclosure of the choir was common to all medieval churches and the choir screen was an architectural statement of the great gulf fixed between clergy and laity. In a monastery it was the monks – those who had taken the triple vow of poverty, chastity and obedience – who alone had the right to worship within the choir. The lay brothers, or *conversi*, worshipped in the rest of the nave and lay*men* were permitted to follow the service from the porch. No woman was allowed within the confines of the abbey. When, in 1205, Abbot Jean received Alix de Champagne, queen of France, he was punished for it by the Chapter General.

All the Cistercian churches were dedicated to the Virgin Mary and over the entrance of Cîteaux itself was the inscription: 'Hail, Holy Mother, under whom the Cistercian fights'. When Dante, in his vision of Paradise, reaches the point at which he is vouchsafed a sight of the Virgin, it is no longer Beatrice, but 'her own faithful Bernard' who does the honours. In another vision of Paradise, Cesare of Heisterbach tells of a Cistercian seeking in vain the monks of his own Order among the blessed until he comes at last to the Virgin Mary who, opening her mantle, shows him all his fellow monks and *conversi* safe within her personal protection. St Bernard even believed that he had been granted a drop of her milk to taste, which was of an ineffable sweetness.

There is a particularly charming statue of the Virgin and Child at Fontenay which dates from the late thirteenth century. By this time the art of the medieval sculptor had reached its maturity. It is a portrait done from the life – some young Burgundian mother holding her child on her left hip in a way which dictates the stance known in French as *hanchement*. The folds of her ample drapery are beautifully arranged and beautifully executed.

There are a number of other medieval sculptures in the church and some well-preserved funeral slabs. Particularly interesting is one to Bishop Everard of Norwich. He was a member of the noble house of Arundel who had been forced to abandon his see. He took refuge at Fontenay and in 1139 he became the abbot and used his personal wealth to finance the building of the church, which was consecrated in 1147. It is thus contemporary with Sens Cathedral, which was started in 1130.

The Abbaye de Pontigny

Another Cistercian abbey in Burgundy has even closer links with the English episcopate – Pontigny, in the neighbourhood of Chablis.

Three archbishops of Canterbury took refuge at Pontigny. The first was Thomas à Becket in 1164. Two years later he moved to Sens when Henry II threatened reprisals against the English Cistercians. The second was Stephen Langton who began a six-year exile here in 1208. He had been to Rome to receive his cardinal's hat and learnt there of his promotion to Canterbury. King John refused to ratify his appointment and Stephen did not deem it prudent to cross the Channel. In 1215 he was to be the chief architect of Magna Carta and helped to bring about a reconciliation between the Crown and the papacy.

The third was Edmund of Abingdon, an academic who was promoted from treasurer of Salisbury Cathedral to archbishop of Canterbury. Assailed by the king on one side and by the monks of his own monastery on the other, he decided to consult the Pope and set out for Rome. On the way back he stayed for a respite at Pontigny, but was taken ill near Provins and died on 16 November 1240. In accordance with his last wishes he was buried at Pontigny and six years later he was canonized. His tomb became the focus for pilgrimages which retained their popularity right up to the French Revolution and even helped to secure the survival of the abbey church at this perilous time. Most of the claustral buildings were destroyed. Pontigny is visited today only on account of its church.

The exterior of Pontigny 'says' very little. It has a simplicity which is not far removed from dullness and a rhythm which is merely monotony. Seen from the outside it is not very attractive, just as the monastic life, seen from the outside, does not appeal to the average spectator. But once inside we feel the full impact of the Cistercian style – a sense of peace and liberation which no doubt was felt also by those who found their vocation fulfilled within the monastic community.

The building follows the Cistercian pattern of a long nave and a short choir, the point of transition being marked by low transepts. The original east end was square, as at Fontenay, but in about 1185 it was rebuilt in the newly developed Gothic style with an apse, an ambulatory and eleven radiating chapels. The construction of these chapels was connected with the fact that by the mid twelfth century at least half of the monks at Pontigny were in priests' Orders; the provision of altars at which they could say the Mass became a necessity. There were at this time about 100 monks and about 300 lay brothers. As the latter were not allowed to worship in the choir, their numbers required a long nave.

Inside, Pontigny offers a combination, not uncommon in Burgundy, of Romanesque construction and pointed arches. This is best illustrated in the side aisles, which have retained their groined vaulting. The nave has a quadripartite vault which appears to have been an afterthought, if not a reconstruction. The evidence for this may be seen at the spring of the arches, where the capital of the tall half-column supports the vaulting arch. It will be noticed that to either side of it two more capitals have been rather awkwardly inserted to receive the transverse ribs. These capitals do not relate to any columns, but merely to a corner of the masonry. In the last bay to be built – the first from the west – this awkwardness has been rectified and the oblique capitals are properly provided with columns of their own. The builders were learning as they went along.

The new choir dates from about 1185. It is a most accomplished piece of Gothic architecture, the creation of a master-builder who knew exactly what he wanted to do and exactly how to set about it.

The whole church looks as if it had just been built; it has a clean-cut purity of style which is greatly enhanced by the pale cream colour of the stone. Its beautiful simplicity conveys a sense of harmony and peace which was the Cistercian ideal. It was not to last. The later history of the abbey follows the same pattern as Cluny.

With the coming of François I, the great days of monasticism were brought to an end. On 15 August 1516, Pope Leo X signed a concordat which granted the king the right to appoint to all high offices in the Church. The revenues of the great abbeys were used to enrich the civil servants and architects of the king. The buildings became richer and the spiritual life became poorer. Unlike Fontenay, which retained its original appearance, Pontigny continued to receive embellishment, first in a complete set of seventeenth-century stalls and secondly by the addition of a magnificent organ loft over the west doors.

The choir stalls, of mid seventeenth century date, were put in by the Abbot Jacques de la Varende. It is clear that the original stalls extended much further towards the west, for the half-columns on the nave arcade end in corbels about 10 feet off the ground. This normally indicates the positioning of stall canopies against the pier. The old stalls were destroyed in 1568 when the Huguenots sacked the abbey. The new stalls were made only to contain 100 monks – a generous, allowance, however, for an age in which vocations were rare.

The whole ensemble of choir screen, stalls and canopies is a masterpiece of the wood carver of a quality which would not have looked out of place at Fontainebleau. The artist has achieved a pleasing balance between the plain panels and the richly ornamented frames and entablature. It is superb, but it is totally at variance with the Cistercian ideal of austerity. One cannot help wondering what St Bernard would have said if he could have seen this voluptuous decoration of the monks' choir, and especially the posturing females, who are most certainly not angels, and who stand like caryatids beside the stalls of the four principal officers of the monastery. The only false note in the whole décor is the lack of proportion between these ladies and the rather larger naked boys playing trumpets in the tympanum above the doorway.

The organ loft, as its style announces, dates from the early eighteenth century, magnificent in its conception and exquisite in its workmanship. This is the more surprising since it was carved by the abbot himself, Joseph Caron. That it was intended from the first to support an organ is proved by the delicate fluting of the pilasters, each of which contains a miniature organ pipe. The present organ was brought here at a somewhat later date from Chalons-sur-Marne.

It is clear from these sumptuous furnishings that the original austerity of the Cistercian Order had been profoundly modified. Donations were continually offered and invariably accepted. These gifts were often in the form of vineyards, such as those of the Clos de Vougeot, offered by landowners 'pour le remède de leurs âmes et celles de leurs prédécesseurs'. At Pontigny there had been a notable example.

In April 1482, Louis XI made a donation to the abbey in the form of a vineyard named Talen, near Dijon. It was not, of course, a disinterested gift. In return for it the monks were to pray 'pour la bonne disposition de notre estomac, que vin et autres viandes ne nous puissent nuire'. Whether this spiritual eupeptic precaution proved effective history does not relate.

It was the monks of Pontigny who introduced the Chardonnay grape to the vineyards of Chablis, and Fontenay has given its name to one of the *grands crus* which is still made today.

The Cistercians, in fact, probably did more than any other people to give to Burgundy the viticulture for which it is famous. 'The extent of monasticism's contribution to wine growing and distilling', writes Desmond Seward, 'is rarely appreciated. Monks largely saved viticulture when the barbarian invasions destroyed the Roman Empire and throughout the Dark Ages they alone had the security and the resources to improve the quality of their wines slowly and patiently.' Continuity of ownership and continuity of memory were the essential conditions. By the end of the Middle Ages the abbey of Cîteaux was producing some of the best wine in the world.

Cîteaux and Clos de Vougeot

I call upon you, and by the virtue of the Holy Cross, armed with the shield of faith, I order and adjure you a first, a second and a third time, all the insects commonly known as *écrivains* and *uribères* and all other worms harmful to the fruit of the vine, that they do cease forthwith from ravaging, nibbling and destroying the branches, buds and fruit; that they shall not have this power in future, that they are to retire to the uttermost confines of the forest where they can no longer harm the vines of faithful people, and that they are to leave the district. And if, by the counsel of Satan, they do not obey this charge and continue their ravages, in the name of God and of the Holy Church, I curse them and pronounce the sentence of malediction and anathema upon them.

So runs an edict sent in 1553 to all clergy of the diocese by their vicar general, Philippe de Berbis. That he should so have acted gives a penetrating insight into the pretensions of the Church and into its attitude towards wine.

It was only natural that a monastery should require a vineyard: it needed wine with which to celebrate the Mass. St Benedict also had made provision for a reasonable ration of wine in the daily menu of the monks. In the first collection of the statutes of the Order at Cîteaux, the Chanoine Marilier assures us, the fifth article permitted the possession of 'lands, meadows, forests and vineyards'. They must therefore have produced wine. That the monks drank it may be inferred from the ruling that any brother who committed the heinous offence of speaking at table should be deprived of his wine.

On Christmas Day, 1098, nine months after the community arrived at Cîteaux, the monks received from the duke of Burgundy a vineyard near the Château de Meursault. A few years later, Gaudri de Chambolle presented the abbey with another vineyard, contiguous with this towards the north, and Hugues le Blanc de Vergy another which joined it in the south. These donations were followed by others at Aloxe, at Corton and les Petits-Musigny. By the middle of the twelfth century some of the great names of the Côte d'Or were already in the hands of the Cistercians and the extensive vineyard of Clos de Vougeot had been established. In 1164 a papal bull, issued by Alexander III, placed the abbey of Cîteaux and its vineyard – *cellarium de Vooget cum appenditis suis* – under the protection of the Holy See.

The group of buildings which go to make up the Clos de Vougeot are among the most attractive and interesting examples of architecture in Burgundy. Both the *cuverie* – a cloister in which the pressing and vinification took place – and the cellar belong to the twelfth and thirteenth centuries. They are severely but beautifully functional. The château, in which the abbot entertained his more important guests, dates from the Renaissance and is a fine example of its style.

Pierre Poupon, who, being both a viticulturalist and a historian, is well qualified to speak on the subject, has sung the praise of the functional buildings.

The ingenuity of the monks who built it is never more clearly shown than in the construction of these two utilitarian buildings. No modern architect, even if not restricted by the site or by the cost of the materials, would manage to achieve the simplicity of the solutions arrived at by the monks to the technical problems of the transport, the storing and the vinification. The most important transport is that of the grapes and of the casks, empty or full. The *cuverie* and the cellar are therefore level with the ground. Vehicles could enter freely into the *cuverie* and leave it, either by the little interior court, or by using one of the galleries, without having to reverse or even make a half-turn. The barrels could be rolled from the *cuverie* to the cellar without any change of level necessitating any considerable man-power. Storage was on the same level and the journeys were reduced to a minimum since only a few metres separate the entrance to the *cuverie* from the door of the cellar. And this cellar possesses none the less all the virtues of an underground *cave*, that is to say a place suited to the conservation of wine, because the isolation and the air conditioning, which are indispensable, are achieved thanks to the thickness of the wall, to the double entrance gates, to the roof which comes down almost to the ground, and to the ceiling insulated with a thick layer of earth . . . We would say today that the vinicultural buildings of the Clos de Vougeot were constructed according to the most rational method in order to obtain the best technical results possible. Everything has been thought of, with regard not only to the ends to be achieved but to the area of the vineyard concerned and the men who were to work there.

Nothing could be more impressive than the enormous presses situated in the corners of the *cuverie*. It would be perfectly possible to make wine here today.

In 1551 Jean Loisier, forty-eighth abbot of Cîteaux, pulled down some of the medieval buildings to make room for his château – or rather his *maison de plaisance*. It was designed by one of the monks and Dom Loisier detected in his attitude to his own design the sin of pride. He therefore had the plans altered by another and obliged the former architect to carry out the instructions of the latter. As the original drawings have not survived it is impossible to judge whether the château gained or lost aesthetically by this essentially punitive approach.

It would not have required any very great architectural skill to have produced such a design. Most of it is in a typical Burgundian vernacular – square towers with low pyramidal roofs; walls of rough masonry inset with mullion and transom windows framed in the finer freestone from the local quarries of Comblanchien; tall French roofs clad in brown Burgundian tiles and pierced by large dormers decorated with rather meagre pediments; all together constitute a building which has much charm but no great distinction. On to these somewhat bucolic façades are attached four porches of a sophisticated Renaissance design which frame the various entrance arches.

No doubt the details, giving the correct proportions of the classical orders, could have been obtained from one of the books of the period. They were adapted with the most complete indifference to the height of the spring of the enclosed arch. The most accomplished achievement is the main entrance to the state rooms. Coupled pilasters mounted on a high podium, and framing between them superimposed niches with scallop-shell hoods, support a carefully correct entablature over the entrance archway. The feature is almost identical with the main entrance to the Château de Lux, north-east of Dijon in the neighbourhood of Fontaine-Française. The version of the design at Lux is slightly more 'advanced' than that of Clos de Vougeot. Either the one copied and improved upon the other, or both made their own interpretation of the same model in the same *livre d'architecture*.

The Grande Salle d'Honneur on the first floor is a magnificent room with a fine fireplace. The architecture of this dates from the reign of Henri II, but in the overmantel, framed between coupled Corinthian columns, is the proud blazon of Andoche Pernot d'Ecrots, abbot of Cîteaux in 1728.

For centuries Clos Vougeot (so spelt when it means the wine) was considered the finest of all burgundies. In 1371 thirty hogsheads (some 228 litres or 50 gallons) of it were sent to Rome to celebrate the election of Pope Gregory XI. Three years later the abbot who sent the gift was made a cardinal. A modern connoisseur, George Saintsbury, was cautious in his praise. 'Clos-Vougeot,' he wrote, 'excellent as it is, seems to me often, if not always, to have the excellencies of claret rather than those of burgundy; it does not "hold to the blood of its clan" quite firmly enough.'

It was not long before the dukes of Burgundy realized that the produce of their vineyards was one of their chief assets. In 1395, Auguste Luchet records, Philippe le Hardi issued an *ordonnance* on the subject. This area, he claimed had of old produced

the best and most precious wines in the kingdom of France and the most befitting for the nourishment and sustenance of the human race ... Nevertheless, since not long ago, some of our subjects in these said places and lands, covetous to have a large quantity of wine, have craftily planted among the good vines a very bad and disloyal plant named *gaamez* [gamay], from which bad plant comes great abundance of wine ... and the said wine from the gamay is of such a nature that it is most harmful to human beings and many, even, who in times past have made use of it have been infected with grievous diseases, as we have heard, because the said wine is full of a great and horrible bitterness and becomes noisesome.

All who possessed gamay stocks were solemnly warned to cut them out within the month. In 1459 Philippe le Hardi confirmed this statute, saying: 'Les ducs de Bourgogne ont toujours été réputés seigneurs des meilleurs vins de la Chrétienté.' It was largely owing to the monks that they were able to make such a claim.

Bibliography

D. Grivot: *Art Roman en Bourgogne*, 1986.
E. Mâle: *L'Art Religieux du 12e Siècle*, 1922.
V. Markham: *Romanesque France*, 1929.
C. Oursel: *L'Art Roman de Bourgogne*, 1928.
J. Virey: 'Les Edifices Religieux de l'Epoque Romane en Saône-et-Loire', in *Congrès Archéologique de France*, 66, Macon, 1899.

Saint-Bénigne de Dijon
M. Aubert: 'L'Eglise de Saint-Bénigne', in *Congrès Archéologique de France*, 91, Dijon, 1928.

Saint-Philibert de Tournus
J. Virey: *Saint-Philibert de Tournus*, 1932.
R. Poinard: *Tournus: l'Abbaye Saint-Philibert*, s.d.

Saint-Martin de Chapaize
D. Ruset: *L'Eglise de Chapaize*, 1985.

Cluny
K. Conant: *Cluny*, 1939.
J. Evans: *Monastic Life at Cluny: 910–1157*, 1938.
J. Evans: *The Romanesque Architecture of the Order of Cluny*, 1938.
P. Lorain: *Essai Historique sur l'Abbaye de Cluny*, 1859.
B. Marguery-Melin: *La Destruction de l'Abbaye de Cluny*, 1910.
Symposium: *Millennaire de Cluny*, 1910.
R. Lloyd: *Abelard: The Orthodox Rebel*, 1947.

Berzé-la-Ville
L. Lex and J. Virey: *La Chapelle du Château des Moines à Berzé-la-Ville*, 1951.

Brancion
M. Rébouillat: *Brancion*, 1981.
J.-L. Bazin: *Brancion: Les Seigneurs, la Paroisse, la Ville*, 1908.

Vézelay
A. Cherest: *Vézelay: Etude Historique*, 1863.

P. Mérimée: *Notes d'un voyage dans le Midi de la France*, 1835.
C. Porée: *L'Abbaye de Vézelay*, 1930.
P. Trahard: *Oeuvres Complètes de Mérimée: Lettres à Viollet-le-Duc*, 1927.

Churches in Brionnais

J. Virey: *Paray-le-Monial et les Eglises du Brionnais*, 1926.
D. Grivot: *Semur-en-Brionnais. Ingrande*, s.d.
D. Grivot: *Anzy-le-Duc. Montceaux-l'Etoile*, s.d.

The Cistercians

M. Aubert and Marquise de Maillé: *L'Architecture Cistercienne en France*, 1947.
Dom M. Lebeau: *Receuil de Textes relatifs à l'Abbaye de Cîteaux*, 1979.

Fontenay

M. Aubert: 'Fontenay', in *Congrès Archéologique de France*, 91, Dijon, 1929.
L. Bégule: *L'Abbaye de Fontenay*, 1984.

Pontigny

Baron Chaillou des Barres: *L'Abbaye de Pontigny*, 1844.
M. Aubert: 'Abbaye de Pontigny', in *Congrès Archéologique de France*, 126, Auxerre, 1958.

Clos de Vougeot

J.-F. Bazin: *Le Clos de Vougeot*, 1984.
C. Rodier: *Le Clos de Vougeot*, 1949.

BURGUNDIAN GOTHIC

The turn of the millennium saw a significant change in the government of Burgundy. Under the Carolingians it had been administered as an apanage to the kings of France by men with the title of duke appointed by the Crown. These dukes, however, did not enjoy sovereign status, nor did they found dynasties. They are known to historians as 'ducs bénéficiaires'. The last of these, Henri le Vénérable, 'homme de bonnes moeurs et plein de douceur', died on 15 October 1002. His son-in-law, Otte Guillaume, attempted to obtain control of the duchy but was defeated by Robert the Pious, king of France.

Robert the Pious made his elder son Henri duke of Burgundy but in practice administered the province himself. On the death of Robert in 1031, Henri became king, the first of that name, and after some hostilities made over the dukedom of Burgundy to his brother Robert. Thus was established the Capetian line of dukes which was to continue until the death of Philippe de Rouvres on 21 November 1361. He was only sixteen when he died; he left no heir and named no successor in his will. Jean II le Bon, who had married Jeanne de Bourgogne, assumed possession of the duchy, but on 1 September 1363 he nominated his third son Philippe as duke of Burgundy in his own right. A new and glorious dynasty, that of the Valois, was to provide Burgundy with its 'four great dukes'. Between them the Capetian and the Valois dukes spanned the Middle Ages.

Robert the Pious issued a manifesto when he took over Burgundy which reflects, reading between the lines, the problems of those troubled times.

Christians, listen to the Covenant of Peace. I undertake not to violate asylum except against malefactors who infringe the present peace. I will not attack clerics or monks or those who accompany them not bearing arms; I will not seize either bulls or cows, pigs or sheep, lambs or goats, donkeys of either sex nor the burdens with which they are laden; it will be the same with birds, with cocks and hens, but only if I have need of hawks and for them I will pay two *deniers* . . . I will not burn or destroy harvests, unless I find my enemy mounted and armed upon them. I will not cut down or tear up vines. I will only make wine from those which I possess . . . I will not destroy mills nor appropriate their produce except in times of war. I will have no thieves in my service and I will not encourage brigandage.

Brigandage needed no encouragement. It was rampant all over the feudal world. It was the direct cause of all proliferation of castles and fortified towns which form the most conspicuous examples of civil architecture of the period.

'The lives of the great and the lives of the lowly were alike centred on the fortress; the latter looked to it for refuge while the former found in it their means of domination', wrote Jean Richard, 'and the policies of princes were bent on obtaining the obedience of the masters of châteaux and depended upon the possession of a large number of fortresses.'

Fortresses, or *places fortes*, could be of three different sorts: the fortified town, the castle and the fortified farm. The Latin word *castrum* can cover all three, and as most of the texts are in Latin, confusion can often result. The first two can designate a place of refuge: sometimes, as at Autun, an inner sanctuary within a city wall; sometimes, as at the smaller Semur-en-Auxois, the whole of the town; sometimes, as in innumerable châteaux, an outer *enceinte* which offered, in times of emergency, a retreat to those in feudal obligation to the château. The fortified farm was merely self-protective.

Burgundy was particularly well supplied with fortresses. Its geological structure provides it with steep slopes and rocky outcrops which often form a natural redoubt. In the early centuries of the Christian era these fortresses may have offered no security other than that afforded by the inaccessibility of the site. The name Semur derives directly from the Latin *sine muros*, 'without walls'. Castrum Sinemurus is its oldest recorded name, but it was not long to remain so called.

Semur-en-Auxois

Perched upon a rocky escarpment and guarding the important road from Auxerre to Dijon, Semur is indeed a site fortified by nature. A long loop of the river Armançon encloses a peninsula which is almost an island. The narrow neck which unites this with the 'mainland' was the most obvious point at which to strengthen the natural defences and it is here that the massive donjon is situated.

It was probably built in the early 1170s when the Duke Hugues III undertook a general improvement of its defensive system. In plan it is roughly rectangular with large towers at each corner. The largest of these, the north-east tower, known as the Tour Lourdeault or Tour de l'Ourle d'Or, stood astride the road from Auxerre to Dijon. The south-east tower was the Tour du Prison, and its use is confirmed by the proximity of a projecting angle of the south wall which contained the Chapelle Saint-Marguerite; this was affected to the use of prisoners. No doubt the chapel connects with the name of the south-west tower, the Tour Margot. The remaining tower, on the north-west corner, was sometimes called the Tour Pordeault, but its more usual name proclaims only too blatantly its real function – the Tour de la Gehenne. *Gehenner* in medieval French meant to torture.

As they stand today, the towers would not have been very effective from a military point of view. The lower parts are of solid masonry, offering no opportunity to the defenders to fire upon their assailants, and the somewhat rare arrow slits of the upper storeys do not provide enough embrasure for the bowmen to cover the base of the tower. It is convincingly argued by the vicomte de Truchis that their only function was to admit a modicum of light and air to the chambers within. There were no machicolations and no battlements, neither on the towers nor on the curtain walls. This confirms the dating of the donjon towards the end of the twelfth century, for at that time it was still the practice, in times of war, to erect *hourds* or hoardings – that is to say, wooden walkways built out from the wall, or round the top storey of a tower, to provide opportunities for dropping projectiles on those immediately below or for shooting arrows at those who were approaching the base of the wall. Viollet-le-Duc notes the construction of stone consoles at Coucy in the early thirteenth century to provide a permanent support to these temporary structures, and dates the earliest proper machicolations towards the end of that century.

The Tour Lourdeault confronts the visitor across the bridge; it is still marked with the great fissure resulting from the siege of Semur during the wars of the League. The old road passed through a tunnel contrived within the base of the tower. In the event of an attack the floor of the guardroom immediately above the tunnel could be lowered into it, providing a platform from which archers could shoot at the intruders. A stone staircase afforded communication between the guardroom and the interior of the donjon. On the inward side of the upper storeys, where the weakening of the structure would not be dangerous, a further stairway was inserted within the thickness of the wall, leading up to the top floor where seven openings gave access to the *hourds*.

To the west of the donjon, starting from the Tour Lourdeault and following the contour of the escarpment, the curtain wall with its eighteen towers – 'tours de grosseur et épaisseur prèsqu'incroyables', wrote Sebastien Munster in the fifteenth century, 'et remparts solides et inaccessibles' – enclosed the area known as the *castrum* or château. To the east a further defensive unit of about the same size, was encircled by walls set about with sixteen towers. This was known as the 'bourg'.

There is a tradition that the bourg was originally peopled by refugees from Alésia, the stronghold of Vercingetorix, after its capture by Julius Caesar. There was a strong sense, in those days, of the duty of hospitality and it was enshrined in the *Lex Burgundionum*: 'Whoever shall refuse his roof and his hearth to the stranger who arrives unexpectedly,' it ran, 'shall pay a fine of three golden *sous*.' It was in the expectation of such hospitality, writes Louis Bocquin, that the Aliziens sought refuge at Semur.

Whatever its origins, the duality created by the division of the town into the bourg and the château led to endless ecclesiastical hostilities, for each of them contained a church.

The first church in the bourg was probably one of the ten pious foundations of Gérard de Roussillon, duke of Burgundy, around the year 830. It was replaced some 200 years later by a new church dedicated to the Virgin by Robert le Vieux, first duke of Burgundy of the Capetian dynasty. He was ordered to found it by the Pope in expiation of the murder of his father-in-law, Dalmace, who was lord of the other Semur, Semur-en-Brionnais.

The church within the château was that of the priory of Saint-Maurice, which Eudes III, duke of Burgundy, regarded as his property along with the château. They formed together part of the dowry which he gave to his wife, Mahaut of Portugal. When she separated from him he gave the château to the priory, which thus exercised the rights of justice – *haute, moyenne et basse*. This conferred upon them considerable prestige.

Both churches, therefore, had strongly ducal connections; both claimed the right to be the parish church. Notre-Dame was supported by the abbey of Flavigny, Saint-Maurice by that of Agaune, of which it was a priory.

A rather typically medieval story is recounted by Bocquin which lay behind the ultimate triumph of Notre-Dame. A citizen of Semur named Girard-le-Riche had been on a pilgrimage to the Holy Land and came back the proud possessor of what he believed to be the Virgin's wedding ring. The fact that he survived the many dangers of the return journey was sufficient confirmation of the authenticity of the relic. Being an inhabitant of the château, he intended to present it to his own church of Saint-Maurice. At the moment of his arrival, however, the bells of Notre-Dame began to ring *à toute vollée* without the aid of any human bellringers and when he placed the ring upon the altar of Saint-Maurice it jumped back into his mouth, its customary place of security. This he interpreted as a sign from the Virgin that she wished her ring to be given to the church which was dedicated to herself. He duly transferred his allegiance.

The possession of the ring greatly enhanced the prestige of the church of Notre-Dame. Unfortunately, however, it was by no means the only church to claim such ownership and in the end Pope Innocent III pronounced that the authentic relic was in Perugia.

In 1225, during the reign of Hugues IV, the church of Notre-Dame was completely rebuilt. Semur was one of his most important fortresses and it was customary for rulers to mark their authority in a place by the erection of a prestigious church. Most of the great Gothic cathedrals in the north of France were affirmations of the ruling presence of the house of Capet.

The new Notre-Dame is one of the finest Gothic churches in Burgundy and has the added advantage of offering almost a history of that style in its successive additions. It was built from east to west, so that the apsidal chapel is the earliest part, and the last three bays of the nave, together with the west front and porch, dating from the early fourteenth century, the latest. The apse itself, finished, according to Viollet-le-Duc, in 1235, is a magnificent example of the Gothic architect's passion for height and *élancement*. It is nearly 98 feet high, which is unusual for a church of this size, but the effect is further enhanced by the narrowness of the nave – 20½ feet – and by the proportions of the three storeys, for the clerestory windows occupy half the total façade.

The sanctuary is set between double side aisles, making a vast vaulted area which gives Notre-Dame the appearance, almost, of a small cathedral. This area was completed by 1250.

Viollet-le-Duc, who restored the building in 1844, draws particular attention to the keystone of the apse vault – 'une des plus belles clefs à sujets'. It is a circular plaque nearly 1 metre across, with a most delicate depiction of the Coronation of the Virgin. Embowered in a circlet of cinquefoil leaves, the figures of Christ and his mother are seated on a bench; an angel descends from above and offers the royal crown at which the Virgin, with a gesture of her left hand, appears to demur. Her whole pose gives a delightful impression of modesty and humility. Two other angels, emerging from the foliage, create a sense of liturgical occasion with their long candles. The tradition of the Virgin's coronation by an angel was first represented in the Porte Rouge of Notre-Dame-de-Paris.

Dating from the late thirteenth century also is the Porte des Bleds (meaning *blé*, 'corn') which gives access to the north transept. It has an admirable tympanum with one of those condensed histories which form a sort of strip cartoon in sculpture. The story reads from the top left but continues from right to left in the lower register. Early historians saw in this the story of Duke Robert murdering his father-in-law, Dalmace, but Emile Mâle is to be preferred in identifying here the legend of St Thomas. The story had been condemned by St Augustine as untrue, but it caught the popular imagination and appears not only here but at the cathedral of Poitiers and in the glass at Chartres, Bourges and Tours.

It starts with Thomas identifying himself by thrusting his hand into the wound in Jesus' side. He is approached by an emissary from Gondoforus, King of India and invited to build him a palace: he crosses the sea to India. The first scene of the lower register depicts a banquet with a tumbler walking on her hands in front of the table; beside her, a dog brings in the hand of the steward who has just been eaten by a lion as a punishment for striking Thomas; the king gives his orders and pays for the building of his palace, but Thomas distributes the money among the poor; Thomas condemned to be flayed alive, is awaiting his execution in the prison, but convinces Gondoforus that, if he will only believe and be baptized, a finer palace will await him in Paradise.

It is difficult to believe that the spectators were expected to infer all this from their reading of the sculpture. We must imagine that groups of pilgrims were treated by some narrator to the full story from the Golden Legend with the tympanum in front of them to provide a visual aid. If their eyes had wandered to the inner column to the left of the doorway, they would have been delighted to see two Burgundian *escargots* climbing up its shaft.

In 1370 considerable repairs were undertaken to the nave and transepts. The vicomte de Truchis, in his examination of the fabric, found traces of a fire which might have necessitated this. It is by no means improbable that the church suffered during the ravages of the English army under Edward III after the battle of Poitiers.

Edward made himself master of Champagne, but failed to make an entry into Reims where he wanted to have himself crowned king of France. Moving south into Burgundy he took the town of Tonnerre, where his soldiers consumed 'six thousand barrels of wine'. He spared Noyers (pronounced *Noyères*), for the lord of Noyers was already his prisoner, but seized Montréal and later Flavigny. These three towns were typical of the fortified sites which played so important a part in the history of those troubled times.

The English found Flavigny so well provisioned that they continued here for six weeks, amusing themselves with hunting, fishing and falconry, 'car le Roi et les Princes anglais avaient force chiens et faucons'.

Flavigny, Montréal and Noyers

'I owe to the Valley of Flavigny', wrote Chateaubriand, 'one of my most vivid and moving memories. It has the appearance of the Valley of Jerusalem. These ancient fortifications, do they not themselves recall the devastated ramparts of the Temple? And these clusters of trees with their luxuriant foliage, are they not the ascetic shades of the Mount of Olives?'

Chateaubriand, with his over-romantic imagination, saw what he wanted to see. Flavigny does not depend on its tenuous resemblance to Jerusalem for its claim to be a holy city. In the year 755 the Abbaye de Saint-Pierre was founded by the Abbé Manassès with the help of Charlemagne. In 864 the relics of St Reine, a young martyr whose real offence was her refusal to marry the Roman governor

Olibrius, were transported here from Alésia, and the monastery flourished. On 28 October 878, it was honoured by a visit of Pope John VIII, who consecrated the altars. It numbered Alcuin among its abbots. But in 1231 it suffered severely from the effects of a fire from which it never really recovered. In the seventeenth century a community of Ursulines was installed in the former Hôtel Couthier de Souhey, to be replaced in the twentieth century first by the Petit Séminaire de Saint-Bernard and later by the monks of Saint-Joseph de Clairval. In the nineteenth century there was a religious revival and in 1848 Lacordaire re-established the Dominican Order here. Their buildings are now occupied by the Petites Soeurs de Saint-François d'Assise. For most of its history Flavigny has enjoyed a strong religious tradition.

But the religious and the secular were never very far apart in the Middle Ages and the abbey was involved in the ceaseless struggle for power between the bishop of Autun and the duke of Burgundy. It was the Abbot Renaud, in 1149, who built the fortifications of Flavigny. Enough of these defences remain today to give the visitor some idea of a Burgundian *place forte*.

The Porte du Bourg, which bars the road from Semur, is a fine example of a fifteenth-century gatehouse. Its design is based on the triple slots for the two drawbridges – from which may be inferred the existence of a dry moat. The machicolations are disposed so as to flank these slots and are diversely spaced accordingly. This gives a pleasing rhythm to what is often a mere monotony. Over the archway a niche, topped with a typically Burgundian arch, the cupid's bow moulding known as *en accolade*, contains an image of the Virgin.

From the west the city could be entered only from the Porte du Val. There are two distant elements to this: an interior gatehouse, dating from the thirteenth century, and another set in advance of it dating from the time of the Wars of Religion. The architecture here is very different from that of the Porte du Bourg, for it is an architecture adapted to small-arms fire. On the towers and parapet the *meutrières*, instead of offering a slit for the archer, provide a round hole for the gunman. The parapet is supported on consoles which are not true machicolations, for there are no downward openings. Each console is complemented by a corresponding projection above the parapet. From the inside these can be seen to be the divisions between five compartments from each of which a soldier could aim his arquebus at the assailant.

The Porte du Val attracted the attention of Viollet-le-Duc, who included drawings of it in his *Dictionnaire*. 'Although very simple,' he wrote, 'this gatehouse is a beautiful example of a military construction at the moment when architects were concerning themselves with the use of fire-arms.'

Viollet-le-Duc was at Flavigny in 1844, when Prosper Mérimée commissioned some repairs. He was back again the following year and wrote: 'The little town of Flavigny is still preserved today more or less as it was in the fifteenth century. Besides its very curious church, for the restoration of which the Minister of the Interior has designated certain funds, this town possesses a large number of houses of the twelfth, thirteenth, fourteenth and fifteenth centuries and two gatehouses passably well preserved.'

Entering Flavigny by the Porte du Val, the visitor has on the left the vast ensemble of the Maison Lacordaire. It dates from the thirteenth century, when it provided the lodgings of the grand bailli de l'Auxois. It was here that the parlement de Bourgogne sat during the Wars of Religion when Bénigne Fremyot took his loyalist government out of Dijon, which was in the hands of the ultra-Catholic League. In 1848 the building became the 'belle, pieuse et chère demeure' of Henri-Dominique Lacordaire. There still stands in the gardens of the convent a charming eighteenth-century pavilion in which he loved to sit and meditate.

To penetrate further into the town is to take a journey back into the past, for Flavigny has been largely spared the fate of modernization. Along its narrow, twisting streets, in none of which would a herd of cows look out of place, the walls of the houses are pierced with Gothic windows or doorways surmounted *en accolade*; staircase towers, some round and some polygonal, project from the façades, some rising from the ground, some built out on corbels; niches containing madonnas or *pietàs* are hollowed out of the stones.

In the rue du Four is a fine thirteenth-century house – a rare and remarkable example of Burgundian architecture in the days of St Louis. In the rue de l'Eglise is the so-called Maison Louis XII, with its large first-floor windows capped *à double accolade* and set to either side of a niche over which the accolade is carried up into an ornate finial forming an ogee. From within its sculptured recess a Virgin and Child look down upon the passers-by. A little higher up the street the visitor comes in sight of the parish church.

Seen from the outside, the church of Saint-Genès is not a very impressive building. Although it is basically a thirteenth-century structure, it has lost its shape. The west front dates from the eighteenth century and is insignificant; the north and south façades have been disfigured by different chapels added at different times; the apse offers a pleasing but not really distinguished example of fifteenth-century Gothic. And yet this was one of the very first churches to be classified as a *Monument Historique* in 1838, the year after the setting-up of the Commission. It attracted the early attention of Viollet-le-Duc who left some of his beautiful drawings of the church and of its more distinctive features. He described it as we have seen, as 'very curious'.

It is only on entering the church that one begins to see why. It is at once apparent that this is a most unusual building. As Charles Oursel puts it, 'it is really without either ancestors or children'. The first two bays of the nave at the west end are only one storey high. This is because there is an entire upper storey with galleries over the aisles. These were needed for any overflow of congregation, such as occurred regularly on the Monday after Pentecost when there was a combined service for the seventy-five churches of the four arch-deaconries which depended on Flavigny. In the last bay before the crossing is a high vaulted gallery – a tribune carried like a bridge across the nave, with a beautiful Flamboyant balustrade and a projecting ambo from which the gospel could be read. This, like the vaults, was built as the result of a campaign of reconstruction undertaken in the fifteenth century.

Beyond the crossing the choir is panelled to the height of the base of the windows with stalls to either side which are enriched with some fine provincial carvings. Many of the figures have been mutilated, but at the far end, on the north side, is an amusing little figure of a man reading a book and holding his nose. Like so much of this sort of carving in Burgundy, it dates from just before the Renaissance.

But the greatest treasure of Flavigny is in the Chapelle Saint-Martin, the easternmost chapel of the south nave aisle. It is a figure of the Angel of the Annunciation, which was found, in 1933, beneath one of the stone flags. One cannot but admire the artist's treatment of the subject – the angel charged to deliver the most momentous message in the world's history. Only a child could have been entrusted with such a message, because only a child would have had the simplicity required; so the angel is represented as a child –

whether a boy or a girl one cannot say, but it does not matter, since angels are sexless. But the robe is ecclesiastical and the figure suggests a little boy, looking pleased but somewhat overawed, when serving for the first time at the altar of a cathedral and who is too small for the capacious alb in which he has been enveloped.

It is not known where the Annunciation group was originally sited, nor what has become of the figure of the Virgin, but there is an excellent wooden statue of her, attributed to the workshop of Claus Sluter, in the westernmost chapel on the south side – the Chapelle des Sept Douleurs. If one could get back behind the destructions of the Revolution, the vandalism of the Reformation and the devastations of time, it seems that these little country churches must have been treasure houses of works of art which any modern museum would be proud to possess. Both in its statues and in its stalls, Saint-Genès de Flavigny is worth a considerable detour to visit.

Another church which is richly endowed in the same way and set within the context of a Burgundian *place forte* is Notre-Dame de Montréal, north-east of Avallon and on the road to Châtillon. The stalls here if anything surpass those of Flavigny. There has been a collegiate church at Montréal since 1068, but the present building dates from the late twelfth century. There was a foundation for a provost and ten canons. Provosts and canons require stalls, but the existing stalls date only from 1522. They are attributed by Courtépée to the brothers Rigolley.

Although in many ways still Gothic in conception, they already show the influence of the Renaissance. The panels are framed between pilasters decorated with arabesques and each has a canopy in the form of a scallop shell. But the figures are in the same spirit as those of Flavigny – holiness expressed as homeliness; religion made contemporary by the simple device of presenting scenes from the Bible enacted by modern Burgundian people in modern Burgundian dress.

There is a delightful Holy Family. Joseph, who receives particular attention throughout the series, is at work on a piece of carving which is a blatant anachronism, for it is a Flamboyant pinnacle. His carpenter's tools are neatly ranged on the wall behind him. Mary is busy with her needle, while the infant Jesus, dressed in the long skirts which would have been worn by a child of that age at that time, stands and watches her. The only intruder is a figure half-way between an angel and one of the *putti* so dear to the

77

Renaissance artist. The Rigolley brothers were obviously not quite at home with such a figure, which is handled without conviction.

Another domestic scene is the Visitation, where Mary puts her hand upon Elizabeth's stomach to verify the pregnancy. To homeliness is added humour in the finial depicting two scholars on opposite sides of a double lectern, each holding his book open with exactly the same gesture. It is answered on the south side, above the Holy Family, by two figures, thought to be self-portraits of the artists, treating themselves to a copious *vin d'honneur* from a capacious *pichet*.

Notre-Dame de Montréal is also remarkable for its reredos which is of English alabaster and of English workmanship. It was originally made as a triptych, the outer panels being half the width of the centre portion and hinged to close over it. Four scenes from the life of the Virgin – the Annunciation, the Adoration of the Magi, the Assumption and the Coronation – are set between figures of St Stephen, to the left, and St Laurence, to the right. Each is surmounted by a beautiful little canopy not unlike those which became so prominent a feature of late medieval stained glass. The central panel, which is taller than the others by the height of a canopy, represents the Mass of St Gregory, at which Christ appeared revealing his wounds.

These alabaster triptyches, according to Paul Biver who made a special study of them, were largely manufactured – probably in Nottingham – for export. 'The brilliancy of these objects', he wrote,

executed in a white, crystalline material, set off by touches of somewhat crude colour and highly gilt, was evidently a factor in their popularity . . . Their profitable production was an easy matter: alabaster is neither rare nor hard to work. In the workshop, one man might be told off to produce Assumptions, another to make Flagellations or figures of Our Lady of Pity, all to a stock pattern. Again, the application of gesso, which gave the carvings their appearance of richness and finish, was a purely mechanical process which could be carried out at a moderate cost. Orders consequently poured in from Flanders, France, Italy and Spain, and even more distant countries.

It is strange to think that the church of St Catherine at Venice, at a time when that city was in the full productivity of the quattrocento, should have purchased from England a mass-produced retable very similar to that at Montréal.

The church of Notre-Dame is early Gothic, dating from about 1170 or 1180, but still retaining the two-storey façade typical of the Romanesque. Here, however, the builder was thoroughly master of his craft and has proceeded with a sure hand. Two different campaigns of construction can be detected; the earlier one, starting from the east end, included the first bay of the nave; the two further bays belong to a later period in the early thirteenth century. The second builder, however, sought to harmonize his additions with the existing structure, and only a sharp eye will note the difference in the mouldings.

It is, however, in the rose windows that the chief architectural interest of Notre-Dame de Montréal lies. Rose windows require to be made of stone of a superior quality and the beautiful limestone of the Ile de France greatly assisted the development of the tracery. Burgundy also has stone of the right quality, and it was here at Montréal that the rose window made its first appearance. There are four of them, marking the four points of the compass. The first to be built – the east window – was described by Viollet-le-Duc as 'remarkable par la naïveté de sa structure'. Three concentric rings are pierced by roughly semicircular openings; a note of variety is obtained, however, by the larger size of the apertures in the middle ring. The north transept shows an advance on this in the design of plate tracery, but its opposite number to the south is Viollet-le-Duc's own design. In the west front, which belongs to the later campaign of construction, the builder has left plate tracery behind and produced a design of eight petals which seems to be a simplification of the first rose window in France, that of the west front of Saint-Denis.

The other particular feature of Montréal is the tribune over the west doors, which is supported by four huge consoles, two at either side of the entrance, and one central one which has the additional support of a slender colonette which is monolithic. The parapet, which has no ornament at all, is equipped with a small table altar, so that the space afforded by the tribune – enough, according to Viollet-le-Duc, to hold some twenty to twenty-five persons – could have served as a private chapel. It has been suggested that this tribune was the seigneurial pew. The only difficulty about this theory is that the staircase which leads to it, contrived within the thickness of the wall, is on the south side of the west doors, whereas the château was situated to the north.

Only the ground plan of the château is known today, but its mere position says much about its importance. Dominating the valley of the Serein, Montréal covered the approaches to Avallon to the west, Noyers to the north and Montbard to the east. The seigneurs de Montréal, who were nearly all named Anseric, occupied an important position in the hierarchy of Burgundy. The last of them, Anseric X, committed a number of atrocities including that of having a priest eaten by flies ('quemdam presbyterum muscis comedi fecerat'). How he secured the co-operation of the flies for this somewhat irregular method of execution is not related. As a punishment, St Louis deprived him of his *seigneurie* and Montréal became the property of the dukes of Burgundy. It was maintained by them as one of their most important fortresses.

The medieval plan, still accessible to Victor Petit in 1870, was typical of a Burgundian *place forte* with its triple division into 'château', 'bourg' and 'ville'. Situated to the north-west of the church, the château itself was built round a courtyard with projecting square towers – the Tour du Roi, the Tour du Logis, the Tour de Beauregard and the Tour de la Cigogne. In the north range was a magnificent Grande Salle, 100 feet long by 36 feet wide. The plan shows only the château and the church, but the area must also have contained the houses of the provost and canons so that the whole enclosure offered the not uncommon mixture of castle keep and cathedral close. The twin powers of Church and State were seen to be in close proximity. Château, church and canons' houses were protected by a curtain wall defended by eight towers, some square, some round. The area thus enclosed was large, for it had to offer security to no less than twenty surrounding villages which enjoyed the *droit de retrayant* – the right to retreat into the château in times of emergency.

By the west front of the church, the Porte d'en Haut gave access to the Bourg d'en Haut, which occupied the long high ridge of the escarpment and was protected by its own wall. From here the Porte du Milieu gave access to the ville or 'bourg nouveau' with a further curtain wall with its two gatehouses, the Porte d'en Bas and the Porte du Bail.

Montréal last served as a fortress during the Wars of Religion. Henri IV, as part of his general policy, had the fortress dismantled in 1597. It bears many traces of its feudal past. It still has something of the fortress and something of the cathedral close about it. The narrow, tortuous streets which climb its contours pass beneath arches which once were gateways. Some of the buildings, judging by the mouldings round their windows, date back to the fifteenth century. But of the triple rings of curtain wall there are few remains.

The opposite is true of Noyers, where the surviving parts of the medieval defences are built into the houses.

On the map the site of Noyers looks rather like that of Semur – an oxbow meander of the river Serein which encloses a peninsula large enough to contain a small town and to provide it with a natural moat. But the contours are totally different, for the peninsula of Semur is a rocky outcrop whereas that of Noyers is level land which lies at the foot of a projecting spur of the surrounding hills. This spur, at the extremity of an escarpment, provides the perfect site for a castle which could overlook and either protect or dominate the town beneath it. The town has survived and is full of interesting and historic houses, but the château has almost completely disappeared. But since it was built by a bishop of Auxerre, Hugues de Noyers, it is described in the chronicles entitled *The Acts of the Bishops of Auxerre*.

In the ascent of the mountain [the word *montagne* in French may designate a steep hill] from the bourg, although on that side the castle is impregnable because of its position, he constructed very big trenches in the rock cut out from the mountain, and strongly fortified gates; on the higher part, where on the summit of the mountain on which the keep is situated there is a wider space, an open site suitable for the erection of machines of war, besides the ancient walls of the fortification, among which was an outer and stronger one built by his brother Clarembauld a little before he died, he built, behind that wall, an inner one of greater height, thickness and solidarity, a very strong tower having been built on the top of it; round the outer wall he made steep trenches, the rocks having been hewn out, and elsewhere put in front cuttings in the mountain which could keep the enemy away from the donjon by multiple obstacles and hindrances; and he made outworks joined to the outer wall and covered over with beams of immense strength, so that those who were underneath need not fear the hurling of weapons or missiles thrown from engines or any other attacks of the enemy, but in security could bar the way to those coming against the lower trenches and the wall to which they were joined. Outside the enclosure of the principal keep, he built a palace of great splendour which was an extra defence to the keep itself, and a dwelling place suitable for the lord.

Hugues de Noyers, according to his biographer Ernest Petit, 'requisitioned all his vassals for nearly ten years to hollow out these very deep, parallel trenches and thus isolate completely the old manor and the new buildings which he constructed'. As they were hewn out of the solid rock it is hardly surprising that the work should have taken so long.

The was little of this left in the 1870s when Ernest Petit was writing his book on the lords of Noyers, but he describes the view from the *emplacement*.

From the summit to which one has arrived one dominates the town to such an extent that it is possible to count the streets, the squares and the houses. One enjoys an enchanting view, but which gives but an imperfect idea of the outlook which presented itself from the top of the crenellated towers of the keep. The prospect of the barren mountains, like bare bones, which limit the horizon offers a conspicuous contrast with the fertility of the valley . . . The extent of these ruins bears witness to the strength of this formidable fortress, which was one of the most esteemed in the whole of Burgundy.

Hugues de Noyers is described as being 'of medium stature, with a handsome face, gifted with a great eloquence, a friend of the arts, hidebound in his opinions, magnificent in his actions, affectionate towards his family but haughty and conceited towards others'. He earned himself the title 'Hammer of the Heretics' by his severities towards the Albigensians. Perhaps his real reason for hostility towards them is hinted by his biographer: 'This sect maintained that all men should be in a condition of equality.'

Enough remains of the medieval walls for it to be possible to picture Noyers as it looked at the beginning of the sixteenth century. Of its twenty-six towers, fifteen remain, though most of them have been incorporated into more recent houses. The two main gatehouses, the Porte Peinte, a fifteenth-century structure guarding the approach from Avallon, and the Porte de Sainte-Vérote the approach from Tonnerre, still confront the visitor. The name of the latter refers to an old custom whereby on 15 August each year the local vignerons hung a bunch of green grapes – *les vérotes* – on the statue of the Virgin and Child over the arch in order to secure divine protection from the thunderstorms which can be so disastrous in this area to the vendanges. In pursuance of this theme the Holy Child is holding a bunch of grapes. The statue dates from the first years of the seventeenth century and probably replaced an earlier one destroyed by the Huguenots, for Noyers was a Protestant stronghold since 1565 when it passed into the possession of Louis de Bourbon, Prince de Condé.

Between the two gatehouses are the city walls, once encircled by a moat, which is now replaced by the Chemin des Fossés to the east and the Chemin des Terreaux to the west. They enclose an area, shaped by the meander of the Serein, which contains a network of narrow streets and small triangular 'squares' – the Place de l'Hôtel de Ville, the Place du Marché au Blé, the Place du Grenier à Sel. Tall gabled houses, with each storey overhanging the one below and built of timber frames and plaster – known in French as *à colombages* – alternate with stone façades of the Renaissance and eighteenth century. A particular feature of the timbered houses is to be seen on some of the larger horizontal beams, which are known as '*sangliers de Bourgogne*'. Each extremity of the beam is carved to represent a monster head which sometimes suggests a wild boar and sometimes a crocodile. These are to be found also especially in Dijon and Beaune.

Originally the only church at Noyers was the priory – a daughter house of Molesmes, situated in the faubourg to the south. On 25 June 1489 it was resolved by the Assembly of the Burgers to build a church in the centre of the town, near the Marché au Blé and on 3 May two years later the first stone was laid. The building was not completed until 1515. It is a good, if simple, example of the last phase in Gothic architecture. Its proportions are generous for a parish of some 2,000 inhabitants, but a strict economy was observed in its decoration. The triforium has been dispensed with, as is not uncommon in Burgundy, and there is an austere absence of sculpture except over the doorway leading to the tower staircase. When the Protestants reigned supreme at Noyers there was nothing for them to smash. The Wars of Religion did not leave their mark upon the building, but once Henri IV was in a position to do so he had the château dismantled. Thus Burgundy lost what had been described as 'le plus bel chastel du royaume'.

The Château de Châteauneuf

The title might well pass to Châteauneuf, which has survived all the dangers to which a *château fort* was exposed. Some 6 kilometres south-east of Pouilly-en-Auxois and perched on the high ground overlooking the valley of the Vendenesse, Châteauneuf occupies one of the natural bastions of the range of hills which forms the watershed between the valleys of the Seine and the Saône. From this advantage point it commands a wide sweep of the countryside bounded to the west by the Mont Beuvray and the heights around Autun.

The new castle – *Novum Castrum* – was built in about 1170 by Jean de Chaudenay in order to create a second *seigneurie* for his younger son, who was able to take possession in 1175. Jean de Châteauneuf, as he was now styled, is chiefly known to history for his pious donations, especially to the Cistercian house of La Bussière, where he died. The younger sons of the family were mostly churchmen and provided the cathedral of Autun with several canons and three deans.

The original castle was just the square keep with a protecting wall and towers. There was no village, but the presence of a fortress soon attracted a small community, seeking work and, no doubt, protection in times of danger. The community grew and in 1267 Jean II de Châteauneuf granted a charter of liberty to what was already described as the 'town' (ville). Right up until the Revolution the inhabitants claimed the title of *Francs Bourgeois de Châteauneuf*.

A century later, Guy de Châteauneuf was one of the few survivors of the battle of Poitiers and brought back to Burgundy the news of the disaster. A period of devastation was to follow. When, in March 1360, Edward III of England signed the Treaty of Guillon with Burgundy, he imposed an enormous ransom – 200,000 *moutons d'or* – and demanded hostages from amongst the nobility and upper clergy of the duchy. Simon de Châteauneuf and his brother Poinçot were among the first to volunteer and Poinçot was duly deported a prisoner to London, together with his neighbour Jacques de Cortiamble, seigneur de Commarin.

In the following year the young duke of Burgundy, Philippe de Rouvres, died. In his will he expressed his gratitude to those who had helped him in this way, naming Poinçot among them. It was not until 1364 that the ransom was finally paid off.

By this time the original fortress had been enlarged and strengthened by the addition of the great towers which form so conspicuous a feature of Châteauneuf today. It is to be presumed that the machicolations which survive on the west façade originally upheld a *chemin de ronde* offering a covered connection between the towers.

Château de Commarin.

Tournus. Église St. Philibert. Lithograph by E. Sagot.

Chapaize. Église St. Martin. Lithograph by E. Sagot.

Abbaye de Cluny. East end. Lithograph after E. Sagot.

Vézelay. West front before restoration. Drawing by Viollet-le-Duc.

Vézelay. Doorway to nave.
Drawing by Viollet-le-Duc.

Autun. Porte St. André.
Lithograph by E. Sagot.

Autun Cathedral. Lithograph by E. Sagot.

Opposite page, left: Sémur-en-Brionnais. Lithograph by E. Sagot.

Opposite page, right: Paray-le-Monial. East end. Lithograph by E. Sagot.

Anzy-le-Duc. Lithograph by E. Sagot.

Paray-le-Monial. Lithograph by E. Sagot.

The last of the male line of Jean de Chaudenay's successors was Guyot, who died in 1441 leaving three daughters of whom Catherine, the eldest, succeeded to the *seigneurie*. She came to a terrible end.

In 1447 she married Jacques d'Haussonville and went to live with him at his Château de Monturent-le-Sec in Champagne. Here she fell passionately in love with his intendant, Giraud de Parmentier, and her one desire was to return with him to live at Châteauneuf.

On 24 November 1455, Jacques d'Haussonville died in agonies under circumstances which gave rise to immediate suspicions of poisoning. His brothers demanded an inquest by the bailli de Chaumont and Catherine was taken to the prison of the Conciergerie in Paris. This formed the part of the old Palais de la Cité which fronts the Seine. One of the three towers was known as the Tour Bonbec. 'Avoir bon bec' is the French for to have the gift of the gab, but here it was used in a more sinister sense – the readiness to talk which is the end-product of the torture chamber. Here Catherine underwent the *question extraordinaire* and made a complete confession. The comte Arthur de Vogüé, who had studied the *procès verbal* of her interrogation 'serré de détails souvent trop précis', tells how she admitted to having purchased realgar (arsenic) at Epinal, cooked it in a special cake (some of which one of her domestics ate by mistake and died) and finally given it to her husband. On 13 March 1456, she was condemned to be burnt alive at the Marché aux Cochons, near the Châtelet, which sentence was immediately carried out.

Her *seigneurie* was confiscated by the duke of Burgundy and on 22 April 1457, by letters patent signed at Bruges, Philippe le Bon made it over to his faithful councillor Philippe Pot, seigneur de la Roche-Pot.

Philippe Pot was one of the most able statesmen of his time. He was godson to Philippe le Bon who made him a chevalier de la Toison d'Or, the Burgundian equivalent of the Order of the Garter. It was he who negotiated the successive marriages of Charles le Téméraire and was responsible for the administration of the Low Countries. When Louis XI reunited Burgundy to the Crown of France, Philippe Pot continued to serve under him and was rewarded by the position of grand sénéchal de Bourgogne, a title revived in his favour. On the death of Louis, Anne de Beaujeu – described by him as 'one of the least silly women in France' – became regent during the minority of Charles VIII; she specially asked that

Philippe Pot should represent Burgundy in the States General of 1484 'on account of his great discretion'. The States General had to deal with an important issue concerning the nature of the French royal family. According to one view the royal power should pass, in the event of a minority, to the princes of the blood. According to the other view the sovereignty reverted in these circumstances to the people, in whose competence it was to appoint a regent.

On 9 February Philippe Pot made a speech on the principles of monarchical government.

History relates that originally the sovereign people created the kings by their vote and that it gave particular preference to those men who surpassed all others in virtue and ability. In fact it is in everyone's interest that he should have a master. Princes are not endowed with their immense power in order to enable them to enrich themselves at the expense of the people, but to enrich the State. If sometimes they act to the contrary, they are tyrants and they resemble those shepherds who, far from protecting their sheep, devour them like cruel wolves. It is therefore of the greatest importance to the people by what law and by what leader they are governed. If the king is good, the nation flourishes; if he is bad, it is impoverished and degraded. Who does not know, who does not repeat that the State is the *res publica*? If that is the case, how could the people abandon its responsibility?

Consequently, what is the power in France which has the authority to regulate the course of events when the king is incapable of governing? Obviously this responsibility does not devolve upon a prince, nor upon a council of princes, but upon the people from whom the power is derived. The people have the right, on two counts, to direct their affairs – because they are the masters and because they are always the victims, in the last resort, of bad government. They do not have the right to rule, but understand this: they have the right to administrate the kingdom by those whom they have elected. I call 'the people' not only plebeians and villeins, but also all men of all orders to the extent that, under the name of the States General, I include even the princes. Thus you, deputies of the three Estates, are trustees of the will of all.

If those words had been heeded by François I and Louis XIV the history of France might have been very different.

Under Philippe Pot Châteauneuf was transformed. While retaining the outward appearance of a fortress it was made into a residence more in keeping with late fifteenth-century standards. In the courtyard, the octagonal staircase tower and the highly decorative dormers were his additions. He also added the chapel to the main *corps de logis* and had the walls boldly and badly painted in vertical stripes of black and red and yellow which were the colours of his livery.

Across the courtyard he built a fine block of lodgings which were, unfortunately, never finished. The huge fireplaces of the upper storey still cling perilously to the walls. To the south of this, towards the church, he planned a new and imposing entrance between the two great towers. The archway was cut and surmounted by a delicately framed panel, no doubt destined to receive his coat of arms or some religious scene such as are to be found on Louis d'Orléans's buildings in the Ile de France – Pierrefonds or La Ferté-Milon. The piers for a new bridge across the chasm of the moat were built up to the level of the entrance. Presumably they were to be doubled by another set of piers, for they are eccentric to the gateway. Presumably, also, he planned some heightened causeway to link the château with the town, which would have curled in an impressive sweep towards the main street.

Philippe Pot had also to some extent modernized his paternal Château de la Roche-Pot. This, too, occupies a superb position, but of greater strategic importance than that of Châteauneuf, for it guards the intersection of two great roads – one from Paris to Lyon and the other from Autun to Dijon. It is the gateway from France to the Côte d'Or.

The irregular shape of the building, which is roughly triangular, is dictated by the contours of the spur on which it is situated. Two capacious cylindrical towers, both capped with conical roofs *en poivrière*, mark the angles of the base of the triangle, which contains the only entrance to the château. The more domestic parts of the building, distinguished by the variegated coloured tiles of typically Burgundian design, range themselves in no particular order round the irregular courtyard. Seen from beneath its walls, the château creates a vivid impression of the strength of a medieval fortress; seen from the hillside opposite, it forms an extremely picturesque ensemble – and here it must be remembered that most of what can be seen today is a late nineteenth and early twentieth century reconstruction.

The views of La Roche-Pot drawn or engraved in the early nineteenth century show a building so completely in ruins that it is difficult to discern even its most prominent features. It was not until 1893 that the property was purchased by Madame Sadi Carnot, widow of the President. She devoted herself to the re-creation of the feudal fortress. She employed the architect Charles Suisse, who carried out the work 'avec un souci passionné d'exactitude'. There is little doubt that what we see today closely resembles the original castle of Philippe Pot.

Châteauneuf and La Roche-Pot are both examples of the great feudal castle which played such an important part in the history of the Middle Ages. There were also innumerable smaller castles, some little more than fortified farms, which are no less important. They are, however, less easy to study for the simple reason that their history is less well recorded. The Revolution was a great destructor of archives, but at least one of these, the Château de Brandon, retains enough of its fabric to provide an illustration.

The Château de Brandon

The Château de Brandon is neither the most beautiful nor the most historic castle in Burgundy, but it is typical of a large number of small châteaux and fortified farms in which the province abounds and it happens to be unusually well documented. The archives survived the Revolution and provided Eugène Fyot with material for his fascinating study published in the *Mémoires of the Société Eduenne*. Both in its structure and in its history, Brandon has a lot to tell us of the way of life of a bygone age.

It was approached by a drive planted with a magnificent lime avenue which looks like a Roman road, but which in fact dates from the eighteenth century – the Pavé du Roi, which linked the priory of Saint-Sernin with the Château de Couches.

Seen from this side the architecture is severe to the point of austerity; the towers which project from the angles are all of them square and unadorned. Originally they would have been seen rising above the battlements of an outer line of fortification, referred to in a description of 1525 as 'avant murailles', which were mounted on a high earthwork. The only survivor of this outer bailey is the round tower of the dovecot or *colombier*. This was first mentioned in a census or *dénombrement* drawn up in 1409.

The entrance pavilion is of about the same date. A broad archway provided for the passage of wheeled vehicles and a narrow one for pedestrians; each was equipped with a drawbridge, from which we must infer the existence of a dry moat. One of the drawbridge slots has been filled in to make space for a large window to be inserted when the requirements of defence began to give place to the requirements of domestic convenience. To the right of this pavilion is a little machicolated projection or *bretèche* which would have served a chiefly sanitary purpose.

At one time in its history this pavilion seems to have been used as a dovecot, for the inner wall is lined with the *casiers* or niches for the pigeons' nests. The reason for their being transferred here from the dovecot tower is suggested by an extraordinary account of two local inhabitants, Claude Vincent and Jean Pelletier who, in 1678, systematically poached the pigeons and, when brought to justice, attacked those who had given evidence against them and burnt their houses. It was two years before they were finally arrested and condemned.

On entering the courtyard, the visitor is confronted by a medley of buildings of different dates and serving different purposes. The whole area is divided into two halves by a terrace wall. The lower area, the Basse Cour, is surrounded by buildings which were mostly stables and cowhouses. Above the terrace is the Cour d'Honneur behind which are the lodgings of the seigneur, built, or rebuilt, in the seventeenth century. Immediately opposite the entrance is a high wall to which there still adheres a capacious fireplace with its chimney. This, together with the proximity of the well, suggests that the original donjon was on this site.

This supposition would also make sense of the position occupied by the chapel in a square tower to the right of this wall. To place a chapel next to a keep is understandable. If the keep was somewhere in the Cour d'Honneur the chapel would have stood oddly alone amid the cowhouses and stables of the Basse Cour.

Although Brandon looks today more like a fortified farm than a castle, it was always described in the feudal age by the word 'châtelet' which always designates the presence of a military garrison. As such it belonged to the duke of Burgundy by whom it was delegated to one of his chief vassals. In due course the position became hereditary and carried with it the normal prerogatives of the châtelain, including those of *haute et basse justice*.

It was only by delegating responsibility for his castles that the duke of Burgundy could maintain the peace and justice of his province. The system did not, however, always work. Mille de Montateaume, seigneur de Brandon, used his position for ravaging the countryside and oppressing the peasants to such a degree that he was successfully prosecuted in 1365 and beheaded at Autun 'le jeudi après la Madeleine'. The bailiff who supervised the sale of his possessions, Robert d'Essertenne, became the next seigneur de Brandon. He must have acquitted himself to the satisfaction of the duke, for it was in his favour that the *seigneurie* became hereditary. This in fact posed more problems than it solved, for Robert had four daughters and no sons. When he died his eldest daughter Jeanne claimed as her heritage 'la moitié du Château de Brandon'. The other half was divided into three lots, so that Isabelle and her other sisters claimed in their *dénombrements* 'la 3ième partie de la moitié de la maison forte de Brandon'.

Such fragmentation threatened the existence of the *seigneurie* and, on 7 January 1376, Duke Philip issued an order by which the integrity of the domain would be maintained. 'La seigneurie de Brandon . . . ne fera dès à present et à l'avenir qu'une seule et même seigneurie sous le nom de Brandon.' At the same time the title of baron was conferred upon its holder.

The finances even of a unified estate, however, were at best precarious and frequent mention is made in the accounts of borrowings against which the *seigneurie* itself was the security. This came to a head in 1414 when Pierre d'Essertenne was obliged to forfeit the possession of Brandon to his creditor, Denis Dumoulin. But the law favoured the hereditary owner by what was called the 'droit de retrait lignager' which provided for the compulsory repurchase of the family estate by the family – if, of course, they could raise the money. This right must have been exercised in this case, for a few years later we find a Guillaume d'Essertenne again owner and baron de Brandon.

From the family of d'Essertenne the barony of Brandon passed, in 1453, to the family of Lugny and from them, in 1521, to that of Bernard de Montessus. In 1575 Melchior Bernard de Montessus increased the family fortunes by his marriage with an heiress named Jeanne de Vintemille. Her father's will begins with a tirade against the times in which he lived: 'Atheism is now valued and honoured under the title of philosophy; women masquerade as men while men become more effeminate than women. We see nothing but impiety and violence among the nobility, avarice in the seats of justice, hypocrisy and superstition among the clergy.' Having unburdened himself of these sweeping accusations, he bequeathed his fortune to Jeanne.

It did not keep the family for long out of financial difficulties and to rescue his estates from jeopardy Charles de Montessus adopted tactics which fully justified what Vintemille had said about superstition. It is described thus by Eugène Fyot. 'Charles de Montessus, to keep his creditors at bay, helped to spread the legend of a hidden treasure . . . He gave to his château the most sinister reputation, certifying that it was haunted by a malevolent spirit.'

At the centre of this conspiracy was a local priest by the name of Philibert Delniau who was, by his own admission, in league with the devil who had appeared to him 'in the form of a very large and terrible man dressed in a black robe which concealed both his arms and his legs and who spoke to him in a loud and very raucous voice'.

On 1 April Delniau was put on trial at Autun for sorcery and made a full confession. He was finally sentenced to be hanged and his body burnt and died in a most edifying state of contrition. The *procès verbal* of his trial gives interesting details of his connection with Brandon.

'In the year 1624', begins the account, 'at the Château de Brandon near Couches . . . a great noise and *tintamarre* could be heard both by day and by night and a ghost could be seen passing lightly as the wind, sometimes in the form of a man, sometimes in the form of a child; at which the seigneur of that place was greatly troubled and disquieted so that he began to investigate the matter.' He had recourse to Delniau who, after certain conjurations of the evil spirit, assured the seigneur of that place that in his château there was a treasure hidden deep in the ground 'since the time when the English occupied a great part of France'. A spirit named Mammon was guardian of the secret, but Mammon was stronger – 'plus grand maître' – than his own spirit and could not be persuaded to be more precise. All that Delniau could do was to give Brandon the reputation of being haunted and spread the rumour of the treasure.

It did gain for Charles de Montessus a respite granted by a treaty with his creditors on 5 January 1626. Seven years later, however, his debts being still unpaid, the estate was put up for sale and bought by the seigneur de Grenelle for 34,000 livres.

A possible reason for the financial embarrassment of Charles de Montessus is that he is thought to have been the builder of the seventeenth-century lodgings on the west side of the Cour d'Honneur. The name of no architect is known, but it is a building which could well date from the days of Louis XIII. It is a plain but pleasing façade which relies almost wholly for effect on the subtle grouping of the doors and windows.

The main doorway, reached by a handsome flight of stone steps, is flanked by two tall windows on either side, thus forming five bays of the ground floor. There are only three windows to the upper storey, which rise above the eaves to become half-dormers, and are capped with pediments of alternately triangular and segmental shape.

To either side of this group, two more doorways each with one window on either side, forming three bays, with only one window in the upper storey. This arrangement creates a gentle rhythm which gives the entrance front its charm. If this was really built by Charles de Montessus early enough to have been the cause of his financial straits it is a precocious example of such an architecture for the provinces.

Brandon provides an excellent example of the transition from feudal fortress to *maison de plaisance*. There is one other form of medieval architecture which was not concerned either with fortification or with domestic convenience, and that is the *hospice* or *hôtel Dieu*. Burgundy possesses two remarkable examples, one at Tonnerre, founded by Marguerite de Bourgogne, and the other, more famous, at Beaune, founded by the Chancellor Rolin.

'It had to be said', wrote Viollet-le-Duc, 'that some of the lords who founded hospices when they were dying had reduced more men to misery during their lifetime than could have been cared for in the houses which they founded.' That is just what Louis XI said of Nicolas Rolin, that 'having made so many people poor and homeless, he could well afford to make his peace with the Almighty by providing for some of them'. Louis XI had reason to dislike Rolin and his accusation may have been unjust. But such a combination of worldly success and magnificent charity would have been typical of his times. 'The Middle Ages were like that', continues Viollet-le-Duc; 'they offer an infinite mixture of good and bad. Therefore it is as unjust to represent this era as a time of continual misery as it would be to represent it as the age of faith, of charity and of wisdom.' It was both, and both were achieved on the grand scale: on the one hand was their ceaseless rapacity, their compulsive brigandage and their callous cruelty – from which the Church was by no means exempt: on the other were their great and noble attainments – the monumental works of intellect and learning which reached their zenith in the *Summum* of Thomas Aquinas – and the magnificence of their great cathedrals. But when St Bernard made his bitter reproach that the Church 'clothes her stones in gold but lets her sons go naked' he did scant justice to her works of charity.

Of these there is no more striking evidence in architecture than those institutions which we would call hospitals but which were more often known in French by the name of 'hospice' or 'hôtel Dieu'.

One of the most famous was the hôtel Dieu built in close proximity to the west front of Notre-Dame de Paris. In 1168 Maurice de Sully, the builder of the cathedral of Notre-Dame, made it a rule that each canon, on his death or on his leaving his canonry for preferment, was to bequeath to the hôtel Dieu 'un lit garni', and a certain Adam, in the household of Philippe-Auguste, left two houses in Paris to provide an income from which, on the anniversary of his death, the trustees were to provide the patients with 'tout ce qu'il leur viendront dans la pensée de vouloir manger'.

There was a fine hôtel Dieu at Angers founded in 1153 and at Chartres another of about the same date. In the early thirteenth century there was a particularly magnificent hospice known, perhaps pessimistically, as the 'Salle des Morts' at the abbey of Ourscamp near Compiègne.

The Hôpital de Tonnerre

One of the finest in Burgundy was built and endowed in 1293 by Marguerite de Bourgogne at Tonnerre. The original charter of foundation has survived and it shows that the inspiration came from the parable of the Sheep and the Goats. There was provision for twenty monks and nuns, whose duty it was to give food to the hungry and drink to the thirsty; to receive the stranger and the pilgrim; to clothe the naked, to visit the sick and to console the prisoner. Convalescents were to be housed and fed for a further week and, on leaving the hospice, were to be provided with shoes, shirt and tunic. A more puritanical and moralistic age would have regarded this generosity as a positive incitement to the thriftless malingerer. Not so the Middle Ages. Architecturally, the hôtel Dieu compares extremely favourably with the workhouse.

The Hôpital Notre-Dame des Fontenilles at Tonnerre is a truly magnificent building. Here the poor and the destitute could be restored to health of body and soul or could die in dignity, thanks to the munificence of the founder.

Marguerite de Bourgogne was one of the three daughters of Duke Eudes IV and the widow of Charles d'Anjou, king of Naples, Sicily and Jerusalem, and, as such, sister-in-law to St Louis. She inherited the comté de Tonnerre from her mother, Mahaut de Bourbon, and here she retired on the death of her husband. As a queen she had witnessed the appalling suffering caused by the endless warfare of the time: as a widow she set out to relieve that suffering on her doorstep.

The hospital took only two years to build, for it was consecrated by the Cardinal de Preneste on 13 March 1295. It consisted of one enormous nave, 328 feet in length and 59 feet in width, the maximum possible to be spanned by a single beam. It was, however, designed to contain only forty beds. There was a spaciousness about it which modern infirmaries might envy. It was lit by twenty-four windows – twelve on each side – which were placed high (the ground level was nearly 20 inches lower than today) so that a wooden gallery could be constructed above the level of the cubicles in which the beds were placed. This gallery enabled the nursing staff to survey their patients and also gave them direct access to the windows, to be closed or opened according to the season. The gallery communicated also with the château so that Marguerite herself could oversee the functioning of her hospital.

The tie beams which crossed from wall to wall had the prodigious length of 60½ feet, still possible before the virgin forests of Europe had been destroyed. These beams support the immense barrel vault of wood which is the distinctive feature of the building. It is pierced at regular intervals with small quatrefoil apertures to ensure the proper ventilation of the room. Medical science was of a primitive nature in those days and many must have died who would not die today; but at least they died in an atmosphere of loving care and religious comfort. To the medieval mind the needs of the spirit were more important than the needs of the body, and this was clearly expressed in the architecture of the hospital.

For the ward was also a church. At the eastern extremity of this long nave a triple archway gave access to the sanctuary. The gallery turned at right angles across the building to form a screen or *jubé*.

The windows of the apse are the full height of the barrel vault and were filled with coloured glass in contrast to the plain *grisaille* in the other windows which tempered the harshness of the light to the eyes of the patients. Both in the chapel and in the ward the architecture is of extreme simplicity, but of great nobility.

From outside, the building appears to be all roof, which today is merely ponderous but which used to present the colourful patterns of Burgundian tiles, like the skin of a reticulated python.

The Hôpital de Tonnerre has had a sad history. The Hundred Years War reduced its revenues to almost nothing. In 1359 the English King Edward III installed himself here, while his soldiers helped themselves to 6,000 barrels of wine. But the fabric survived. In 1556 Tonnerre was devastated by a terrible fire; but the hospital survived. It was not until the twentieth century that its value as a *Monument Historique* was fully recognized. But its chequered history somehow preserved it from any serious mutilation or restoration and today it speaks to us directly of the great concern of the Middle Ages for charity and of the noble donation of Marguerite of Burgundy. It was not, however, the hôtel Dieu de Tonnerre but that of Saint-Jacques at Valenciennes which was to inspire the most famous of all Burgundian hospitals, the Hospice de Beaune.

The Hospice de Beaune

The Hospice de Beaune was the foundation of two of the most remarkable figures in Burgundian history, Nicolas Rolin and his wife, Guigone de Salins. Nicolas was the outstanding figure of his age and served Philippe le Bon much as Colbert was to serve Louis XIV. 'En France', wrote the chronicler Chastellain, 'on ne savait pas son pareil.' Philippe le Bon had been quick to recognize his ability and 'in all matters relied upon the wisdom, understanding and management of this prudent chancellor. Therefore the good duke, wishing to recompense him for such labours, made him rich by more than forty thousand livres in income and gave high preferments to his children and relations.'

Guigone, descended from the two noble houses of Vienne and Salins, was a wife to match so capable a spouse. Such was her reputation at Rome that, in 1441, Pope Eugenius IV made a dispensation in her favour of the strict rules of enclosure of religious orders and not only allowed her access to such houses, but relaxed, for the duration of her visit, the rule of silence.

Rolin was called to administer Burgundy at a time of great difficulty and poverty. In 1435, by the Treaty of Arras, the duke of Burgundy and the king of France had united to expel the English, but in doing so they had unwittingly created an even deadlier foe. The disbanded soldiers formed themselves into companies of brigands – *les écorcheurs* – who terrorized the countryside to such an extent that the peasants were obliged to abandon their fields and take refuge in the fortified towns and châteaux. The abandonment of the crops bred famine and famine bred pestilence. There is no more deadly combination of misfortunes.

In 1438, writes one chronicler, 'fut grande famine par toute la Bourgogne et grand' faute de vin'. The poor were reduced to eating a kind of 'bread' made of acorns and clay. They were dying by the thousand. Wolves, accustomed to eating the dead, grew bold enough to attack the living and in the very streets of the towns.

Attempts were made to alleviate their suffering. 'There were so many poor in Beaune, Chalon and Macon', continues the chronicle, 'that the townsmen made communal houses in which to lodge them and engaged themselves by weekly turns to look after them.' It was unlikely that such charitable measures could have dealt adequately with the problem. Beaune was at this time one of the hardest-hit areas in Burgundy. Of 465 hearths, Rossignol informs us, only 27 were solvent.

It was probably for this reason that Rolin chose Beaune for the foundation of his hospice. A letter from the Pope applauding his intention mentions the possibility of Autun as an alternative to Beaune. Autun was Rolin's natal town and his eldest son was currently the bishop, but the need was greater at Beaune. For Beaune, therefore, the Act of Foundation was solemnly drawn up.

I, Nicolas Rolin, knight, citizen of Autun and seigneur of Authume, Chancellor of Burgundy, on this Sunday, the 4th of August in the year of Our Lord 1443, setting aside all worldly considerations and in the interest of my salvation, desirous of exchanging, by a happy commerce, against treasures in Heaven the temporal possessions which I owe to the goodness of God, and of the corruptible to make the eternal; by virtue of the authorization of the Holy See, in gratitude for the possessions which the Lord, source of all goodness, has heaped upon me; from now and for ever I found and endow in the city of Beaune, a hospital for the sick and the poor.

Rolin immediately set about the realization of this undertaking, and the building which resulted is one of the most famous in Burgundy. The name of Jacques Viscrere – a name otherwise unknown – is linked in a poetic eulogy with the building of the hospice. The Latin word *peractorem* is an unusual one which suggests more the entrepreneur who undertook the construction than the designing architect, but the building itself is evidence enough that there was a highly skilled architect behind the design.

The façade towards the market-place is simple and austere and dominated by the huge slope of the roof. The windows to the left of the entrance mark the Grand' Salle which was the hospital ward – four small lights set rather widely apart followed by two larger windows filled with Flamboyant tracery which mark the chapel at the east end. Reasons of security no doubt account for the somewhat forbidding architecture of the exterior. It is only to those who penetrate the courtyard that the full glory of the Hospice de Beaune is revealed. As Viollet-le-Duc said, 'it would tempt one to be ill. Whatever the squalor in which the poor had lived their lives, the moment that they entered the Hospice they were lodged in the most princely grandeur.'

In the façade across the court, the ground-floor windows and doorways, each surmounted by an elegant *accolade*, are set behind a long colonnade which gives the effect of a cloister. The colonnade supports a gallery at first-floor level which forms a covered way providing communication between all the rooms. The shorter columns of this upper colonnade do not correspond with the columns below, but are set at irregular intervals which are dictated by the large windowless dormers or *louvres*. Some of these contain three archways and some two, which creates a pleasing rhythm rather than a symmetrical array. Between these are true dormers with mullion windows, set higher in the roof, which provide another rhythm to the roofscape.

A particular feature of the decoration of this façade is the multiplicity of weather vanes or *girouettes* which surmount the complex and beautiful finials at the point of each gable or the summit of each tower. The *girouette* was one of the hallmarks of nobility. 'Only gentlemen had the right to *girouettes* on their houses', wrote Le

Laboureur in his book on the origins of heraldry; 'they are either pointed, like a pennant, for the simple knight, or square, like a banner, for the knight banneret.' Those at the hospice are square and bear the three golden keys of Nicolas Rolin and the battlemented tower of Guigone de Salins. These, together with the delicate cresting of the roof ridge, are the special ornaments of the building and evidence of the minute attention to detail of the founder.

But it is the roof which is the particular glory of the whole building, one of the most perfect examples of the typically Burgundian use of coloured tiles. Let the name of Baudechon Courtois, who laid out these complex, interlacing patterns, be held in honourable remembrance.

'This delightful "palace of the poor"', wrote the traveller Montégut, 'recalls, in its elegant originality, the municipal buildings of Flanders; it is the art of Flanders at its most brilliant period, transported to Burgundy.'

The Flemish influence was the direct result of the marriage, in 1369, between Philippe le Hardi and Marguerite, heiress to the vast and opulent estates of Louis de Male, count of Flanders. On his death in 1384 all this territory passed into the possession of the duke of Burgundy. It was to have a considerable effect upon Burgundian art.

Rolin was among the first patrons of the great Flemish artists of his time – Jan Van Eyck and Roger Van der Weyden. Portraiture before Van Eyck, as Kenneth Clark has pointed out, was concerned to emphasize the status of the sitter rather than to penetrate his individual personality. Of Van Eyck he writes: 'No one has looked at the human face with a more dispassionate eye and recorded his findings with a more delicate hand.' Van Eyck was the first of the great portrait painters who used the physiognomy of the face to mirror the psychology of the sitter.

There is no better example of this than his painting of Rolin in the Louvre. Van Eyck depicts the great chancellor in prayer. The face, which is almost in profile, is the very picture of shrewdness and of that watchful suspicion which is the foundation of shrewdness. He might be engaged in a penetrating scrutiny of some foreign plenipotentiary with whom he is negotiating and whom he is deciding not to trust. He is in fact directing his gaze at the Virgin Mary. She has her eyes on the child on her knee who looks as if he is on his best behaviour when in the presence of the Chancellor of Burgundy.

The picture was presented by Rolin to the church in which he had been baptized, Notre-Dame d'Autun, but in the days of the Consulate it was transferred to Paris.

The other great picture commissioned by Rolin is the retable of Roger Van der Weyden in the Hospice de Beaune. It originally stood behind the high altar in the Chapel of the Grand'Salle. The subject is the Last Judgement and the technical excellence of the painting is beyond praise. Its greatest interest – since this was its most obvious purpose – is as a theological statement. Van der Weyden was no less skilful than Van Eyck in the portrayal of facial expression and here he used this skill to great effect.

The central panel depicts the Weighing of Souls. The faces of Christ the Judge and of St Michael wear expressions of perfect impassibility. The figure of St Michael holds the scales, on the cups of which are engraved the words 'peccata' and 'virtutes'. His whole stance, with his weight on his right foot as he bends slightly to the left, and the delicate poise of his fingers are indicative of the nicety of the balance on which depends the eternal destiny of the soul. One feels that half a milligramme could make all the difference.

Above him the face of Christ appears, like the Law, to be 'deaf and inexorable' – deaf even to the entreaties of his mother, who is the only figure in the whole scene whose expression betokens compassion. She seems to be imploring mercy and to be imploring it in vain. Such was the medieval belief in the character of God.

In many of the great treatments of this theme in stone the elect are shown as decently clothed. Here they are ushered naked into Paradise as the condemned tumble naked into the abyss. This nakedness was the cause of offence in 1802 and resulted in an act of bowdlerization. 'To conceal the nudity of these little figures, which are treated with a rare finish,' wrote Fontenay, 'someone had spread a layer of brown paint applied with a bad paintbrush.' It was not until 1878 that the painting was restored at the Louvre to its original condition.

It was probably also in 1802 that a ceiling, since removed, was inserted beneath the great barrel vault of the Grand'Salle and a fireplace contrived at the west end. The problem of heating so vast a space was not tackled directly by Rolin, but the inventory of 1551 mentions an 'eschauffeur' which was placed on the table. This may have been a container for charcoal such as is recorded in the study of Charles V at Vincennes, and was used for warming the hands. Besides this *eschauffeur* an extra red blanket was provided in winter and each patient had a hot-water bottle of pewter.

Between 1874 and 1878 the Grand'Salle was carefully restored by the architect Oradou. The thirty beds, each designed for two occupants, were remade to the original design as well as the little tables and chairs which accompanied them.

It was specified by Rolin that the inmates of the hospital should be cared for by a team, usually twenty-four, of young ladies 'droites et de bonne conduite'. Their elaborate head-dresses – *les hennins* – suggested that they were nuns, but they never formed a religious order. They therefore survived the abolition of religious orders in the Revolution. They continued until as recently as 1971 to serve the purpose for which Rolin had endowed his charitable foundation.

The survival of a medieval hospital is perhaps surprising enough. The survival of a town house is even more so. But at Dijon there is a remarkably well-preserved town house of the late fifteenth century in the Hôtel Chambellan, now the Syndicat d'Initiative and therefore readily accessible to the public.

The Hôtel Chambellan

Thanks to the researches of Eugène Fyot, enough is known of the history of the Chambellan family for us to have a rare opportunity of watching the rise in their fortunes from the position of a merchant draper to the ranks of the aristocracy of the town.

In the year 1386 we first hear of a Jean Chambellan, *marchand drapier*, living in the parish of Notre-Dame, lending money to impoverished noblemen and supplying red and green cloth to the 'Dorenlots' – the performers in something akin to a student rag which was authorized in Advent. In 1404 he was buying land from the Dame Jeanne de Mont-Saint-Jean. Two years later he bought a vineyard. In 1408 he was rich enough to found a chapel in the church of Notre-Dame. In 1416 his name appears among the aldermen, the echevins de Dijon. Two years later his son Etienne obtained the controllership of the Grenier à Sel. Etienne was to be six times elected mayor of Dijon.

In 1450 his son Guillemot was in his turn elected mayor and the family tradition was continued. Of Guillemot's two sons, Richard became abbot of the wealthy monastery of Saint-Etienne and was able, in 1416, to pay out of his own pocket for the repair of the church after the fall of one of the bells. His brother Henry left the ranks of the drapers for the more lucrative trade in salt.

In 1460 Henry Chambellan married his neighbour and childhood friend, Alix Berbisey. The Chambellans lived in what is now the Maison Milsand in the rue des Forges. The house next door to this on the eastern side belonged to the Berbisey family and passed through Alix to the Chambellans.

In 1491 Charles VIII conferred upon Henry Chambellan 'les titres, prérogatives, dignités et privilèges de noblesse' and he was able to put up his coat of arms 'd'azur à deux pattes de griffon d'or en chef, et en pointe une tête de léopard arrachée de même, lampassée de gueules'.

This escutcheon used to ornament the Flamboyant doorways to the transepts of the church of Saint-Michel until they were defaced by the Revolution. The Chambellan family, chiefly in the person of Antoine, the abbot of Saint-Etienne, were considerable patrons of Saint-Michel.

Finally, on 5 June 1500, Henry Chambellan realized his life's ambition and took his seat in the Chambre des Comptes. He had become one of the ruling aristocracy of Dijon. He died three years later. Among the many items of his will figured 'la grosse maison de Berbisey' now known as the Hôtel Chambellan.

The date of the ennoblement of the family is probably the date also of the reconstruction of their new house. The doorway which confronts the visitor on entering the court – a lovely piece of Flamboyant architecture – used to carry in the niches to right and left of the central arch miniature statues of Henry de Chambellan's benefactor Charles VIII and his queen, Anne de Bretagne.

The most important blocks, which front the courtyard, are set at right angles and joined by a staircase tower, and have survived more or less intact. The north block is entirely of stone and its ornaments are confined to the window surrounds with the *accolade* and *double accolade* above them. The ground-floor window sills are supported by charming little twisted columns. But the main feature of the façade is the great dormer window, comprehending two storeys in a single architectural composition. These are comparatively rare. Examples have survived at the Château de Josselin in Brittany and at the Palais de Justice at Rouen, but none, apparently, in Burgundy.

The cage of the staircase tower, sometimes called the Escalier du Jardinier, is open for the first two storeys and twice crossed in an oblique spiral by the ascending ramp and handrail – 'like a double ribbon of lace', says Eugène Fyot, – 'des merveilles de grâce et d'ingéniosité'.

On arrival at the top of the staircase the visitor discovers the reason for the name Escalier du Jardinier – the figure of a gardener, stooping to support a basket out of which splays a sort of palm tree whose branches provide the ribs for the vault, its crown the central newel.

Behind the staircase is the chapel or oratory – always the mark of opulence in a private house – where the vaults meet in an elaborate pendentive. Viollet-le-Duc complained that these baubles 'fatiguent les voûtes au lieu de les maintenir dans une juste équilibre' – but these have shown no signs of fatigue in the course of nearly five centuries.

The civil buildings of the Middle Ages, whether castles or fortified towns or hospitals or houses, have much to tell us of the way of life of those turbulent times. But the Gothic style was first and foremost ecclesiastical. Its proper place is in the cathedrals and the churches. Although the Romanesque style was the one which found its finest expression in Burgundy, the Gothic also – a term defined by Victor Hugo as 'parfaitement impropre mais parfaitement consacré' – has an important place in the ecclesiastical architecture of the province and often takes a recognizably Burgundian form.

The cathedrals of Sens and Auxerre

Just as Canterbury, for remote historical reasons, had become the seat of England's southern primacy, so Sens was the archbishopric which numbered Paris and Chartres among its suffragans. The new cathedral was the first to be built in the Gothic style.

We know from the chronicler Geoffrey de Courlon that there was a fire at Sens in 1128 and that the archbishop, Henri le Sanglier, 'began to renovate the great church'. This suggests a possible date of 1130. The cathedral was built very much under the influence of St Bernard.

It is clear that from the very start it was intended to cover the nave with a sexpartite vault, for at the base of the great piers the columns destined to receive the thrust of the transverse ribs are set obliquely in anticipation. This was the first building of this size to be covered with a sexpartite vault. It was something of a pioneer enterprise and the architect has proceeded with understandable caution. The nave is wide – 49 feet from column to column – so that the span to be vaulted was considerable. It would have been foolhardy, at this stage in the development of Gothic construction, to have attempted any very great height. The vault ribs meet their keystones at just over 80 feet above floor level.

The proportions dictated by this combination of width and height may have occasioned a further distinctive feature – the omission of tribunes. These great vaulted galleries, which formed the first floor over the aisles in so many Gothic churches, served a dual purpose. They offered extra accommodation for any overflow of congregation, and they provided abutment to the nave vaults. In most of the early Gothic cathedrals, such as Noyon or Laon, the tribunes were surmounted by a triforium and clerestory, thus making a four-tiered façade. At Sens there is a three-tiered façade of great arcade, triforium and clerestory. This was to become the classical formula for the great cathedrals from Chartres onwards.

The sexpartite vault creates a strong rhythm caused by the alternation of two sorts of piers, known in French as *pile forte* and *pile faible*. At Sens this rhythm is dramatically pronounced. The *pile forte* is made up of a cluster of five colonettes which receive the thrust of the two wall ribs, the two transverse ribs and the vaulting arch. Between the two *piles fortes* the bay is divided into two by the *pile faible*, which here takes the form of coupled columns of almost Corinthian proportions with almost Corinthian capitals. From the square abacus there rises a single colonette to receive the thrust of the intermediary cross rib. Since the cathedral, as originally built, had no transepts, this rhythm was continued without interruption from the west end to the apse.

In the early fourteenth century, during the episcopate of Etienne Bécard, the choir was separated from the nave by the construction of a stone screen or *jubé* and the grand perspective from west to east was lost for 400 years. Abbot Suger also omitted the choir screen at Saint-Denis 'in order that the beauty and magnificence of the church should not be obscured by such a barrier'.

Although the Gothic 'skeleton' is here for the first time apparent, the original windows were comparatively small – so small that in the thirteenth century it was found necessary to enlarge them. In the bay between the western towers, to the north of the organ loft, can be seen the original vaulting and the smaller, round-arched windows (which here are blind) which show how the cathedral was originally roofed and lit. By comparing this with the first bay in the nave, one can see immediately how the windows were enlarged by adjusting the vaults to what is aptly named a 'ploughshare' vault. The extent to which the clerestory windows were increased is nowhere more evident than in the three eastern lights of the apse. Here a kink in the containing wall rib shows very clearly the spring of the original arch.

It is not difficult to imagine Sens as it was originally conceived. It possessed that somewhat austere grandeur which, in a religious person, may often accompany an ascetic life. In this it reflected the character of the man under whose influence it was built – St Bernard of Clairvaux.

The beauty of Sens is based upon a severely intellectual theory of proportion. Bernard was a disciple of St Augustine and as such was deeply interested in the connection between musical harmony, visual proportion and ultimate truth. It is significant that music and architecture were the only two art forms which appear to have interested him. Alone among the fine arts, music found its way into the syllabus of the great cathedral schools.

The distinctive fact about music is that harmony is a matter of objective truth. The human ear is so constituted as to register the octave. Augustine was deeply impressed by the observation that harmonic intervals can be represented as intervals of length along the string of a musical instrument. From here it is an easy step to the theory that these intervals of length constitute harmonic proportions which are as pleasing to the eye as their equivalents in sound are satisfying to the ear. This theory is stated most clearly by Boethius, but he put it the other way round: 'The ear is affected by sounds in exactly the same way as the eye is by optical impressions.'

It had already been suggested by Plato in the *Timaeus* that this harmony lay at the very root of Creation. So, to Augustine, beauty was a quality which derived from metaphysical reality. Audible and visual harmonies were intimations of a fundamental harmony between the Creator and his Creation. The platonists of Chartres believed that the structural coherence of the universe was the result of the perfect proportions on which it was constructed. From this they derived their belief that the principles of sound construction coincided with the formula for perfect beauty.

Such was the aesthetic theory embraced by St Bernard. A church building was no longer conceived as a canvas to be covered with mural paintings or as an area of stone to be covered with carvings. Its beauty was regarded as belonging to the very bones of its structure. The skeletonic system of Gothic architecture proclaims that a beautiful building is a building which is structurally sound; it would be structurally sound if it were firmly based on the musical proportions which owed their authenticity to divine precedent. The builders of Sens would have agreed with the saying of Friedrich von Schelling that 'architecture is frozen music'.

The application of this theory to the new cathedral was extremely simple. The square bays of the nave and choir are divided into two equal halves by the middle rib of the sexpartite vault. They are thus twice the width of the bays in the aisles, giving the ratio 1 : 2, which is the octave. Owing to the adoption of the three-storey façade, as Otto von Simson pointed out, 'it was possible to give the same proportion to the relative heights of nave and aisles. The elevation of the nave, moreover, is subdivided at the level of the arcade imposts into two equal halves: the octave ratio of 1 : 2 permeates the whole edifice.'

The scholars of the Middle Ages, and notably those of the school of Chartres, were, in von Simson's words, 'obsessed by mathematics, especially geometry'. They naturally saw a metaphysical significance in figures. The square, resulting from the multiplication of a number by itself, expressed the relationship of God the Father to God the Son. Mathematics provided the link also between music and architecture, for if the scholars of Chartres thought of the Creation as a symphony, they thought of the Creator as an architect. It is not uncommon in medieval illumination to find God the Father represented as the *Elegans Architectus* holding a large pair of compasses.

St Bernard's influence on Sens Cathedral was largely exerted through his friendship with the archbishop, Henri le Sanglier, whose early behaviour had earned him the name of 'the Boar' and had brought down upon him the rebuke of St Bernard. The rebuke was accepted and the reformed bishop became the lifelong friend of his former critic. Bernard's treatise 'On the Conduct and Office of a Bishop' was written at the request of Henri le Sanglier, who submitted to the ascetic requirements in it. One of those requirements was 'moderation in building'.

Henri le Sanglier was succeeded by Hugues de Toucy. We learn from the chroniclers that he 'bestowed much work' upon the cathedral. In 1163 he was able to receive the Pope Alexander III 'with a great concourse of bishops and cardinals of the Holy Roman Church' and on 19 April 1164 Alexander consecrated an altar 'in ecclesia nova'. This act suggests that in all important respects the main structure of the choir, and possibly the nave also, had been completed. In the following year the Pope solicited the generosity of the faithful for the completion of the great task.

This chiefly meant the building and carvings for the west portal. Like so many of these sculptural ensembles, the carvings suffered badly during the Revolution. But they had already been damaged in 1268 when the south tower collapsed. Enough remains to show that the subject-matter must have been the Last Judgement. The figures of the Wise and Foolish Virgins can still be identified and in the roundels to the right and left of the central arch are represented the open and closed doors which pointed the moral of the parable and connected it with the theme of the Last Judgement.

All the statue columns have gone, but the beautiful figure of St Stephen in the long, simple dalmatic of a deacon and holding the gospel, which it was the function of the deacon to read at Mass, had a lucky escape. On 7 November 1793, when the *enragés* were smashing the statues, somebody capped St Stephen with the *bonnet rouge* and inscribed his gospel with the title *Livre de la Loi*. With these certificates of citizenship he escaped destruction.

Inside the cathedral the stained glass fared rather better than the statuary. There are some fine survivals from the late twelfth century in the choir and ambulatory. 'The atmosphere which they create', wrote Bishop René Fourrey, 'by the interplay of their colouring, has something magical about it. It is a display of precious stones. It calls to mind the walls of sapphires, of rubies, of topaz and emerald of the Heavenly Jerusalem.'

They seem to form a group with certain windows at Canterbury and Chartres. It has been suggested by von Simson that the same team of glaziers may have travelled from Canterbury to Sens and from Sens to Chartres. One of these windows – the first in the north ambulatory – is dedicated to St Thomas of Canterbury. He was well known at Sens, having spent much of his exile at the abbey of Sainte-Colombe.

It is therefore not surprising that the architectural impact of Sens should have been felt, not in any French cathedral, but upon Canterbury. Here, after the disastrous fire of 1175, it was William of Sens, 'a man active and ready and as a workman most skilful both in wood and in stone', who was put in charge of the rebuilding. The architecture of Canterbury does not afford any overall likeness to that of Sens, but round the hemicycle the coupled columns of almost Corinthian proportions bear a distinct resemblance to the *piles faibles* of their Burgundian prototype.

On 23 June 1184, another fire devastated the city of Sens and left its traces upon the walls of the ambulatory of the cathedral. It may have been the damage occasioned by this fire which necessitated the repairs in the course of which the flying buttresses were added. In 1230 the clerestory windows were enlarged and the vaults adjusted accordingly. Thus, with a few modifications, the cathedral of Sens was completed, except for its towers, according to the original inspiration of its master-builder. It represents the dawn of the new style. It was destined also to represent its sunset.

Marius Vachon, in his study of the architects of the Chambiges family, has drawn attention to the great revival of Gothic architecture at the end of the fifteenth and beginning of the sixteenth centuries – 'a period of renewal of Gothic architecture which, at the hour of its declining, seems, like the sun, to emit the same radiance and to shine with the same brilliance as at its rising'. Cathedrals, whose completion had been interrupted by a century of warfare, were again *en chantier*. Their spires were erected, their façades, especially of the transepts, were completed and their dilapidations were restored. 'The Flamboyant style', wrote Vachon, 'seems to reflect the new flame of genius of the old master-masons.' Camille Enlart has listed 647 buildings thus brought to their perfection, among them the Tour de Beurre at Rouen, the porch at Albi and the Tour Nouvelle at Bourges. But the most distinguished of all were the works of Martin Chambiges at Sens, Senlis and Beauvais.

At the end of the fifteenth century the archbishopric of Sens was held by Tristan de Salazar, a man who combined in his person the qualities of a great churchman and of a distinguished patron of the arts. In 1489 he invited Chambiges to draw up the design for the transepts.

Fortunately the chapter accounts for the period have survived and provide some interesting details on the progress of the work. In 1491 the chapter made a contract with Pierre Gramain, *tailleur d'ymages* from Auxerre. He received twenty-one livres for eight statues. It is clear that the elaborate façades of niches, both here and at Beauvais, were originally peopled with miniature statues. In 1496 the south portal was nearing completion for it was possible to dispense with the *gruat* – presumably some sort of crane. On 8 July in the following year the expenditure of five francs is recorded for a ceremony which always marked the completion of any particular feature – the *vin d'honneur* for the workmen, 'for the wine on the day that the finial and the statue of Our Lady were set up on the gable of the transept'.

In 1501 work began on the north transept. It was carried out by Hugues Cuvelier under the supervision of Chambiges. The statuary on the north porch was more lavish than that on the south, presumably because it was for public use. The south porch, opening into the courtyard of the episcopal palace, was private to the archbishop. Accordingly, in April 1503 Pierre Gramain signed a contract for twenty-six 'images' for the architraves of the door 'according to the plan provided by Canon Hodoard'. In this we see the clergy still dictating the themes to the artist. In 1516 the carpenter was paid for dismantling the scaffolding. The work of Martin Chambiges was complete. In all, 22.000 livres had been expended – 9.710 on the south transept and 12.290 on the north.

At about the same time Tristan de Salazar erected the monument to his parents which stands against the second *pile forte* on the north side of the nave. It is, in miniature, an exquisite example of the style in which the cathedral had been completed. In the tiny intricacy of their interlacing arches and the chiselled precision of their execution, the three canopies represent Flamboyant decoration at its perfection. Here we can see in stone what the stalls of Amiens so miraculously provide in wood – the last realization of the dream that found its first expression at Saint-Denis and here at Sens Cathedral.

Saint-Etienne de Sens thus shows the first dawn and the last sunset glow of the Gothic style; Saint-Etienne d'Auxerre offers examples of most of the intermediary phases of the style. It has the merit of being, for a Gothic cathedral, well documented. Its history is known to us from a series of chronicles called the *Gesta Pontificum Autissodorensium* – 'The Acts of the Bishops of Auxerre' – and from the memoirs of the Abbé Lebeuf, published in 1743. Writing as he did before the Revolution, Lebeuf had access to documents which have since disappeared. Between them these two sources enable us to see the progress of the building often in sharp focus and to date some parts of it with precision.

The Gothic cathedral of Auxerre replaced a Romanesque one of some distinction, of which the crypt, started in 1035, is the only survivor. The crypt attracted the attention of Prosper Mérimée who described it, in a report of 9 February 1844, as 'a monument of immense interest'. The cathedral seems to have been in a Romanesque style which came from the Ile de France or Normandy. With its twin towers mounting guard to either side of the apse, it sounds like a larger version of Morienval. It had been modernized by Hugues de Noyers, who was bishop from 1183 to 1206, 'in order that the church, which, according to the former custom, was always badly lit [*subobscura*], should be illuminated with a more ample brightness'.

Hugues de Noyers was a great builder. Not only did he renovate the cathedral – he built or rebuilt the castles of Varzy, Toucy, Regennes, Beauretour and Noyers. It is probable that he bequeathed to his successor, Guillaume de Seignelay, a cathedral church that was in a good state of repair. But it was out of date.

Lebeuf recounts an amusing story about the election of Guillaume de Seignelay to the bishopric. In 1194, at the age of thirty, he was elected dean of Auxerre. His elder brother, Manassès, was archdeacon of Sens and of Auxerre. So devoted to each other were the two brothers that they always shared not only the same house but the same bed. When Hugues de Noyers vacated the see it was offered first to Manassès, who turned it down, protesting that his brother the dean was more suited to the post. The offer was then made to Guillaume, but he, 'with tears in his eyes', protested that his brother was not only the elder but had led a more exemplary life. The archbishop of Sens had to be asked to intervene. He had a candidate in mind for the deanery and prevailed upon Guillaume to accept. On the feast of the Purification, 1206, he was duly elected bishop of Auxerre. In the following year Manassès was elected to the see of Orléans and the two brothers had to part company. The election of Guillaume was of no small importance for the future of Auxerre Cathedral, for he was determined to be abreast of his times. 'Seeing that his church was suffering from the age of its construction and badly put together' – and we may doubt the honesty of that description – 'whereas all the bishops around him were raising cathedrals of new and most splendid beauty, he did resolve to order a new edifice, with the help of specialists skilled in the art of building, so that it might not be wholly different from the others in its appearance and its design.'

With this intention, Guillaume de Seignelay pulled down the Romanesque choir but retained the crypt which he used as the foundation for his new building and thus determined its proportions. In pulling down the old choir the builders made what could have been a dangerous miscalculation, for the towers which flanked it collapsed. The event is recorded in the *Gesta Pontificum*.

Now in the year of Our Lord 1217, on the Sunday before Advent in honour of the Holy Trinity, we were starting the solemn day. There were on either side, in the old church, two towers of no considerable height and of great thickness of wall, one on the south, the other on the north, containing between them the whole breadth of the choir and the stalls of the canons. These towers began to crack open when the roof beams of the old work, by means of which they used to stand firm, were removed to make way for the new fabric – the soundness of their structure having earlier been impaired by a small rift. Yet it was not foreseen that they would threaten so quick a ruin. On the aforementioned feast, therefore, in a solemn manner as is the custom with such things, not only the small but even the great bells were rung; in their progressive clanging, it was feared, not without reason, that they would fall and crush all those who had gathered at the church in even greater numbers than usual on that day, on the pretext of the feast . . . Furthermore, the south tower was opening up in a major fissure. Seeing this, some people began to gather round to discuss it, and the word reached the canons. The master of the work was called, hard on the third hour, and was asked if the fall of the towers was imminently to be feared, and if the congregation could safely celebrate the divine offices beneath them. As he affirmed over and over again that there was no reason to be afraid, one of his apprentices, who was present, said it was not safe to remain beneath them for an hour. The master began to object, as if this were pressing an unnecessary fear on the canons, while pointing to some beams extending to the tower, which were keeping the whole apparatus from falling.

When he was pressed even more urgently on the question of their security, that he should make no pronouncement but the most certain, as if overcome by the importunity of his questioners, he replied: 'I mean nothing is at all certain; I do not know what the future may show.' At these words, as if in some presentiment of the spirit, the common feeling of all was that, when the impending procession was over (for it was the third hour), in the chapel of the Blessed Mary which is among the annexes of the great church, the solemnities of the Mass would be celebrated, which was done. Nevertheless all the bells were solemnly rung in the usual manner, as if there was nothing to fear . . . and when the Mass was over and the canons were sitting down to dinner together, lo, the south tower fell with a sudden crash against the north one, whose base was crushed deep within.

It is to be presumed that the master of the work referred to was the man in charge of the rebuilding of the choir. The anecdote reveals him as someone a little over-confident in the power of a structure to remain standing with the least possible support. Such an attitude might well be inferred from the architecture of the Gothic choir.

It creates a wonderful impression of spaciousness and lightness. The masonry dividing the lights of the clerestory windows is reduced to what is strictly necessary; the clustered columns of the great piers have been slimmed down to an absolute minimum; the triforium arcade is upheld by the most slender of colonettes; the columns at the entrance to the eastern chapel seem dangerously thin. Nowhere is there an ounce of superfluous stone. The skeleton of the shafts and vault ribs appears to stand free from the outer wall; the triforium forms an openwork screen in front of it, so that there are open walkways passing behind the supports both at triforium and at clerestory level, and this is repeated in the side aisles. These superimposed interior passages are identified by Robert Branner as 'the outstanding characteristic of Burgundian Gothic'. The feature first appeared in the Trinity Chapel at Canterbury and later at Lausanne and Geneva. Both these latter were completed in 1215 just at the time when the choir at Auxerre and the church of Saint-Martin de Clamecy were started. 'There can be little doubt', writes Branner, 'that Lausanne and Geneva played an important role in the design of Auxerre and Clamecy.'

The architecture has also certain affinities with Chartres – the three-storey façade, the clerestory windows composed of two lancets surmounted by a large rose, and the use of piers, one on each side of the choir, with a central cylinder flanked by four smaller columns. But although the choir has an obvious unity of style, there are certain features which imply a change of plan in the course of construction.

The choir itself was obviously intended to have a sexpartite vault. There are two double bays of which one retains the alternation *pile forte – pile faible*, but some weakness in the structure caused the builders to alter this. The second *pile faible* has been rebuilt as a *pile forte* and the vaulting is quadripartite. A sectional drawing shows that the capitals of the piers have been raised one by one and the vaults are now higher than those of the apse.

The new choir was well advanced by 1220, when Guillaume de Seignelay was translated to the see of Paris. His ambition that the choir, 'having shaken off its ancient form, should be resplendent in all the beauty of its renovated youth', was almost realized. It was finished by his successor at Auxerre, Henri de Villeneuve, who left his signature – the *Agnus Dei* – in one of the windows of the clerestory. This gives us a date not later than 1234 – the year of his death – for the completion of the first campaign. One has only to compare the choir at Auxerre with Sens to see how far the Gothic style had travelled in the space of seventy years.

In 1308 Pierre de Grez was consecrated bishop of Auxerre. We learn from his correspondence with Pope John XXII of his desire 'to replace with a richer and more elegant architecture that part of his church which was in a gross style [*rudi schemati*]'. The word '*rudis*', meaning something rough and uncultivated, is not one which we would apply to the Romanesque today. It referred, in this instance, to the nave.

Pierre de Grez's first move was to instigate an inquiry into the authenticity of the cathedral's most treasured relic – the body of St Amâtre, a bishop of Auxerre who was martyred in 418. Satisfied with the result of his enquiries, he detached the saint's head and placed it in a silver reliquary. Such a procedure was frequently the prelude to a fund-raising campaign in which the relic was taken round the diocese, or even further, by *quêteurs* or collectors of alms. Pope John also accorded indulgences and by 1321 we know that work had begun on the nave. In 1341 Jean de Valenfroy, 'master of the fabric' at Sens Cathedral, purchased a large quantity of stone from the quarries of Ivry, near Paris, for the chapter of Auxerre.

To walk from the choir of Auxerre into the nave is to pass from the thirteenth century to the fourteenth. The accent here is on the vertical lines and the presentation of a single vertical plane by the façade. This is achieved by the almost total elimination of capitals.

Viollet-le-Duc, in his great *Dictionnaire Raisonné de l'Architecture Française*, traces the gradual disappearance of the capital from the composition of the pier. First it lost its function, as at Limoges, of which he writes: 'It carries nothing; it is only an ornament, for the profiles of the arch which rest upon the abacus are exactly those of the pier.' The next stage, which is that reflected in the nave at Auxerre, is the reduction of the capital to an insignificant minimum. 'At the end of the 14th century the capitals assume so little importance that one hardly notices them. Then, any horizontal line, any sculpture which arrests the eye and prevents it from following without interruption the vertical lines of the architecture, embarrassed the Masters.'

The buttresses of the nave are internal and enclose between them four chapels to north and south of the aisles. This part of the church has therefore the width of a nave with double aisles and this width dictates that of the towers. The aisles, however, connect with the secondary arches of the west portal, but, because of the increased width, these doors are not central to their façades. The spaces to the right and left of them have been made use of to contain what might be called the overflow of the sculpture from the portals, set within a blind archway, but the aesthetic effect of this is not altogether happy.

But what the west front lacks in architectural coherence it makes up for by the excellence of the statuary. Much of this, and of the stained glass, suffered when Auxerre was occupied by the Huguenots in 1567. But Viollet-le-Duc drew attention to a petty vandalism of a different sort – the vandalism of children 'who, to this day, are allowed to do as they will although there are laws for the punishment of those who mutilate public buildings'. He then proceeds to a diatribe against those learned societies which protested against his own acts of restoration. 'Would it not be more useful', he asked, 'if they were to obtain from their magistrates a more attentive policing on the sites of these ceaseless mutilations of monuments which are unique and of the greatest value? Of the two centuries, which are the true Goths from the point of view of art? Is it the one which was capable of inspiring these sculptures and which possessed, in small provincial capitals, artists capable of executing them, or the one which allows these works to be destroyed by a few naughty children?'

He goes into raptures about the figure of Bathsheba on the right-hand portal. 'Never has the naked figure been so well rendered beneath the draperies . . . all the statues of this portal, and most notably the Sibyls, have the same merit. It is clear that these sculptors did not seek their draperies from the Antique; they did not drape their models with wet linen. This is cloth on the living nude . . . clothing worn and revealing all the delicacy of movement of a supple body.'

Marcel Aubert adds his praise of 'these charming personages and, beneath them, the little bas-reliefs carved in the beautiful Burgundian stone with its fine, close grain, in a style which is rich, firm and delectable, in the best Burgundian tradition'.

A feature of the portals at Auxerre is the exquisite architectural detail of the canopies which surmount the figures. It has the crisp precision of metalwork and it has survived extremely well. This is because the valley of the Serein, in Auxerrois and in Tonnerrois, furnishes some of the best limestone in France. The quarries of Montillot provided the beautiful white stone for Vézelay, and those of Tharoiseau the darker, ferruginous stone which offers so striking a contrast. Saint-Bris supplied the stone for Pontigny and later for the *collégiale* of Chablis. Next door to it are the quarries of Bailly which provided much of the stone for the cathedral of Auxerre.

The high quality of Burgundian limestone accounts also for the possibility of that slimming down to a minimum of the stonework of the structure which is so much a feature of the choir at Auxerre. It is evident also in one of the most important churches deriving from Auxerre – Notre-Dame de Dijon, a triumph of Gothic construction in a strongly Burgundian style. It was praised by Viollet-le-Duc as 'a masterpiece of reason in which the science of the builder is concealed beneath an apparent simplicity'.

Notre-Dame de Dijon

Viollet-le-Duc was the first architect since the Middle Ages to reach a profound understanding of the principles of Gothic construction and he devoted his careful scrutiny to the structure of Notre-Dame. The tall, monolithic and incredibly thin colonettes which support the apse vaults he describes as 'slender pins, as strong as if they were of cast iron, thanks to the quality of the stone employed'.

The building dates from the second quarter of the thirteenth century. A single reference, in 1229, to a bequest from the widow Améline le Riche 'for the construction of the said church' shows that work was in progress by that date. A rather unusual anecdote related by the Dominican Etienne de Bourbon gives the date of 1240 for near completion. A certain usurer of Dijon, walking beneath the west façade, was killed by the fall of one of the 'gargoyles'. The other usurers of the city clubbed together and obtained the removal of all these dangerous objects, of which the Dominican was an eyewitness.

The present 'gargoyles' were placed in the façade only in 1881. They are none of them gargoyles in the proper sense of the word, for they play no part in the water drainage system. They form the most striking and original feature of the church, for the west front takes the unusual form of a vast screen of masonry.

The west front of a Gothic church usually expresses the interior architecture, the divisions between nave and aisles, arcade, triforium and clerestory being clearly articulated on the façade. The screen at Notre-Dame de Dijon merely conceals the church. The horizontal divisions between its superimposed arcades do not correspond with either the triforium or the clerestory.

At first-floor level it contains a large chamber or tribune which now houses the organ. The floor of this tribune is several feet higher than that of the triforium and the difference in level is marked by a number of steps which could be useful to musicians. There is no evidence, however, that the tribune was intended for such a purpose, but it was clearly an important part of the designer's intention. Its presence directly affects the vaulting of the porch below.

This porch continues the sexpartite vaulting of the church, creating a double bay corresponding with the nave and four smaller bays corresponding with the side aisles. Owing to the level floor of the tribune above, the vaults of these bays are all the same height. Logically those of the side aisles should be lower. In order to keep the larger arches the same shape as the smaller arches, the architect has had to lower the spring of the larger ones and the difference in the height of the capitals is the distinctive feature of the porch.

The origins of the porch or narthex go a long way back into the history of the early Church, when it was thought proper for those as yet unbaptized to be segregated from the community of the faithful until they were ready for full admission. The narthex was the architectural expression of this segregation. With the advent of infant baptism the original *raison d'être* of the narthex became obsolete, but the practice of building it continued. The monastic Orders found a new necessity for this area of segregation as the nearest into which they dared to invite women.

In the days when public buildings were scarce, a church porch offered a convenient covered space for certain civil or judicial purposes, such as the hearing of causes. The regularity with which these practices were forbidden is only evidence for the frequency of their occurrence. To make secular use more difficult the porch or narthex was often entirely enclosed – as at Tournus. It was recognizably part of the church, from which it was separated by a partition. Later porches – of which one of the most beautiful is that of Saint-Germain-l'Auxerrois in Paris – were open on all sides. But Burgundy affords a rare example of the transition from closed narthex to open porch in the church of Saint-Père-sous-Vézelay.

Saint-Père-sous-Vézelay

The porch at Saint-Père is a late thirteenth-century addition to an early thirteenth-century church, opening towards the west by three arches like the *portail* of a miniature cathedral. The windows to the north and south were originally glazed, which would have made the porch more enclosed than it feels today.

But the church of Saint-Père is chiefly remarkable for its tower and its gable. As Viollet-le-Duc said: 'Burgundy, unfortunately for Art, only possesses a small number of bell towers of the thirteenth century.' The influence of the Cistercians was largely to blame for this, and behind their influence was that of St Bernard. He had forbidden the building of towers as 'contrary to the humility of the Order'. It may be inferred from this that St Bernard knew, or deeply suspected, that these towers served as monuments to civic, or even monastic, pride. His opinion was endorsed at the time of the Revolution, when the hostility of the *enragés* was often focused on towers and steeples as '*contraires à l'égalité*'.

Cluny, however, did not share the asceticism of St Bernard and it is chiefly among churches of the Order of Cluny that belfries were to be found. They are mostly of the twelfth century, but one of the first and finest of thirteenth-century steeples is that of Saint-Père-sous-Vézelay.

A particular feature of this tower, which is of course square, is an awareness on the part of the architect that it is going to become octagonal in order to support a spire; square spires do not succeed. At first-storey level he marks each corner of the square with a colonette; the capital of this colonette is set obliquely to the façades. At second-storey level the colonette is replaced by a statue, also facing obliquely. At the topmost storey the final transition from octagon to square is masked by four airy pinnacles, one at each corner, upheld by slender columns and set, as at Laon, obliquely to the corners of the tower. They were clearly destined to carry little steeples which stood as foothills to the central spire.

'Looking at this elegant construction,' wrote Viollet-le-Duc, 'beautiful by its happy proportions and by the charming details of its decoration, one might believe that the Burgundian school, in spite of the Cistercians, was not at the experimental stage.' He knew, however, of no Gothic tower in Burgundy of an earlier date.

There were to have been two such towers, but only the northern one was built. They would have framed the tall gable which is the second most impressive feature of Saint-Père. This gable, which rises high above the western façade, was built as part of a project to elevate the whole nave. The project was never realized, so the gable is free-standing.

It stands so high that the artist of the statues has taken perspective into account. Seen from their own level, the figures look slightly elongated; seen from ground level they are properly proportioned. It is not, however, a well-thought-out scheme. The architect has just squeezed in a maximum of nine narrow arches into which he has managed to insert ten figures by the expedient of making Jesus Christ and St Stephen share the same niche. A line drawn through the points of the arches over the figures' heads would bear no relationship to the outline of the gable. The result is an immediate impression of overcrowding and confusion. A more detailed inspection reveals that the figures are not all done to the same scale.

This gable has clearly provided the inspiration for that of the church of Sainte-Madeleine at Vézelay itself and is in all probability by the same artist. Here he corrected the errors of which he was guilty at Saint-Père. First of all he has relieved the congestion by taking the Apostles out of the gable and placing them between the five lancet windows beneath it. This leaves the whole area of the gable to the figures of Christ, the Virgin, St Anne and two attendant angels, who are all comfortably accommodated in spacious niches. But whereas at Saint-Père the sides of the gable are straight, here at Sainte-Madeleine they form a pointed arch – a disposition which Viollet-le-Duc believed to be unique. It would be difficult to find two churches in such easy proximity which afford between them such a wide range of Romanesque and Gothic architecture as the two churches of Vézelay. Both were nearly in ruins at the beginning of the nineteenth century; both were saved and restored by Viollet-le-Duc.

It is not always possible to determine what were the causes of the deterioration of the fabric. Sometimes, as at Sainte-Madeleine de Vézelay, it was due to faulty construction with faulty materials. More often it was simply due to lack of upkeep. One of the saddest examples of this is the church of Saint-Thibault-en-Auxois.

Saint-Thibault-en-Auxois

One of the most astonishing architectural experiences afforded by Burgundy is the first sight of the church of Saint-Thibault. It lies about half-way along the road between Semur-en-Auxois and Pouilly, but the best approach is from Vitteaux which brings the visitor in from the west so that he is confronted by the magnificent apse, rising high above the rooftops of a rather undistinguished village. It looks like a cathedral, or one of the great churches of the Ile de France – Saint-Sulpice de Favières or La Chapelle-sous-Crécy. One would expect a nave and transepts of the same height as the apse, but what nave there is – two bays of eighteenth-century construction – is only half as high. The apse is finished off so as to look like a polygonal tower, rising in solitary grandeur above its attendant chapels.

That there was a nave, accompanied by transepts but not by side aisles, is known from a plan of 1748, but the plan tells a sorry tale; everywhere, except in the apse and chapels, is written 'ruines: ruines: ruines' and the draughtsman has tried to represent the rubble on his plan. He has also shown the remains of monastic buildings to the south of the church. It cannot have contained a numerous establishment, for the refectory is hardly larger than one of the chapels, but the church of Saint-Thibault was a priory and only a priory until 1379 when it had to assume the double role of parish church as well.

It was unfortunate that it remained a priory, for when François I instituted the system of *commende*, which entitled him to appoint to all the lucrative posts in the Church, abbots and priors usually became absentees and the religious life of the Orders declined. The parishioners of Saint-Thibault were neglected to such an extent that they actually took their prior to law in 1579, but such was the cumbersome incompetence of the Church courts that it was not until 1616 that judgement was finally made – in their favour.

But if the spiritual needs of the people were neglected, so was the fabric of the church. On several occasions during the next century the parlement had to order the parishioners to contribute half the cost of upkeep. But the building continued to deteriorate until, in 1712, the tower fell in, causing great damage to the rest of the building. A year later the prior referred to the 'debris and almost total ruin of the church'. He recalled that the nave had collapsed previously.

In 1723 the parish obtained royal permission to hold a lottery in aid of the fabric fund. It raised 16,000 livres, but owing to the corruption of the system it was not until 1748 that the money reached the parish, and it was not 16,000 livres that they received, but 10,000. Prior Piget could only wring his hands in despair. 'If the payments had been made in 1734', he wrote, 'the church could have been re-erected and the poor inhabitants would not have been obliged for fourteen years to hear the Mass out in the cemetery in the rain and the cold and the snow, there being in this place only a chapel 15 feet deep.' He ended with an expression of appreciation of the Gothic style which must have been rare at that time: 'an order of architecture as beautiful and as exquisite as any in the kingdom'.

The existence of such a church in such a place demands explanation. All that can be said is that the priory of Notre-Dame, as it was first known, was able to obtain two ribs of St Thibault when his body was returned to France after his death near Vicenza. Devotion to the new saint, encouraged by a number of alleged miracles, made the priory a popular place of pilgrimage and the funds became available for the construction of a large and magnificent church.

The story of Thibault is told twice in the iconography of the church. The north transept is entered by a *portail* typical of the third quarter of the thirteenth century. It is a distinguished example of a feature common at the time, but it is outstanding in its possession of two doors, covered with carvings and in a remarkable state of preservation. The left-hand door tells the story of Thibault. It is fairly clear that the artist has drawn his inspiration entirely from the retable within the church, while adapting his compositions to fit the upright panels of the door. The story is easier to follow on the retable.

Thibault was born in Provins in 1017 to Arnulph and Willa, close relatives of the comte de Champagne. In the first scene his great-uncle Thibault, bishop of Vienne, is seen foretelling the glorious destiny of their child, as yet unborn. At his birth a huge hand of God descends to bless the boy. There follows a delightful pose of the mother and child, like any village madonna, with the baby Thibault chucking her under the chin. In the next scene he is a young man with a falcon on his wrist and accompanied by his friend Gauthier. They meet the hermit Burchard, before whom Thibault kneels and once again receives a blessing from on high. The two are then depicted on horseback, accompanied by their servants, going to join the community of Saint-Rémi de Reims.

The upper register begins with a scene in which Thibault and Gauthier change clothes with two poor pilgrims. Having renounced the world and its wealth, they are next seen, barefooted, carrying stone for the building of a church. In fact at this point in his career Thibault became a hermit in Luxembourg. The sequence is interrupted in the centre of the composition to depict a crucifixion, which is interesting in that it shows Adam, who was traditionally buried at Golgotha, rising to receive the mercy of the dying Christ. To the right of this is what appears to be an exorcism, followed by the death of Thibault. His soul is represented in the usual way as a little child being received by an angel; the scene thus bears a certain resemblance to that of his birth in which the infant Thibault is received by the midwife.

His popularity as a saint may be inferred from the magnificence of his shrine and this in turn reflects the munificence of the donations. The first of these that we know of were from Elizabeth de Charny, dame de Thil, and from Hugues de Toucy, vicomte de Tonnerre, in 1257. More were recorded in 1263 and all were earmarked for the fabric fund for they were made to the *oeuvre* – 'operi ecclesiae Sancti Theobaldi'. When in 1290 Robert II duke of Burgundy made a contribution it must have been to a building already of advanced construction, but gifts are recorded as late as 1321. In 1323, when the Duchess Agnès, daughter of St Louis, made a donation, it was to the 'oeuvre du monastère'. Perhaps the church was now completed and funds could be diverted to the monachal buildings of the priory. At least these acts of piety give us the approximate dates of the building.

The design has many distinctive features and the building is best thought of as a casket of stone and glass, a vast reliquary rather than a conventional church. Since there were no side aisles, there was no need for a main arcade. The façades are always the inner faces of the outside wall. As was usual at that time, the architect has sought to slim down the stone skeleton to an absolute minimum, acclaimed by Viollet-le-Duc as being 'd'une légerté incroyable', which gives an air of slightness if not of fragility to the apse.

Each bay is treated as a single, traceried screen divided into four horizontal sections. At the lowest level the screen takes the form of a blind arcade decorated with the slightest of cusps. Above this is a passageway, glazed on the outer side and contained within the openwork screen on the inner side. It is noticeable that the tracery of the screen differs from the tracery of the windows behind. The result is a confusion to the eye which must have been deliberate. Above this the triforium contains the one inelegant feature of the whole – a solid parapet or *garde-fou* which forms an unsightly band round the apse. The clerestory windows are on the same plane as the screen and continue its vertical lines. The apse was described by Marcel Aubert as 'one of the most elegant constructions raised by the architects of Burgundy at the end of the thirteenth century or the beginning of the fourteenth'.

The church is fortunate still to possess the reliquary of St Thibault, for, as Viollet-le-Duc records, 'the numerous pilgrims who visited it believed that they would be cured of all manner of diseases if they ate a morsel of the wood of which it is made, with the result that today this reliquary seems to have been nibbled by an army of rats'.

More interesting, from the point of view of the history of art, is the memorial to a knight on the south side of the sanctuary. He dates from the late thirteenth century and is thought to be the founder of the priory. He lies in front of a recessed arch on the back wall of which is a bas-relief depicting a funeral procession. It is described by Viollet-le-Duc in a letter to Mérimée dated 8 August 1846.

To either side of his head are two angels who are censing him; at his feet is a lion; two monks are reading the liturgy for the departed. The little bas-relief represents a procession of monks holding candles; they are followed by women in tears; one of them, supported by a man, has apparently succumbed beneath the weight of her affliction. Nothing could be more pathetic, nothing more gripping than this bas-relief of such an impeccable execution.

They form a significant contrast: the reliquary of the saint and the memorial to the great man of the world. Here at Saint-Thibault they are held in balance, but as the Middle Ages declined the accent was placed more and more upon the latter. The great men of the early Middle Ages tried to purchase eternity by pious foundations; those of the late Middle Ages seem more concerned to perpetuate their memory on earth. The monument came to replace the reliquary as the focus of artistic activity. Burgundy possesses no clearer witness to this change of emphasis than in the tombs which it raised to two of its greatest dukes.

Ducal monuments

It was the desire to perpetuate one's memory after death, the same desire that raised the pyramids, which led to a particular flowering of art in Burgundy. The late Gothic here was more distinguished in its monumental statuary than in its architecture. This flowering coincided with the century covered by the dukes of the Valois dynasty and owed a great deal to their patronage.

After the death of the last of the Capetian dukes, Philippe de Rouvres, on 21 November 1361, the succession was disputed between Jean le Bon, king of France and Charles le Mauvais, king of Navarre. Of these at least the latter merited his title in the eyes of France and Burgundy. The devastations of the English under Edward III in the vicinity of Flavigny and Semur, 'as if', wrote Joseph Calmette, 'they had set themselves the task of making the duchy a hotbed of anglophobia', had been abetted by the king of Navarre. Although technically his claim to the ducal coronet was the better, neither the French nor the Burgundians were prepared to support his candidature. The death of Philippe de Rouvres was even kept a secret while the negotiations were taking place. But although the title of duke of Burgundy was assumed by the king of France, there was no annexation. Burgundy retained its independent status. Two years later Jean le Bon conferred the dukedom on his youngest son, whose intrepid behaviour at the battle of Poitiers had earned the title of Philippe le Hardi.

Thus was inaugurated the dynasty of the Valois who were to be acclaimed by Brantôme as 'the four great dukes of Burgundy'. They were: Philippe le Hardi (1364–1404), Jean sans Peur (1404–19), Philippe le Bon (1419–67) and Charles le Téméraire (1467–77). With the death of the last-named at the siege of Nancy the line was extinguished and Burgundy once more reverted to the Crown of France. This time it was not to be separated.

The reign of Philippe le Hardi was distinguished by his patronage of the arts. He surrounded himself with architects, sculptors, painters, goldsmiths, silversmiths and weavers of tapestry. Among the architects were Jacques de Neuilly and Philippe Mideaul who were responsible for important additions to the ducal palace at Dijon, and Drouet de Dammartin, who had assisted Raymond du Temple with the construction of the Louvre for Charles V. Drouet de Dammartin was the builder of the Chartreuse de Champmol, on the outskirts of Dijon.

The Chartreuse de Champmol

It was on 10 September 1377 that Philippe le Hardi first inspected the site. A year later he bought the land with the intention of settling here a community of twenty-four Carthusians together with five lay brothers and a prior. Their church was to be the Saint-Denis of the dukes of Burgundy – their last resting place and the mausoleum which housed their memorials. On 20 August 1383 the first stone was laid by Marguerite, duchess of Burgundy and the second by her twelve-year-old-son, Jean, comte de Nevers, later to be known as Jean sans Peur.

A team of sculptors and painters, mostly of Flemish origin, was assembled at Dijon to realize the sculptural decoration of the church and to create the monumental sepulchre for the duke. Three great names succeeded each other as leaders of this team and in each case the succession went from uncle to nephew. First was Jehan de Marville; he had been on the payroll of the duke since 1372. On the death of Marville in 1389, Claus Sluter, the greatest name of the three, took charge of the works. Sluter died some time in January 1405 and his nephew Claus de Werve solemnly undertook to complete the sepulchre 'according to the terms of the agreement made with the late Claus Sluter'.

The details of the construction of the Chartreuse de Champmol were carefully recorded in the accounts. They yield an interesting picture of the close relationship between patron and artist.

The position of valet de chambre was accorded to the most distinguished practitioners. Under Philippe le Hardi we find Jehan de Marville and Claus Sluter '*ymaigiers*' (makers of statues) and 'varlets de chambre à Monseigneur'. The painters Beaumez, Maluel and Broederlam had the same position together with a master-glazier, a goldsmith, a silversmith, a tapestry weaver, an armourer, a harpist and the duke's barber. The title of valet de chambre conferred upon its bearer freedom of access to the duke and always implies a personal relationship. It was not unknown for the duke to stand sponsor to their children.

The accounts refer continually to the house in which first Marville and then Sluter lived and worked. It is described as 'la maison de Monseigneur le Duc où demeure Claus' and its situation can be accurately identified. It was within the outbuildings of the ducal palace next to the Chambre des Comptes. Philippe le Hardi had only to cross a narrow street to enter the courtyard of his master-sculptor. He must have been a welcome as well as a frequent guest, for his visits are recorded in the accounts because of the wine offered to the workmen on these occasions. The stables were converted into workshops for the craftsmen who assisted the *ymaigier*.

These formed a team of ten '*ouvriers*'. Four had the title of *maîtres sculpteurs*, three that of *dégrossisseurs* – those who rough-hewed the blocks of stone or marble – and three that of *tailleurs de pierre* – dressers of stone. The hierarchy is revealed by the salaries. Jehan de Marville was paid eight *gros* per diem; Drouet de Dammartin six and the *maîtres sculpteurs* four. In addition to his higher salary, Marville had the services of two valets and a horse, and his free lodgings.

The fact that the sculptor was more highly paid than the architect was born out by the fabric of the Chartreuse. The church had the simplicity of style which befitted a Carthusian chapel, but this austerity was offset by the richness of the retables and the excellence of the carved figures.

The Chartreuse de Champmol was destroyed as the result of the Revolution. It was sold to a private owner, Emmanuel Crète, who had represented Burgundy on the States General. Crète pulled most of the buildings down, including the church, but he carefully preserved the west portal. It was probably the only part worth preserving; architecturally, the Carthusian chapel was undistinguished. Its chief claim to merit was in the sculptures of Claus Sluter with which the portal was decorated.

The architecture of the doorway, with its empty architraves and undecorated tympanum, is of the simplest Gothic design which throws into relief the five figures which are its only ornament. To left and right of the double doors are kneeling figures of the duke and duchess, their attention focused upon the central group of the Virgin and Child. Each is backed up by a further figure; St John the Baptist behind the duke and St Catherine behind the duchess, who seem to reinforce their petitions. As Eugène Fyot says: 'Philip knew better than anyone how an entreaty stands a greater chance of being accepted if it is presented with eloquence by persons of influence.' John the Baptist is there, no doubt, in the first place as patron saint of the Carthusians, but also as a great preacher, skilled in presenting his case. Sluter has obviously taken a real Jew as his model. St Catherine, who converted the philosophers sent to argue her into abjuring her faith, performs the same role; her whole stance is suggestive of eloquent persuasion.

Claus Sluter was both a realist and a portraitist. There can be no doubt that the likeness of Philippe le Hardi is a faithful representation of the ageing duke. He is depicted not so much as a humble penitent but as 'the head of a State conversing with the Virgin', so Cyprian Monget puts it, 'and to whatever the substance of the prayer which is being formulated behind his closed lips, the success of the politics of the duchy could be no stranger'. As he said himself, he had chosen the Carthusians because 'it was their mission to pray for the people and for those entrusted with their government'.

The treatment of the face is ably seconded by the treatment of the robes. 'No school', wrote Joseph Calmette, 'has taken to such lengths the art of rendering the folds of a material and of making it serve for the expression of movements and even of sentiments, than the school of Sluter.'

In the figure of the duchess Sluter has taken his realism to the point of frankness. The face, with the downward turn of the mouth, is grim and sulky. It exactly illustrates Froissart's observation: 'Madame de Bourgogne était fort absolue et assez méchante' – she was very peremptory and pretty ill-natured. It has even been suggested, by Eugène Fyot, that Duke Philippe never qualified more truly for the epithet *le Hardi* than in taking such a woman as his wife.

The next task allotted to the great sculptor was a Calvary, placed in the centre of the cloister. The Calvary was destroyed during the Revolution, but the huge hexagonal base, with its six figures of the Prophets who predicted the Passion, has survived. It took the form of a fountain and derived from this and from its most prominent personality the name of 'les Puits de Moïse'.

The figure of Moses is probably Sluter's masterpiece – the face of the man who had beheld the face of God. An odd convention, which owes its origins to the *Drame de la Passion* of Rouen, provided the forehead of Moses with projections like the first growth of a stag's horns – 'cornuta facie' – in an attempt to render in three-dimensional form how 'the skin of his face shone' when he came down from Mount Sinai.

There is an apparent touch of humour in the juxtaposition of Daniel and Isaiah. Daniel turns towards the aged prophet and indicates a phrase on his phylactery, while Isaiah, his regard downcast and discouraged, stands in an attitude of petulant rejection of whatever he is saying.

These statues were originally all coloured and some of them were adorned with ornaments of brass. On 2 January 1402, Hannequin d'Att, 'goldsmith of Dijon', was paid 4 livres and 10 sols for one 'diadème de cuivre' for the figure of Mary Magdalene and for a 'bésicle' – that is to say, a pair of spectacles – for Jeremiah.

With all this work on the Calvary and its support, progress was slow on the sepulchre of Philippe le Hardi. On 28 December 1402, a breach had been made in the apse wall to bring in the great slab of black marble on which the recumbent figure was to lie, but on the death of Philippe on 27 April 1404, the work was very far from finished. The design, however, had been agreed and, as we have seen, after the death of Sluter, Claus de Werve undertook to execute it faithfully.

Claus de Werve, interpreting his uncle's inspiration, has brought to life the concept of a funeral procession, which elsewhere had been reduced to a formula. The forty little figures of the mourners – *les pleurants* – are each highly individual, not only in the distinctive realism of their expressions, but in the seemingly inexhaustible variety of their draperies, which were accomplished, according to André Michel, 'with an artistry which is infinitely ingenious, which turns to good account the costumes themselves, so that the draperies contribute to the expression of the state of mind and the dramatic situation'.

The architectural setting takes the form of a gallery in the finest Flamboyant tradition. To break the monotony of an uninterrupted arcade, a rhythm has been introduced between broad double archways and narrow triangular niches. In the shelter of these openings the figures of the *pleurants* are grouped, as if the funeral procession had halted and was standing at ease. The alternation of the niches dictates the disposition of the figures, the triangular apertures containing only one figure and the double archways two. These juxtapositions play an important part in the composition; 'as they turn towards one another', wrote Pierre Quarré, 'to exchange a few words or to make some gesture of consolation, or are turned in upon themselves in spiritual recollection, meditation or in an exalted moment of prayer, each one manifests his own grief with an astonishing variety of attitudes'.

One of the greatest compliments to the work of Claus de Werve came from Philippe le Bon when he, in his turn, wished to erect a similar memorial to his father, Jean sans Peur, murdered on the bridge of Montereau on 10 September 1419. In 1435, when Claus was still in office, an order was placed for twenty-two large pieces of black marble from Dinant, but four years later Claus died. Philippe le Bon chose as his successor Jehan de La Huerta, a native of Aragon who was currently working at Chalon-sur-Saône. He was commissioned to produce something 'as good if not better and of the same and as fine a stone as that of the late most excellent prince of noble memory'. The tomb of Jean sans Peur is little more than a copy of that of his father.

Jehan de La Huerta, having made a start, abandoned his work at the end of 1456. It took five years before his successor was appointed, and in 1461 the good duke gave the commission to Antoine le Moiturier of Avignon, with an obligation to complete his task in three years. It was not, however, until 1470 that the tomb of Jean sans Peur and his wife was finally installed in the Chartreuse de Champmol, which thus became the proud possessor of two of the greatest masterpieces of Burgundian art.

It is interesting to read the praise bestowed upon these two tombs by the Cistercian Joseph Meglinger in 1667. It was not an age conspicuous for its capacity to appreciate Gothic art. He describes them as being superior to anything which I have seen, not only on this journey, but in the whole of my life. The alabaster is hollowed out with such delicacy that it might be the work of a goldsmith, and in the recumbent figures art has really triumphed over nature; above all I admired the faces on which the pallor of the marble expresses in so striking a manner those traces left by life at the moment when it has just departed from the body, so that you would have called it a peaceful slumber.

Here they were to sleep until the Revolution.

In 1791, when all religious Orders were suppressed, the chartreuse was sold and the tombs were removed to the Cathedral of Saint-Bénigne. The entrepreneur, named François Guillemot, estimated 2,100 livres for transferring them. Once again it necessitated the breaching of the walls. He specifies: 'one of the black marble slabs, being of a single block of 10 feet long by 7 feet 9 inches broad, it would be impossible to pass it through the doors, which are too small; it will be indispensable to make a breach in the north wall of the church and to close it up after the work is finished'. The interesting fact is that the monuments were still valued sufficiently highly to warrant such expensive treatment. Guillemot, in his estimate, described them as 'two monuments of great value to the arts in a country which has always cultivated these with success, and whose honour it is to have produced artists of the highest merit'.

On 2 July 1792, another entrepreneur named Duleu removed the tomb of Jean sans Peur from Champmol and set it up in a side chapel at Saint-Bénigne and on 16 July that of Philippe le Hardi – 'fort difficile à défaire' – was successfully placed in the adjoining chapel. On 31 July Guillemot was able to report that the monuments had been positioned perfectly, 'M. Duleu having taken great care'. It looked as if the preservation of these masterpieces was assured.

It was not for long. Already on 25 July the Duke of Brunswick had published his ill-conceived manifesto offering military help to the enemies of the Revolution. The reaction was immediate. On 1 August the Conseil Général of Dijon decreed the erection of a scaffold 'destiné à reçevoir la machine à décapiter'. The guillotine was to be established in permanence. On 4 August the statue of Louis XIV in the Place Royale was overthrown. On 10 August in Paris the mob invaded the Tuileries and the monarchy was abolished.

With the fall of the monarchy, the position of the Church became even more precarious. On 24 November the new bishop of Dijon, Jean-Baptiste Volpius, an *assermenté* – that is to say, a priest who had taken the oath of allegiance to the revolutionary government – celebrated his first Mass in Saint-Bénigne. He gave an immediate indication of his political position by having the *Marseillaise* played during the Offertory.

The abolition of the monarchy led to a movement which penetrated deep into society. Kings and queens were banished from the chessboard and replaced in packs of cards lest their appearance there 'might recall to players the spectre of despotism'. Even the very syllable 'roi' was expunged from place names by the fanatics, so that Rocroi was rechristened Roclibre.

An ideology which could go to such lengths could hardly be expected to tolerate real and deliberate memorials to monarchy. On 31 July 1793 Barère proposed the celebration of the anniversary of the fall of the monarchy by the destruction, at Saint-Denis, of their sepulchres, which, to his mind 'semblent encore, même dans la tombe, s'enorgueillir d'une grandeur évanouie' and he demanded that 'the strong arm of the Republic must efface without pity these proud epitaphs which recall the dreadful memory of kings'.

What Paris did one day, Dijon did the next. On 8 August a motion was put before the Conseil Général to remove the tombs of the dukes from Saint-Bénigne and destroy them. Bishop Volpius was himself behind the move. The recumbent figures were to be replaced by 'emblems of Liberty and Equality'. The order was given that the marble figures were to be reduced 'en bloque brutte', in other words to be squared off into blocks. This order was not carried out.

It was recorded on 29 November 1794 by a certain M. Baudot that a caster of metal named Bonnin was given the job. He and his assistants 'set aside and spared the little Carthusians [the *pleurants*] and the Gothic architecture which formed the surround of both the tombs . . . They partly sawed through the hands of the dukes and duchess and did not break them . . . the heads were spared.'

There are other records of workmen refusing to carry out the destructions ordered by the Revolution. On 18 February 1795, a Monsieur Robert, administrateur du département de la Côte d'Or, protested against the vandalism at Dijon in a long letter to the Comité de l'Instruction Publique. 'One of the most sumptious monuments in Europe', he claimed, was the west front of Saint-Michel. Its bas-reliefs had been condemned to mutilation – 'the ladders were already erected for the destruction and pulverization of these masterpieces, when the workmen, overcome with respect for these monuments, refused to commit the outrage which was commanded of them, and the alert thus given to those who were friends of the arts saved them from the ignorant ferocity of a few stupid men'.

Great efforts were made also by the artist Devosge to arouse public opinion and to halt the vandalism, but it was not until 1817 that a museum was created at Dijon for the preservation of works of art. Ferret de Saint-Mesmin, the first conservateur, obtained a grant of 25,000 francs for restoring the tombs of the dukes and in January 1828 they were set up in the Grande Salle built for Philippe le Bon in 1450. It would be difficult today to detect that they had been vandalized in any way.

Robert, in his passionate appeal, had placed the tombs of the dukes of Burgundy second only to those of the Medici in Florence. Neither those of Marie de Bourgogne in Bruges, nor of the princes of Nassau in Delft, nor those of the house of Orange in Breda, could be compared to those of Dijon. To this list he makes one significant addition: 'the tombs of the House of Savoy in Notre-Dame de Brou'. Few critics today would be disposed to invert that order, but it must be conceded that the late Gothic, not only in Burgundy but in France as well, produced no more astonishing examples of architectural virtuosity than the three sepulchres of the Eglise de Brou.

L'Eglise de Brou

The church of Brou has exercised a strange fascination on both poets and writers of prose. Moyria sang its praises in a long and mostly tedious eulogy; Matthew Arnold, who sites it in a mountainous landscape far removed from the flat but fertile plains of Bresse, made it the subject of one of his more mediocre poems; Hilaire Belloc, in a letter to Mrs Raymond Asquith, credited it with 'a beauty beyond this world and smiling like an early spring morning in Paradise, dumb with beatitude'. But nothing in either poetry or prose has gone to such lengths as the panegyric of Edgar Quinet. In one of the most purple of purple passages he sentimentalizes over this church which was rightly described by Robert Speaight as itself 'a purple passage in architecture'.

'The Middle Ages were dying', wrote Quinet; 'they were dying on their feet . . . the sixteenth century was drawing near and mounting the doorsteps; it was knocking on the door; it was coming like a gravedigger to take the corpse from the bed on which it was lying in state.'

Christopher Columbus was already afloat; Luther was already studying the Epistle to the Romans at Wittenberg; Michelangelo was already doing to art what Luther was doing to doctrine.

Gothic architecture had suspended its work. It had arrived at its summit together with the society which it represented. It lacked the strength to rise any higher . . . The art of the Middle Ages, abandoned and dying, rallied itself for a final effort and constructed its own tomb for itself in the church of Brou. There it was, in the earth of France, that it registered its final thought and laid itself down in the coffin. Ah! those marble mourners which surround the tomb of Marguerite, may they never wipe away their tears! For it is not only Marguerite and the duke of Savoy who sleep in the grave; it is a thousand years of history; it is the old belief, the old love, the dust of all the fallen faiths; it is the lost tradition, the lay of the last minstrel which the coming of the sixteenth century was to reduce to ashes.

It is entertaining, but it is stark nonsense. The Gothic in France was by no means moribund in 1513 when the church of Brou was started. The stalls of Amiens, the finest and most fantastic expression of the late Gothic in wood, were started a few years earlier and finished later. The beautiful Gothic transepts of Sens and Senlis and Beauvais, conceived and realized by Martin Chambiges towards the end of the sixteenth century, were still to come. The fall of the spire at Beauvais in 1573 is a much more plausible date for the demise of the Gothic style than the beginnings of Brou. The church of Brou is a mausoleum – not of the Gothic style or of the Middle Ages, but of three persons: Marguerite d'Autriche, her husband, Philibert de Savoie, and his mother, Marguerite de Bourbon.

Marguerite de Bourbon had married Philippe, comte de Bresse and later duc de Savoie. In 1480 he was seriously injured in an accident on the hunting field, and Marguerite made a vow that, if he recovered, she would found a monastery at Brou. He did recover but she died three years later without having fulfilled her vow.

Philippe de Savoie died in 1497 and was succeeded by his son, Philibert le Beau. Philibert and his sister, Louise de Savoie, had been brought up in the court of France. Louise was later to marry Charles d'Angoulême and to become the mother of François I. Philibert le Beau married Marguerite d'Autriche who was the granddaughter of Charles le Téméraire and the last heiress of the Valois dukes. On the death of Charles le Téméraire, Louis XI had asserted his rights over the duchy of Burgundy, but to make doubly sure of his position he arranged a marriage alliance between his own son, the future Charles VIII, and Marguerite, who was only two years old at the time. To prepare her for her position as queen of France she was brought up at the Château d'Amboise in the Loire Valley, together with Louise and Philibert de Savoie. Philibert was eventually to be her third husband.

For the marriage between Marguerite and Charles VIII never took place. In 1491 he married Anne de Bretagne and Marguerite was sent back to her father, Maximilien, emperor of Austria. Rousselet records the story that, soon afterwards, she was offered some extremely sour wine. On enquiring what country it came from, she was told it was from France. 'Je ne m'étonne pas,' she replied, 'les serments n'y valent rien.' It was a pun which does not translate into English: *serment* means an oath; *sarment* means the branch that bears the grapes.

Marguerite's marriage to Philibert – by all accounts a happy one – did not last for more than three years. One day he was out hunting at Lagnien-en-Bugey. A picnic had been prepared by the palace servants in a shady spot on the banks of the Rhône. He was overheated by the chase and the coolness of the atmosphere brought on a pleurisy of which he died on 10 September 1504 at the Château de Pont d'Ain where he had been born.

Marguerite now determined to realize the vow of her mother-in-law and to build at Brou a monastery with a church which was to provide a mausoleum for herself, her husband and his mother. The building was entrusted to a Flemish mason, Louis van Bogen. Beginning in 1513 he completed his task in 1532, just short of twenty years. In 1530 Marguerite died without ever having seen her church. She had, however, kept a very close control over the designs. The cartoons made by Jan Van Room for the sepulchres were drawn 'as large as the life'. In 1526 Conrad Meyt was commissioned to execute the statuary.

The difficulties under which Van Bogen worked can be illustrated by a single example. The bringing of the Carrara marble to Brou was no mean undertaking. From the nearest point on the Rhône at

Neyron it is a distance of only some 50 kilometres, but it took nine horses fifteen days to carry the three largest blocks for the wheels of the cart were continually breaking and the cart itself broke twice.

In spite of such obstacles, the building of the church progressed at an astonishing speed. Speed of construction naturally results in unity of style and the nave of Brou exhibits this unity to perfection. There is no variety to be detected; it is beautifully designed, beautifully executed and beautifully lit. The pale, near-white stone of Ramasse looks as if it was quarried yesterday.

And yet, in spite of this perfection – or possibly because of it – there is something unsatisfying. Perhaps André Maurois was expressing something deeply true when he admitted: 'J'aime mieux les fautes vivantes qu'une perfection morte' – 'I prefer faults which are alive to a perfection which is dead.'

But it is not in its architecture that Brou is chiefly distinguished. The work of the mason is the necessary precondition for the work of the carver. The three sepulchres – Duke Philibert with his mother on one side and his wife on the other – have taken the tradition of Champmol to its ultimate extreme. For, strictly speaking, the Eglise de Brou is not a church; it is a mausoleum, a gigantic chantry, a place where the dead were to be eternalized in stone and Masses multiplied for the salvation of their souls. Nevertheless it takes the form of a church – of a very large collegiate church with stalls for the monks or canons.

It is in the statuary and carved decorations that the distinctive character of Brou lies. It is probably the most elaborate sculptural ensemble that the Gothic age ever produced. The visitor cannot fail to be amazed at its richness, bewildered by its complexity and overwhelmed by the exuberance of its conception.

The richness of the decoration forms a striking contrast with the clean-cut lines of the architecture and is used to emphasize certain focal points in the church. It occurs first in the portal of the west front which marks the entrance; it occurs in the choir screen which marks the entrance to the place of worship; it is used, in the woodwork of the stalls, to mark the whole of the choir area, and it culminates in the three sepulchres and in the exquisite retable which faces the tomb of Marguerite d'Autriche.

Where the sepulchres themselves are concerned, one cannot help being struck by the contrast between the peace and repose of the recumbent effigies and the restless movement of the surrounding architecture. We are never allowed to see a pure form or a plain surface; all the lines are broken and all the spaces filled; arches grow out of arches and lose their shape in meaningless projections; cusps curl in upon themselves and break forth, like Aaron's rod, into the writhing tendrils of some budding plant; pinnacles cluster together to canopy niches crowded with posturing figures. But the architectural forms – cusps, arches, ogives, canopies and crowns – all disappear beneath the brittle incrustations of a carved ornament which defies description.

This is particularly true of the ponderous baldachino raised over the effigy of Marguerite d'Autriche. Opposite to her, on the east wall of the chapel, is the retable of the Seven Joys of the Virgin. At least this retable can be seen as a conscious and coherent composition. There is an airy lightness about the whole to which the lacelike decoration of the architecture is entirely appropriate and provides a proscenium for the little tableaux – an open screen of bright, Flamboyant Gothic.

The miniature scenes are delightful, but Victor Nodet, the author of an important monograph on Brou, takes exception to the little angels – or are they cupids? – who flit like bees about a flower-bed 'with their affected expressions, their emphatic gestures, the tortured lines of their draperies which adhere to their bodies revealing a thick anatomy of soft fat . . . accentuated by a talented technique, light and brilliant, which one can only regret to see used in the service of such Italianized Flemish'.

For the Italianate has made its intrusion into the background of the scenes within the niches, such as the Annunciation, which credits the Virgin with the possession of an uncommonly fine Renaissance bedstead. It has to be said that wherever the Renaissance has invaded the decoration – most notably in the large babies, with their ugly rolls of fat, who surround the tomb of Philibert – its effect is wholly deplorable.

The Renaissance did not come, as Edgar Quinet appears to have thought, like a gravedigger to the bedside of a dying man, nor as a cuckoo ousting the Gothic chick from the nest. It began with a number of rather timid little appearances, mostly in the form of decorative details applied to a church that remained faithful to the structural methods of the Middle Ages, or a touch of the Italianate stuck on to the façades of a château which remained impregnably feudal and French.

In the late fifteenth century Corinthian columns and cornices had already provided the backgrounds to the miniatures of Jean Fouquet and Etienne Chevalier and had put in a modest appearance in the chapel of Saint-Lazare in the church of La Major at Marseille. The first years of the sixteenth century saw the application of pilasters and arabesques to the gatehouse at Gaillon; Chenonceau was started in the same year as the Eglise de Brou. In Burgundy the Renaissance details of Pagny-le-Château date only from 1536 and those of the west front of Saint-Michel de Dijon from the following year. It was not until 1546, with the building of Ancy-le-Franc, that Burgundian architecture was to receive the full impact of the Renaissance.

Bibliography

J. Richard: 'Châteaux, Châtelains et Vasseaux en Bourgogne aux 11e et 12e Siècles', in *Cahiers de Civilization Mediévale*, 1960.

Semur-en-Auxois
Vicomte de Truchis: 'Semur-en-Auxois', in *Congrès Archéologique de France*, Avallon, 1907.
L. Bocquin: *Esquisse Pittoresque, Morale et Historique de la Ville de Semur*, 1977.
A. de Vaulabelle: *Histoire Générale de Semur-en-Auxois*, 1927.

Flavigny-sur-Ozerain
P. Levantal: *Flavigny*, 1978.
Vicomte de Truchis: 'Flavigny', in *Congrès Archéologique de France*, Avallon, 1907.

Montréal
E. Petit: 'Seigneurie de Montréal-en-Auxois', in *Bulletin de la Société des Sciences de l'Yonne*, 1865.
F. Salet: 'Montréal', in *Congrès Archéologique de France*, Auxerre, 1959.
Comte P. Biver: 'Some Examples of English Alabaster Tables in France', in *Architectural Journal*, 1910.

Noyers
E. Petit: *Les Sires de Noyers*, 1874.
M. Alméras: *Noyers*, 1975.
J. Vallery-Radot: 'Noyers', in *Congrès Archéologique de France*, Auxerre, 1959.

Châteauneuf-en-Auxois
Comte A. de Vogüé: 'Châteauneuf et ses Seigneurs', in *Mémoires de la Société Eduenne*, Vol. 41, 1915.

The Château de Brandon
A. Dessertenne: *Le Château de Brandon*, 1986.
E. Fyot: 'Le Château et les Seigneurs de Brandon', in *Mémoires de la Société Eduenne*, Vol. 28, 1900.

L'Hôpital de Tonnerre
F. Salet: 'L'Hôpital Notre-Dame des Fontenilles à Tonnerre', in *Congrès Archéologique de France*, Auxerre, 1959.

L'Hospice de Beaune

J. Boudrot: *L'Hospice de Beaune*, 1881.

A. Perier: *Nicolas Rolin*, 1904.

A. Rhein: 'Beaune: l'Hôtel Dieu', in *Congrès Archéologique de France*, 91, Dijon, 1929.

Baron Verhaegen: 'Le Polyptique de Beaune', in *Congrès Archéologique de France*, 91, Dijon, 1929.

L'Hôtel Chambellan

E. Fyot: *L'Hôtel Chambellan*, 1925.

La Cathédrale de Sens

O. von Simson: *The Gothic Cathedral*, 1956.

R. Branner: *Burgundian Gothic Architecture*, 1960.

I. Dunlop: *The Cathedrals' Crusade*, 1982.

La Cathédrale d'Auxerre

J. Lebeuf: *Histoire d'Auxerre*, 1743.

C. Porée: *La Cathédrale d'Auxerre*, 1926.

J. Vallery-Radot: 'Auxerre: La Cathédrale de Saint-Etienne', in *Congrès Archéologique de France*, 118, Auxerre, 1958.

Notre-Dame de Dijon

J. Vallery-Radot: 'Notre-Dame de Dijon', in *Congrès Archéologique de France*, 91, Dijon, 1928.

Saint-Père-sous-Vézelay

Y. Bruand: 'L'Eglise de Saint-Père-sous-Vézelay', in *Congrès Archéologique de France*, 118, Auxerre, 1958.

Saint-Thibault-en-Auxois

M. Aubert: 'Saint-Thibault', in *Congrès Archéologique de France*, 91, Dijon, 1928.

A. Colombet: *Saint-Thibault: L'Eglise at ses Oeuvres d'Art*, s.d.

E. Viollet-le-Duc. 'Eglise et Châsse de Saint-Thibault', in *Annales Archéologiques*, 1846.

Ducal monuments

J. Calmette: *Les Grands Ducs de Bourgogne*, 1949.

M. Aubert: 'La Chartreuse de Champmol', in *Congrès Archéologique de France*, 91, Dijon, 1928.

C. Monget: *La Chartreuse de Dijon*, 1898.

P. Quarré: *Les Pleurants des Tombeaux des Ducs de Bourgogne*, 1971.

L'Eglise de Brou

V. Nodet: *L'Eglise de Brou*, s.d.

M. de Moyria: *L'Eglise de Brou* (introduction by Edgar Quinet), 1835.

Le Père Rousselet: *Histoire et Description de l'Eglise de Brou*, 1767.

THE RENAISSANCE

One of the most striking forms of late Gothic ornament was the pinnacle or canopy which surmounted a niche or formed the framework of a stained glass figure. By the sixteenth century pinnacles appear to be merely ornamental. Viollet-le-Duc observed that they had become something extraneous – 'hors d'oeuvre' – not properly bonded into the masonry but simply stuck on to it, 'des édicules plantés sur des contreforts', decorative survivals of a forgotten function. Perhaps it was because they played no role in the structure that they were the most easily replaced with something else. For these were the first features of the Gothic style to be translated into Italian idiom. In place of the cusps and crockets and gables and finials, there appeared a series of little superimposed cupolas or temples of diminishing size, known in Italian as *tempietti*. They made their first appearance in Burgundy in 1530 in the Chapelle de Bouton in the church of Notre-Dame de Beaune.

Jean-Baptiste de Bouton, seigneur de Suze and du Thillot, became a canon of Notre-Dame in 1511, but he seldom if ever exercised his functions there, for in the following year he was appointed chancellor of Rouen Cathedral. An amusing little anecdote illustrates his attitude towards his canonical duties at Beaune. Every Christmas one of the canons was expected to play the part of King Herod in the Mystery of the Nativity. In 1522 this role fell to the Chanoine Bouton. To atone for declining it he offered a gold embroidered cope, costing 100 écus d'or. In thanking him for this munificent gift, the chapter stated that 'Aaron himself would not have blushed to wear such a vesture before the altar'.

As chancellor of Rouen Cathedral, Bouton was in close touch with the archbishop and was a frequent visitor to his Château de Gaillon, where the Renaissance had made one of its earliest appearances in France. He died at Rouen on 7 November 1532. But Bouton never forgot that he was a Burgundian and a canon of Beaune, and it was here at Notre-Dame that he wished to be interred. He started to construct his mausoleum two years before he died and it was still unfinished at his death. In his will he decreed that 'the money which is in my chest shall be used to complete the work which I have begun in the Chapel at Beaune.' On 16 January 1534 the first Mass was said in the chapel, from which we may conclude that the work was finished.

Notre-Dame de Beaune is one of the darkest and most ill-lit churches in Burgundy and the Chapelle de Bouton does not escape the general obscurity. Its chief interest is in the six *tempietti* which, before the Revolution, used to contain six alabaster statues of the four Evangelists together with Moses and David, who traditionally represented the Old Testament. The beautifully coffered ceiling, possibly inspired by that at the Palais de Justice at Dijon, is very difficult to see in the semi-darkness of the chapel.

From the outside the one important feature is an attractive though apparently useless gallery just beneath the roof of the south-west corner of the church. The pillars of the gallery rise from a parapet which is in a purely Italian style – as Henri David says: 'the most Lombardic of all Renaissance friezes in Burgundy'. On the west side the gallery is supported by a double recessed arch, divided by a pilaster ending in a pendentive. These twin arches, together with the detail of the parapet, form an unmistakable connection between the Chapelle de Bouton and the chapel at Pagny-le-Château. It is clear that both were conceived by the same mind.

Pagny-le-Château

One of the most tragic losses to Burgundian architecture was undoubtedly that of Pagny-le-Château, some 35 kilometres to the east of Beaune. It was pulled down in 1774 by the duc de la Vallière. In 1835, Henri Baudot published a long description of it; he quotes no source for his information, but we know that he had at his disposition the notes made by his uncle. It is quite possible that his uncle knew the château before it was demolished and was describing what he had seen. Henri Baudot's account is so detailed that it is hardly possible to believe that he was romancing.

There was an ancient fortress here since the tenth century. It belonged to the great Burgundian family of Vienne. In 1436 Jeanne de Vienne, dame de Fontaine-Française, married Jean de Longvy, seigneur de Givry. In 1526 Françoise de Longvy, the heiress to their estates at Pagny, married Philippe Chabot, comte de Charny, grand amiral de France and the childhood friend of François I. Françoise de Longvy had an uncle, Claude, Cardinal de Givry, who was one of the great figures of the French Renaissance.

With his father a Longvy and his mother a Beauffremont, he came from the bosom of the Burgundian aristocracy. At the age of thirty he succeeded his uncle as bishop of Macon, and eighteen years later, in 1529, he was offered the diocese of Langres. Claiming that 'he felt too weak for the charge', he nevertheless accepted it 'so as to conform with the will of God'.

Langres was one of the bishoprics which carried with it a dukedom and the dignity of being one of the Twelve Peers of France. Together with the evêque-comte de Beauvais, it was his function to 'uphold' the king on his throne on the *jubé* of Reims Cathedral after his coronation. In addition to the dukedom, the bishopric of Langres was endowed with 150 seigneuries, including the titles of comte de Mont-Saulion, marquis de Coublans, baron de Luzy, Mussy and Gurgy-le-Château, and the rich abbacies of Saint-Bénigne and Saint-Etienne de Dijon. The combined revenues of these were enormous. They put him in a position to exercise an extensive patronage of art, which seems to have been his major interest in life. One of his finest creations was the chapel at Pagny.

In about the year 1530 the comte de Charny began to rebuild the château. 'The whole northern range', writes Baudot,

which formed the principal block or donjon, was completely reconstructed. It was in the form of a rectangle, one hundred paces long, three storeys high, with many towers and two large square pavilions, one of which, on the left-hand side, became known as l'Ancienne Tour and that on the right as the Tour de l'Amiral.

Access to the château was by a grand flight of marble steps; the walls, faced with stucco, framed in their niches the busts of the most recent kings of France . . . The apartments of the king and queen were ablaze with gilding; the salon was hung with crimson velvet and incorporated in its decoration many masterpieces of sculpture . . . A terrace overlooking the moat bordered the château to the north; the courtyard, situated to the south and surrounded by fortifications, was a real Place d'Armes; a numerous garrison could easily manoeuvre there.

In its mixture of military strength and magnificent apartments,

Pagny-le-Château suggests something like Chantilly in the days of the Montmorency, after the embellishments of Pierre Chambiges. More than this we shall probably never know.

Beyond the moat and within the confines of the outer court of the château was the chapel, the only remnant of the vast ensemble today. It offers one of the most perfect examples of a seigneurial chapel at the moment of transition between the late Gothic and the early Renaissance styles. Inside it is of a rather restrained Flamboyant architecture. The beautiful lierne and tierceron vaulting is not overcharged with pendentives and other baubles; the tracery of the windows is no riotous profusion of intersecting arcs; the exterior is as plain and pleasing as the interior is dignified and simple.

The ground plan at once suggests its purpose as the chapel of a château, for its two 'transepts' are right up by the sanctuary, providing on the north side a private chapel for the seigneurial family, 'qui ne voulait pas se mêler au vulgaire', and could worship in comfort with the warmth of a fire in winter. It is connected with the first bay of the choir by an oblique passage and opens into the sanctuary by a means of a large archway; this, however, is encumbered by the monument of Jeanne de Vienne and her husband Jean de Longvy, who died in 1463 and 1472 respectively. It is quite clear that this monument was not made to fit this space, for the two angels who uphold the helmet, and were clearly designed to kneel on the slab behind the recumbent figures, have had to be placed upon the wall above them.

The chapel was designed also to accommodate the memorial of Jean II de Vienne, who died in 1436. He is placed in a deep embrasure within a heavy architectural frame, like a huge fireplace against the wall. The four-centred arch – *en anse de panier* – is framed between two flat pilasters which support a heavy entablature. The whole is delicately carved with Italian arabesques.

This juxtaposition of a richly Renaissance feature in a frankly Flamboyant construction has suggested to some historians that the church was built in the fifteenth century and the decorations added later. Henri David rejects this theory. 'Just as much in the exterior, in the brickwork, the windows, the buttresses, as in the interior in the vaulting and profiles, the whole work has a strict unity. It indicates a short and quick campaign of building made possible by powerful financial backing.' He puts the beginning of the campaign at about 1530.

The juxtaposition of Flamboyant and Renaissance was therefore deliberate and part of the original design. Where construction was concerned the conception is still wholly Gothic; where decoration is concerned most of it is imported from Italy and probably from Florence.

On the west front there is a monumental entrance in the form of a frontispiece of stone against the diapered brickwork of the wall. It bears the date 1533. This frontispiece, which in some ways resembles that which marks the entrance and staircase of Azay-le-Rideau, is of the finest workmanship and the most fanciful design; the capital of one of the columns incorporates horses' heads in place of volutes. But it is overcharged with ornament. Pillars, pilasters, architraves and entablature are all encrusted with carved arabesques and *putti* in high relief.

A lot of information about Pagny comes from the accounts of the abbey of Saint-Etienne de Dijon, of which Givry was the abbot. A large part of the revenues were devoted to the construction of the chapel at Pagny and it is clear that Givry was the real builder. Some of the accounts are missing, but the first entry leaves no doubts about his authorship. On 23 July 1535, twenty livres were paid to the accountant Jean Barat for 'la chapelle que mon dit Seigneur faisait alors faire à Pagny'. It is not usually stated to what particular purpose the sums mentioned were affected, but in 1536 travelling expenses were paid to two master-glaziers, Pierre Fleury and Jean d'Orain of Dijon, 'who had been to visit the windows at Pagny'.

The windows have not survived, but we may infer something of their appearance and style from the magnificent set of windows at Champigny-sur-Veude, near Richelieu. These windows were the gift of Givry to his other niece, Jacqueline de Longvy, who had married, in 1538, Louis de Bourbon, duc de Montpensier.

It is a strange coincidence that Givry's two nieces should have been mistresses of two of the most important early Renaissance châteaux in France, both of which were demolished without leaving any pictorial record of their architecture, and both of which had superb private chapels, which are still standing. But Champigny alone has retained its glass.

The windows of Champigny were in the new style of the Renaissance, which made use of enamel. 'We are here in the presence of windows', writes Eugène Marcel, 'which are veritable pictures, according to the Italian fashion, with skies, and landscapes with foreground and background stretching away into the distance.' The figures, carefully posed and grouped, represent, in the lower and more accessible lights, the members of the house of Bourbon with some of their more distinguished collaterals. 'Jamais famille français', wrote Emile Mâle, 'n'étala aussi orgueilleusement sa noblesse dans la maison de Dieu.' Above them are depicted a number of episodes in the life of a saint. It is, however, St Louis. The subject-matter was still within the family, for it was from his sixth son Robert that they were all descended. In the upper registers are scenes from the life of Christ. It is mere conjecture, but it seems likely that the windows at Pagny were of a similar character.

In 1539 the accounts of the abbey of Saint-Etienne show that the chapel was once more in use for the service of God, which must mean that the builders had left the site. On 17 October a payment of 49 livres was made to Claude Vérizet, 'prêtre, maître des enfants de choeur de la Chapelle de Pagny'. A further 19 livres was recorded for Pierre Cuvelier, organist. Either there was a quick turnover of the personnel, or there was some doubling of roles, for in the following year Messire Etienne Thieulley, chaplain, was 'maître et recteur des enfants de choeur' and two years later Jacques Barat figures as 'ayant le gouvernement des enfants', and again in 1542 'Jehan de Chemarin, prêtre, maître des enfants de choeur'. It is possible that there were two posts, one of 'gouverneur' which usually indicates general oversight and discipline, and the other of 'maître' which could imply 'choirmaster'. It suggests a resident choir of no small size.

It was not unusual for these seigneurial chapels to have a large establishment. At Champigny there was a dean and ten canons. The dean, with papal approval and a concordat signed by the bishop of Poitiers, was granted the right to wear a purple soutane, a mitre and a pectoral cross and to carry a crook; in other words he was allowed to dress as a bishop and he took precedence over abbots and other deans. Of a canon it was required that he should be 'honest, but not lame or hunchbacked, nor one-eyed nor deficient in any limb and not a bastard'. He was not to grow his hair long or to wear red, yellow or 'Persian' shoes.

The Cardinal de Givry knew all about this and it is probable that his chapel at Pagny-le-Château was as well served as that at Champigny.

Henri David had drawn attention to the almost exact similarity between the *tempietti* on the frontispiece at Pagny with those which ornament the buttresses on the west façade of the church of Saint-Michel which was the first important Renaissance structure in Dijon.

Saint-Michel de Dijon

Saint-Michel de Dijon is really the chapel of Pagny writ large. Here we have a sizeable church in the late Flamboyant style with a Renaissance screen, not just an elaborate doorway, but forming the whole of the west front. Since the entire front is comprehended within a unified design, the adherence to medieval form is all the more remarkable. For at Saint-Michel there is a triple *portail* such as would have been built on any thirteenth-century cathedral in France. The three cavernous recesses, corresponding respectively with the nave and its aisles, present to the visitor a perspective of diminishing arches, their imposts and architraves offering the usual series of statues and carvings in the truest Gothic tradition. But the style of the decoration is pure Renaissance. The façades of the towers are composed of pillars, pilasters and pediments, the four storeys divided by the correctest of cornices and the entablatures carved with curling acanthus scrolls.

Work on the west front began in 1529. The sculptures were probably the work of Jean Damotte, who certainly carved the Retable des Trespassés inside the church. Two angels of his have survived in the south transept and are very similar to those of the porch. The south arch of the porch bears the date 1537 and the central arch 1551. The Last Judgement in this is by Nicholas de la Cour. He came from Drouai, but the inspiration is obviously Florentine.

But it is not just in the style that these decorations announce the arrival of the Renaissance; it is in the subject-matter also. The long frieze which surmounts the *portail* and separates it from the façade above is decorated with scrolls and grotesque figures interwoven with texts from the Apocalypse, but at either extremity of the frieze is a bas-relief; the scenes depicted are from the Labours of Hercules. In the centre of the porch, on the pier between the double doors, is a statue of St Michael. The console which supports him is covered with carvings which show the same mixture of sacred and secular subjects. David slaying Goliath, the Judgement of Solomon, John the Baptist preaching in the wilderness, Christ appearing to Mary Magdalene are represented together with Leda and her swan, Cupid at the toilet of Venus and Hercules carrying off the cattle of the monster Geryon – a strange assortment for the decoration of a Christian temple.

Hugues Sambin

One of the names traditionally attached to the building of the west front of Saint-Michel is that of Hugues Sambin. But the archives are silent and any attribution to Sambin must remain largely conjectural and based on similarities of style.

Sambin was a man of many parts. His father, also Hugues, is known to have graduated 'Maître Menuisier' at Dijon in 1549. His son and grandsons also earned that title. They were workers in wood. The Hugues Sambin with whom we are concerned was employed in a wide variety of activities; he was as much an engineer as a woodcarver and concerned himself with fortification, the redirection of the river Suzon and the general water supply of Dijon; he built abattoirs, he built mills. In 1564, when Charles IX visited Burgundy, Sambin designed some of the triumphal arches for his entry into Dijon. In his words he puts architecture as his chief employment – 'à laquelle je me suis adonné des mes premiers ans, avec diligente application de mon esprit, sans avoir discontinué'.

It is, however, as a woodcarver and as maître menuisier that he is best thought of. One of his few documented works is the screen and doors to the Chapelle du Saint-Esprit at the Palais de Justice, for which he was paid 80 écus. The heavy pediment is upheld by free-standing columns, but these are supported upon projecting consoles. This is more typical of elaborately architectural furniture than of architecture itself. A trained architect would have been more likely to stand his columns firmly on the ground or mount them upon a podium.

There is enough similarity of style – especially in the slender caryatids which decorate the mullions – from which to infer that the great entrance doors to the palais are also from the hand of Sambin.

They show him to be a lover of bizarre shapes and to have a tendency to over-ornamentation, but the ornament is mostly in shallow relief.

There is not much common ground between the screen and doorway of the palais and the façade of the Maison Milsand in the rue des Forges, commonly attributed to Sambin. Its decorations might well look more in place if carved in walnut upon some monumental *armoire*. They are heavy and in deep relief; their tendency is to clutter the wall space. Some of the motifs are similar to those on Sambin's woodwork, but this alone would not establish authorship. Sambin's one fully attested work of architecture was the Palais de Justice at Besançon. Its façade is illustrated in Bernard Prost's article; it bears no resemblance to the Maison Milsand or to any of the other façades in Dijon loosely attributed to Sambin.

In 1572 Sambin produced a book on caryatids – *Oeuvre de la diversité des Termes*. He was at the time resident at Pagny-le-Château and dedicated his book to Léonor de Chabot. It is difficult to imagine that Sambin spent a year and a half in the most important Renaissance château of the age without contributing to its decoration, but unfortunately no records have survived.

The example set by Givry as a patron of the arts was soon followed by others. Many of the earliest achievements of the Burgundian Renaissance were in the form of chapels – either inserted into the structure of a cathedral or church or incorporated in the building of a château. In one case the same patron built a mausoleum for himself in Langres Cathedral and a chapel for his family château. His name was Jean d'Amoncourt, seigneur de Piépape, a friend and relative of Givry's and his archdeacon of Langres. He was nobly born; the blood of the Beauffremonts and the Châtelets ran in his veins; he held several seigneuries as well as a plurality of ecclesiastical benefices. Appointed in 1551 bishop of Poitiers, he did not visit his diocese until four years later and continued to spend most of his time at Langres.

The Château de Montigny and the Amoncourt chapels

In 1537 the archdeacon's brother – rather unimaginatively also called Jean – began the rebuilding of the Château de Montigny-sur-Aube, between Châtillon-sur-Seine and Chaumont. He appears to have retained the outer walls of the old fortress, for

Nesle, writing in 1851, describes them as 'de lourdes bâtisses des 11e et 12e siècles'. But the rooms were reconstructed and the inward façades rebuilt in Renaissance style – a rather monotonous repetition of coupled pilasters, Ionic above Tuscan. It has, however, the particular interest of being the earliest example of a complete Renaissance front in Burgundy to have survived. It antedated Ancy-le-Franc and Jours by several years, but was certainly started later than Pagny-le-Château, the architecture of which it may have reflected. The buildings were ranged round three sides of a quadrangle, but in 1817 the north and east wings were pulled down, leaving only the south range of the courtyard and the north-east tower which contains the chapel – 'une des plus admirables chapelles seigneuriales', wrote Yvan Christ, 'de toute la France'.

Unlike the Chapelle de Bouton, the entire conception here is in Renaissance style. The whole is proportioned by a double order, Ionic above Doric, with three cartwheel roundels in the upper storey which are so large as to cause the cornice to arc slightly in order to contain them. To the right of the altar, the *lavabo* affords an opportunity for a delightful little niche framed between fluted pilasters and carrying a pediment which reflects in miniature the doorway to the chapel.

But it is the ceiling of the chapel which is its greatest glory. It is in the form of a barrel vault. Three vaulting arches enclose the two bays of the main nave; two radiating arches divide the half-dome of the apse. The whole is carved with a lacelike delicacy into patterns of alternate rounds and squares, each framing within itself a smaller pattern, either armorial or naturalistic, which suggests the complexity of a snowflake. The chapel was consecrated on 1 May 1552. It is therefore contemporary with Jean d'Amoncourt's mausoleum in Langres Cathedral of which it is clearly a smaller version.

The Revolution did not leave Langres Cathedral untouched and d'Amoncourt's chapel had its share of vandalism. The bas-reliefs which lined the walls and recounted the episodes of the Passion have disappeared; so have the statues from the niches. The stained glass, in which was depicted the discovery of the true cross, has vanished without trace. It has left only a memory in the name of the Chapelle de l'Invention de la Sainte-Croix. More often it was known as 'La Pothière', a name derived from d'Amoncourt's diocese of Poitiers.

Even without its statues and its stained glass this is a very fine piece of architecture, but as at Montigny, its coffered ceiling is its

Abbaye de Fontenay.

Sémur-en-Auxois. Lithograph by E. Nesle.

Flavigny. Église St. Gènes. Upper Tribune. Lithograph by E. Sagot.

Flavigny. Angel of the Annunciation.

Montréal. The Holy Family. Carved pew end.

Château de Châteauneuf. Lithograph by E. Sagot.

Château de Brandon.

Hospice de Beaune.
Lithograph by H. Clerget.

Hospice de Beaune. Detail
of retable. The weighing of
souls.

Dijon. Hôtel Chambellan. Lithograph by H. Clerget.

St. Père-sous-Vézelay.
Lithograph by E. Sagot.

Church of St. Thibault.
Lithograph by E. Sagot.

Église de Brou. Retable of the Seven Joys of the Virgin. The Annunciation.

Église de Brou. Retable of the Seven Joys of the Virgin.

Pagny-le-Château. Chapel. Entrance in its original state.

Dijon. Église St. Michel. Lithograph by E. Sagot.

finest feature. 'It is a real marvel', wrote the Chanoine Marcel, 'this composition so beautifully designed; complexity without confusion, simplicity with so much diversity, elegant in its sobriety, clarity and grace. These are essentially French qualities.'

The snowflake patterns of the ceiling are reflected in the porcelain tiles of the floor. This type of flooring is understandably vulnerable, and not many examples have survived. This one at Langres was in fact renewed in 1885, but enough was left of the old for the reproduction to be faithful. We see today what d'Amoncourt intended us to see. 'Each one of these tiles', writes Marcel, 'would merit a study. Not one is the simple replica of another. It is an extraordinary richness of decoration which stretches out across the fifty-four square metres of the floor, beneath the feet and beneath the eyes of the visitor. One thinks of those illuminated manuscripts in which each page is a surprise and brings a new enchantment.'

Here at Langres, and in the smaller version of it at Montigny, we have a building which is no longer an application of Italian detail to a Gothic structure, but one conceived and executed throughout in the full style of the French Renaissance. The question imposes itself: who was the architect? For such a building must have been the work of someone trained in the techniques and inspired by the ideals of Italy, and yet who has managed to assimilate and to acclimatize the style into something subtly French. Montaiglon suggests the name of Jean Bullant.

The churches of Ligny-le-Châtel and Cravant

The influence of Langres as a centre of radiation for the Renaissance style was partly through the family connections of Givry and d'Amoncourt and partly through the patronage which the cathedral chapter exercised among the parish churches of the diocese. This patronage usually entailed responsibility for the choir, the upkeep of the nave and transepts being left to the parishioners. But since chapters were rich and parishes were poor, this division of responsibility sometimes left the church with a magnificent Renaissance choir set at an awkward angle to an old and undistinguished nave, for, as the new choir presupposed a new nave, the opportunity was often taken to correct the orientation.

This is particularly evident at Ligny-le-Châtel, near Pontigny, which was, up till the Revolution, within the diocese of Langres. In the middle of the sixteenth century the chapter decided upon a rebuilding and on 7 August 1554 the first stone was laid for the new choir. The old nave, a building of the twelfth century, was devoid of any architectural contrivance, a defect which might pass unnoticed since the lack of windows makes it almost invisible.

In contrast with the obscurity which reigns in the nave, the choir was flooded with a new light. A complete set of clerestory windows encircles the sanctuary and the slender columns of the great arcade allow the aisle windows to illuminate the altar.

Although this choir was built by the chapter of Langres Cathedral at about the same time as the construction of d'Amoncourt's chapel, there is little or no similarity of style. Ligny-le-Châtel is chiefly Renaissance in its absence of Flamboyant features, in place of which shallow pilasters crowned with meagre capitals provide a rather dull and featureless façade.

A much more interesting and exciting variation on this same theme is the church of Cravant, some 16 kilometres along the road from Auxerre to Avallon. Cravant is almost contemporary with Ligny – it was started in 1551 and finished in 1578 – and was built under similar circumstances, only here it was the chapter of Auxerre Cathedral who were the patrons. They rebuilt the choir and the parishioners never rebuilt the nave.

At Cravant the skeleton of the choir, with its side aisles and chapels, is still that of a Gothic church, but the visible body of the architecture is in wholly Italianate form. The piers of the great arcade are adorned on each face with a Corinthian pilaster with a fully foliated capital; the arches are rounded and a properly proportioned entablature divides the wall from the ceiling, which is still in the form of a sexpartite vault.

'Constructed of the choicest of materials, a limestone of a very fine grain which lends itself to all the delicacy of a most carefully executed decoration,' writes Jean Vallery-Radot, 'this particularly successful ensemble is the work of an architect nourished in the solid traditions of the Gothic but at the same time right up to date with the innovations of the Renaissance.' The twelve piers of the choir and apse each carry a finely chiselled *tempietta* above the capital, destined no doubt to provide a canopy for a statue of one of the Twelve Apostles.

Vallery-Radot draws attention to the similarities between the plan of Cravant and that of Saint-Pierre d'Auxerre, but here the whole of the church was reconstructed and its particular glory is in its west façade.

The Eglise Saint-Pierre d'Auxerre

Saint-Pierre was one of those churches, not uncommon in the Middle Ages, which was shared between a parish and a monastery. It was a formula for failure which gave rise to endless bickerings and quarrellings of a somewhat unchristian nature. The monastery had the choir and the parish had the nave. But this gave the monks exclusive access to the bells. In 1536 the parishioners decided to build themselves a tower in order to have their own bells. The foundation stone was laid on 6 June and on it could still be read, in the eighteenth century, the inscription:

En mil cinq cens et trent six
Au mois de juin sixième jour
Les fondements furent assis
De cette magnifique tour.

The tower is certainly magnificent and clearly owes a lot to the north-west tower of the cathedral, which was still unfinished at that time and only to be crowned with its belfry in 1543. The tower of Saint-Pierre was completed in 1557 and in August the bells were finally installed. An anonymous manuscript, dating from about the year 1640 and possibly written by one of the canons who replaced the monks in 1635, states that the tower had cost 22.000 livres.

But one thing leads to another. The excellence of the tower showed up the inferiority of the church. 'The said parishioners, seeing that the church did not match the magnificent tower which they had built, being very narrow and lying very low on the ground, and the great age of it rendering it ruinous, they formed the design of building a new one.' They even consented to rebuild the choir and hand it over to the monks. This was agreed before the notary Taffineau on 15 June 1561. But they were unable to start before 1575, for Auxerre was one of the trouble centres of the Wars of Religion. It was too near the route between the prince de Condé's château at Vallery and his fortress at Noyers and d'Andelot's château at Tanlay to keep out of the fighting. In 1567 Protestant troops surprised the town when most of the inhabitants were gathering their grapes for the vendanges. They attacked the cathedral, burnt the abbot's lodging and refectory at Saint-Pierre and tried to set fire to the new tower, 'à dessein de la ruiner'.

Six years later it was decided to proceed with the reconstruction of Saint-Pierre. It began with the choir; 'it was marvellous', continues the account, 'how they have built so quickly, without having any other funds but their collections, for in less than forty years it had been rebuilt.' This brings us to 1623, a date which is marked on one of the choir vaults. The nave was started in 1627 and three years later, two masons, Isaac Gillot and Blaise Chériot, signed a contract for the west front. It was built storey by storey with a new contract for each stage; 1635 for the first floor; 1656 for the top.

The façade of Saint-Pierre is a delightful piece of architectural composition and compares favourably with that of Saint-Michel de Dijon. This latter has a certain massive grandeur, but it is rendered top-heavy by the fact that the windows in the two upper storeys are broader than those of the lower storeys.

At Saint-Pierre the central section of the façade forms an elegant frontispiece proportioned by a triple order, Ionic, Corinthian and Composite, with two columns on either side of each door or window separated by a niche. It recalls the elaborate features which marked the entrances to such châteaux as Anet and Coulommiers. But although the architectural detail is almost entirely Renaissance, the structure is still essentially Gothic, with flying buttresses supported by pinnacles which are translated into Italian idiom in order to harmonize with the rest of the front. In the half-gables which mark the ends of the aisle roofs, the little windows beneath the segmental pediments are still quatrefoil and the central light above the west door retains the pointed arch. Here, on the very threshold of the Grand Siècle, the Gothic is still in evidence. This survival is chiefly found in ecclesiastical buildings; it is less common in the domestic architecture of the period. A great advance towards the Italin style had already been made in the building of Ancy-le-Franc.

The châteaux of Ancy-le-Franc and Jours

It is not often that we are permitted to look over an architect's shoulder at the time of the Renaissance and see him producing a series of designs in which the project of a house is brought nearer and nearer to his patron's wishes. What would an art historian not give to be able to observe the evolution of Chambord or to follow the successive stages of Fontainebleau? Ancy-le-Franc is one of the rare buildings of the French Renaissance where this is possible.

Some 20 kilometres south of Tonnerre, by one of the wide meanders of the river Armançon, the château of Ancy-le-Franc occupies 'a very beautiful position, surrounded by woods and hills, with springs of living water all around. The hills form an amphitheatre which embraces a very fertile plain in which the building is situated . . . encompassed by a deep, capacious moat nourished by the springs, which discharges its waters into the river.'

Thus wrote Sebastiano Serlio, the author and architect of one of the first and finest buildings of the High Renaissance in France. It was an achievement of which any architect could be justly proud.

The house stands four-square around a central *cortile*, its façades set between massive square towers which give it something of the castle air. It is built of a beautiful white freestone not unlike that which comes from the valley of the Loire. The façades are of two storeys and the towers of three; each façade is regularly divided by attached pilasters into a series of equal bays. It is an arrangement derived from the Palace of the Chancelry in Rome, but it had already been used in France, notably at Chambord and Villandry. On three of the façades there is a window to every bay, but on the towers the central bay only is opened.

The tall slate roof is clearly a last-minute alteration, for it cuts across the cornice of the towers. It can be seen inside the roof that the cornice in fact continues all the way round. There is but one possible explanation: that the first intention had been a roof of lower pitch that left the towers standing clear of it. This raising of the roof-line was the last of a whole series of modifications to an original, more severely Italianate design by Serlio.

Serlio was one of the important figures of the French Renaissance. Born in Bologna in 1475, he went to Rome, where he became a pupil of the architect Peruzzi, but he was clearly influenced also by the buildings of Raphael and Bramante. From Rome he moved to Venice, and from Venice, in 1541, he came to France, where he was appointed 'Peintre et Architecteur Ordinaire' at Fontainebleau. Exactly what 'ordinaire' meant in terms of status and authority is not clear, for there is no part of Fontainebleau which can be attributed to him except, possibly, the Grotte des Pins. His designs for the Salle de Bal were altered out of all recognition by Philibert de l'Orme and he complained that he was never even consulted.

Serlio, in fact, is more important for his writings than for his buildings. His influence upon French architecture was indirect but none the less considerable. His most important building is here in Burgundy at Ancy-le-Franc. In the evolution of its design can be traced the development from an original and typically Italian conception to something deliberately 'acclimatized'.

The same development can be observed in Serlio's books. In his earlier writings he takes purely Italian buildings for his examples, but his experience of working in France opened his eyes to the fact that different lands need different styles of architecture.

'I would certainly say', he wrote, 'since there are beneath the sky countries that differ in their air, in their water and in their land, an architect, who has just arrived in a place which he has not yet seen, has good reason to take note of the opinions of those who were born and have grown old in that country.' He resolved, on coming to France, to practise what he preached. 'I intend in my manner of proceeding to unite what is suitable to France with what is customary in Italy.' In particular he came to value those high-pitched roofs encircled with a 'coronet' of ornamental dormers which often formed the most impressive feature of a French château. Although he was sixty-five and described as 'bon vieillard' when he came to France, he was remarkably adaptable and his style became more and more French. This process is illustrated in the genesis of his design for Ancy-le-Franc.

It is unusually well documented. A whole series of drawings and plans has survived which gives us a rare and fascinating record, enabling us to watch the process whereby the first draft was altered, in accordance with the patron's desires, until it became the building which we see today.

It was begun in about 1544 for Antoine de Clermont-Tonnerre, who had married the sister of Diane de Poitiers. A few years later Serlio wrote the sixth volume of his treatise on architecture, which was never published. Two manuscript versions of it have come to light in the course of this century, one in Munich and one in Columbia University. They both contain a detailed description of Ancy-le-Franc together with plans and elevations. The plans are nearly identical, but the elevations are significantly different.

What Serlio says is extremely interesting and deserves to be quoted at some length.

Here in France gentlemen, and especially those of the greatest houses, live outside the towns, and although in this kingdom there are no factions and all live in obedience to their king, nevertheless, from old custom, they build their houses in the form of fortresses [in modo fortrezza], surrounded by water if the site permits, and by means of drawbridges and other defences they can resist at least a raid [battaglia da mano]. Thus the house in question [Ancy] is accommodated to this custom, having the form of a castle, according to the wishes of its master.

In pursuance of this aim the vestibule is flanked by two guard rooms from which 'the enemies who enter there are attacked from both sides by arquebuses or pikes'. There are also little rooms contrived within the thickness of the tower walls with meutrières which would enable a raking cross-fire to be brought to bear on any unwelcome guests.

Of the two manuscripts, that of Columbia University gives the earlier design. There are two drawings: one an external elevation and the other a section showing one of the façades of the courtyard. It is this external elevation which concerns us first. Its features are quickly listed. The towers contain two windows on each floor and except for their enormous quoins they are devoid of ornament. The central block, by contrast, is almost elaborate. The façade divides horizontally into two equal halves, of which the lower, which is of two storeys, is heavily rusticated. At piano nobile level it offers an attached colonnade with an alteration of windows and niches set within a blind arcade. Above the cornice a parapet, treated as a miniature arcade, completes the design. To this was added a low-pitched roof forming squat pyramids over the towers; neither roof nor pyramids would have been visible to anyone standing at all close to the façades. The effect is ponderous and alien to the ethos of French architecture.

The Munich manuscript shows what is clearly a revision of this project. On the ground floor the rustication has been restricted to the quoins and window surrounds and the blind windows have been replaced by niches surmounted by pediments. At first-floor level the rustification on the towers has been replaced by a decoration of pilasters resembling the actual arrangement except that there are two windows to each floor and the pilasters at the corners are

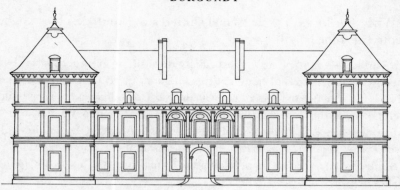

The Château of Ancy-le-Franc as built.

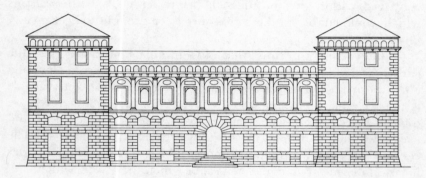

The Columbia design.

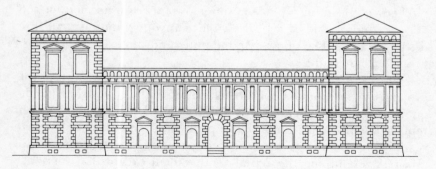

The Munich design.

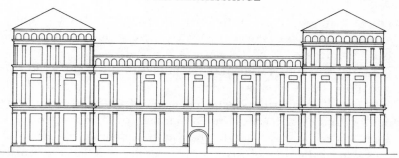

The Albertina design.

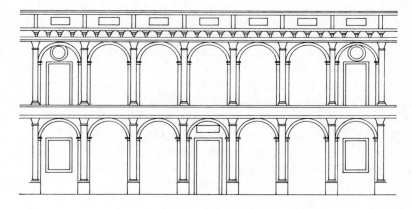

Courtyard, Albertina design.

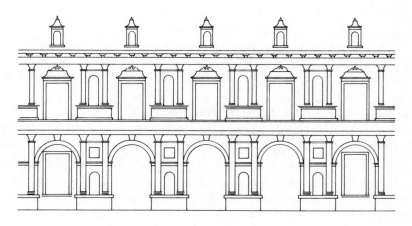

Courtyard as built.

coupled. The treatment of the central façade has been simplified; the rectangular panels over the niches have gone and the arcading has been omitted.

Some of these alterations are explained in the text. Serlio states that Antoine de Clermont-Tonnerre was from the first involved in the design. 'To obtain a richer effect, he decided to put pilasters from top to bottom.' The Munich manuscript seems to represent a suggestion of how this might look at first-floor level. Serlio also states that at the time of writing the building was 'entirely finished as to the exterior, and as to the interior was for the most part habitable'. He does not, however, show the final form of the design as we see it today. Two further phases in the development can be detected.

There has recently been discovered in the Albertina Museum in Vienna a collection of drawings by Serlio. It includes a façade of Ancy-le-Franc which is intermediary between the Munich drawings and the façades as built. Here rustication has disappeared altogether and has been replaced by pilasters throughout. These, however, are coupled on each storey of the towers, which still have two windows on each floor. On the central façade the niches have gone, leaving the alternate bays blank. The wishes of the patron have been respected but, clearly, he was still not satisfied. There is something rather dull and monotonous about the Albertina project.

It looks as if at this point the comte de Clermont-Tonnerre turned away from Serlio in search of something more suited to his native land, for there comes now an injection of new ideas from an unidentified but almost certainly French architect. It appears in a series of rather sketchy drawings and plans recently discovered in the Bibliothèque Nationale. These sketches are clearly the originals behind du Cerceau's engravings in his first *Livre d'Architecture* which he published in 1559. It is not stated that this is a project for Ancy-le-Franc, but the ground plan is unmistakable.

Here, in the 'French' design, the towers appear for the first time with a single, central window to each floor, but the designer has abandoned pilasters and reverted to quoins. The arcaded parapet has finally disappeared and the typically French feature has been introduced of a high-pitched roof pierced with large dormers. The design also provides for statues to replace the pilasters on the first floor.

But it is in the design for the façade of the courtyard that this project is of special interest. To appreciate its importance we must now go back over the same ground and compare the drawings of these inner façades in the respective manuscripts.

The Columbia drawing provides for a rusticated arcade to the ground floor surmounted by an arcaded colonnade to the first floor. It is not unlike Serlio's design for the Salle de Bal at Fontainebleau. Both the Munich and the Albertina drawings show an identical treatment of both storeys – a superimposition of arcaded colonnades. Du Cerceau, interpreting the sketch in the Bibliothèque Nationale – the 'French' design – shows a new concept altogether and much nearer to the façades as built. It provides an alternation of broad and narrow bays – *la travée rythmique*. The broad bay contains an open arch at ground-floor level surmounted by a large window on the first floor; the narrow bay is composed of a niche framed between two pilasters. It was a rhythm used by Bramante at the Belvedere and it also appears in Burgundy at the Château de Jours-les-Baigneux. There is no accurate date for Jours but it seems probable that Ancy-le-Franc was the prototype.

The final design of the courtyard at Ancy is a refinement of this earlier one. The superimposition of two colonnades of the same height is top-heavy and rather monotonous. At Jours this is overcome by making the first-floor windows lower than those of the ground floor. But at Ancy the architect wanted to make his first-floor windows taller than those of the ground floor, for the rooms of the *piano nobile* were the more important. He has solved his problem delightfully, making the pilasters of the upper storey smaller by mounting them on a podium. Thus the windows come down to the top of the cornice but the pilasters do not. This creates an 'up-down, up-down' rhythm which is very pleasing to the eye.

One more change was made at the same time. In all three of the earlier projects there is a small attic storey shown with little horizontal windows. This is replaced in the 'French' drawing by a high-pitched roof pierced by tall dormer windows. The decision by Antoine de Clermont-Tonnerre is recorded by Serlio: 'He also decided not to have the little windows above the topmost cornice, which were his own invention and contrary to my wishes, thanks to which the building stands better and is more worthy of praise.'

It is clear that Serlio is talking now of the finished design as we see it today, and he describes the external shell of masonry as being finished at the time of writing – that is, about 1550. It seems probable that Serlio himself was asked to incorporate some of the features of the 'French' design and was the author of the finished building. But in spite of his attempts to frenchify, Ancy-le-Franc still looks like something imported, whereas Jours, which in many ways reflects the design, is more in harmony with its countryside; it is built of a warmer stone which matches its brown roof and the brown soil of Burgundy.

The dating of Jours can be determined approximately on heraldic grounds. Over the door, Nesle records, was the escutcheon of Claude d'Anglure and his second wife, Isabeau de Joyeuse. He married her in 1542 and died in 1566. It is therefore reasonable to place the building of the château within that period.

The arms of d'Anglure incorporate the crescent of Islam. There were also, before the Revolution, two leaden figures which ornamented the roof ridge – one of Jehan d'Anglure and one of the Sultan Saladin, both 'armed at all pieces'. The story behind these is not without interest.

Saladin had recaptured Jerusalem from Guy de Lusignan and the Third Crusade was organized to win back the Holy Places. Jehan d'Anglure went with the expedition and distinguished himself to such an extent that Saladin sought him in single combat. Saladin unhorsed him and he was sold into slavery. Some years later Saladin came across him again and offered him his freedom, imposing, however, a stiff ransom. D'Anglure said that he could not raise so large a sum unless he could return to his estates. He was asked what surety he could offer and answered: 'My Lord, you have made me poor, naked and miserable, but I still have one jewel far more precious than all the riches of your empire.' When asked what this jewel was he proudly replied: 'Ma foi de chevalier.' The surety was accepted and he returned to France, but being unable to raise the sum demanded, he went back, like Regulus, to offer himself once more as a slave to Saladin. The latter, however, was so moved by his sense of honesty that he allowed him to return, requiring only that he should include the crescent in his coat of arms and that his successors should bear the name Saladin before that of d'Anglure.

What is chiefly remarkable about Jours is the very high standard of execution. The Corinthian capitals are the work of a sure and experienced hand. But Jours is only a fragment – one wing of a project which must have encompassed at least two more. Nesle records a monumental fireplace in the Salle des Gardes. It occupied a square of just over 29.5 feet and was divided into two storeys with each entablature upheld by caryatids – masculine on the lower storey and feminine above. A frieze of arms and armour ran above the fireplace aperture and an elaborate heraldic achievement dominated the upper panel. 'The chimney of the Salle des Gardes', wrote Nesle, 'can give us some idea of the luxury and richness of the ornamentation which reigned throughout this beautiful building.'

It is unlikely, however, that Jours can ever have rivalled the interior decoration of Ancy-le-Franc. This offers the same mixture of Italian and French influences which we have seen in the exterior architecture, but here there is almost no documentation to illuminate the process. There are few certainties. The magnificent and unrestored ceiling of the Salle de Diane obviously owes something to the work of Raphael in the loggias of the Vatican. It bears the date 1578, but not the name of the artist.

The provision of galleries, so numerous at Fontainebleau, was a necessity for a house of the magnitude of Ancy. The finest of them, the Galerie de Pharsale, occupies the first floor of the south range overlooking the courtyard. It records the battle between Julius Caesar and Pompey in the year 48 BC, inspired, no doubt, by Lucan's poem *Pharsalia*, and painted in monochrome in a rich yellow ochre. It is a gigantic composition of endless scenes of violence in which the chief casualties seem to be the wretched horses. It is of Italian inspiration but of unknown authorship. By contrast the Chambre des Arts, which treats of love and not of war, is set about with large oval cartouches and recalls unmistakably the styles of Primaticcio and the influence of Fontainebleau.

The style, however, becomes more French in the Cabinet du Pastor Fido and the chapel, with mural paintings by Philippe Quantin and André Ménassier, both of them Burgundians. The work of the former, clearly influenced by Caravaggio, was particularly admired by Poussin.

The chapel is a magnificent achievement. The lower half is beautifully panelled in walnut enriched by gilding: the upper half is entirely painted by Ménassier, who has obligingly signed his work and added the date of 1596. As an example of a seigneurial chapel, that of Ancy-le-Franc has come a very long way from that of Pagny-le-Château. It is no longer a free-standing church, but is, as at Fontainebleau, one of the 'rooms' in the house. Its decor does not at first sight differ greatly from that of the other rooms. There are, however, certain indications that this particular room was used for divine worship, including, of course, the altar.

Beside it a marble slab records a grant of indulgences to all those who 'devoutly visited the chapel of the Château of Ancy-le-Franc on the day of St Peter and St Paul, between the first Vespers and the end of the following day, who prayed for peace between Christian princes, the extirpation of heresy and the exaltation of the Church'. It is dated 31 October 1603. A year later another indulgence was granted of 'quarante jours de vrai pardon' for all those who came on the feast of the consecration of the chapel and prayed for the comte de Tonnerre, his wife and his children. Consonant with this noble theme is the painting to the left of the altar of Catherine-Maria d'Escoubleaux at prayer before a table on which are set three coronets, one with the strawberry leaves of a duke and two with the raised pearls of a count. Whether the gesture was one of laying aside her earthly coronets in hopes of a heavenly crown, or whether she has put them on display to remind the Almighty that she was no ordinary penitent, it is impossible to say.

With the decoration of the chapel the creation of Ancy-le-Franc may be regarded as having been completed. It was no mean achievement in an era of civil and religious warfare. But, apart from Jours, this great Renaissance building had little effect on the architecture of Burgundy. It stands in splendid isolation. It is possible, however, that the 'French' design is connected with another important château which, had it been completed, might well have rivalled Serlio's masterpiece – the Château de Vallery.

The Château de Vallery

The authorship of the 'French' design for Ancy-le-Franc has been the subject of much learned speculation. The use of heavy quoins as the only ornament on all but the entrance front suggested to Jean Guillaume a possible analogy with the Château de Vallery, on the western confines of Burgundy, a house qualified by Brantôme as 'une des plus belles et plaisantes de France'.

Vallery was started some four years later than Ancy for Jacques d'Albon, Maréchal de Saint-André. He was a person who stood in much the same relationship to Henri II as the duc de Luynes was to stand to the young Louis XIII two generations later. History accords to him the unbecoming title of 'Favourite'. In 1523, when he was eighteen, Albon was appointed by François I as governor to his second son, Henri, duc d'Orléans, who was then only four. Henri had been taken to Spain as a hostage against the release of his father after the disaster of Pavia and spent two sombre years in the castle of Pedrazza de la Sierra. He returned to France the victim of a taciturnity which it took him a long time to outgrow. He was described by a Venetian ambassador as 'melancholic and satur-nine'. His whole delight was in manly exercises – hunting, jousting, swordplay and tennis – and in this Jacques d'Albon was a more than able instructor. He so attached his young pupil to himself that when Henri became king in 1547 (his elder brother had died in 1536) there seemed to be no limit to his generosity to his former tutor. D'Albon was created Maréchal de France and loaded with lucrative posi-tions; he was well placed to indulge in the costly art of building.

In April 1548, he purchased the domain of Vallery, some 38 kilometres east of Fontainebleau. It is widely accepted, though not proven, that Pierre Lescot was the presiding architect. He certainly worked for Saint-André and the building bears sufficient similarity to Lescot's external façades of the Louvre to support the theory.

As at the Louvre, the building consisted of two wings set at right angles with a taller pavilion marking the corner. At the Louvre this 'Pavillon du Roi' contained the king's private rooms. It is clear from the ground plan of Vallery, which shows the typical grouping of three rooms of different sizes, that the pavilion contained the principal *appartements*.

It is also clear that Vallery was never finished. The south front adjoined the gatehouse of the old château, its archway set between tall towers roofed *en poivrière* with two little projecting *échaugettes*, as at Chenonceau, overhanging the drawbridge. This was presumably used by Saint-André as his main entrance. But the west front was clearly intended to replace it. Du Cerceau, in his aerial view, includes a bridge in anticipation. The large central archway gave access to a vast and imposing vestibule, its walls scalloped into niches, which in turn opened into the Cour du Seigneur by a loggia of five arches. That this façade was meant to be extended by a further corner pavilion to complete its symmetry must be beyond doubt. That another wing at right angles to this was to have projected eastward would have been wholly consistent with the architecture of the time. Beyond that we cannot guess. Saint-André may well have wished to retain the towers of the former château as evidence of his new nobility.

We know what Vallery looked like chiefly from a series of drawings and a ground plan by du Cerceau, now at the British Museum, and from the mutilated remains of the château today. But, misleading and degraded as these remains are, they do give us a sense of the grandiose proportions of the buildings and the colossal scale of the lay-out, which could by no means be inferred from du Cerceau's drawings.

Architectural historians have learnt to mistrust du Cerceau. He combines a minute recording of detail with a somewhat cavalier approach to larger issues. He will shorten a façade by one or more bays in order, one supposes, to get it into the picture. His views of Ancy-le-Franc, already referred to, are a good example of this foreshortening. He does the same for Fontainebleau. But at Vallery his accuracy can be cross-checked. There exist at Chantilly four drawings by Sengre which give a complete picture of the château as Saint-André left it, which corroborates du Cerceau's.

Of the interior we can only form a general impression of high quality and extreme opulence. We know that Primaticcio, heavily involved at Fontainebleau, was summoned to Vallery, but we do not know for what purpose. The painters Pierre Sturbe and Jean du Breuil, also from the Fontainebleau team, were employed at Vallery. Du Cerceau, in likening the interior of Vallery to that of the Louvre, states that 'il n'y a rien que beau et bon'. Brantôme says much the same: 'For the superb and beautiful adornments of fine furniture, both rich and rare, he surpassed even our kings . . . principally at Vallery.' After his death, Brantôme concludes, the contents of Vallery were sold at an auction which seemed to go on for ever. More significant is the fact that Catherine de Medici had bought the most important items before the sale. In a 'mémoire présenté à la Reine' some of these were listed. There were 'large and beautiful silver pieces from the sideboard'; there was a large silver basin 'which is so beautiful and excellent that there is nothing to match it in France' and which alone cost 2,000 livres; there were great tapestries , façon de Bruxelles, with the highlights picked out in gold and silver; there were Turkish and Persian carpets and hangings of cloth of gold and velvet. Most famous among the tapestries were those depicting the career of Scipio, woven by François de la Planche, which later were to belong to Mazarin. Even the linen was mentioned for its luxurious quality.

The death of Henri II on 10 July 1559, as the result of a jousting accident, put an end to Saint-André's ambitions. One of the first acts of Catherine de Medici on becoming queen mother was to make her son, François II, revoke all his father's donations from the crown domain. In March 1561, the provincial assembly of the Ile de France passed the resolution that 'Monsieur le Maréchal de Saint-André is no longer a member of the Council and shall render accounts of the excessive gifts which he has received and will pay the balance'. In his reduced circumstances the Maréchal de Saint-André was prudent enough to leave his building unfinished.

One of his methods of repairing his fortunes was to confiscate the property of Huguenots in those provinces of which he was governor. On 19 December 1562, at the battle of Dreux he was unhorsed and had to surrender himself a prisoner to a man whom he recognized, too late, as one whom he had ruined. He tried to transfer his surrender and was shot in the face.

He left a widow, Marguerite, and a daughter, Catherine, aged sixteen. She was betrothed to Henri de Guise, a leader of the Catholic party. Marguerite, however, had been carrying on an affair with the prince de Condé, a leader of the Protestant party and next in succession to the crown of France after Henri de Navarre. Three months after the death of her husband, Marguerite became a Huguenot. She broke off the engagement between Catherine and de Guise and offered her to the duc d'Enghien, Condé's eldest son. Just before the signing of the contract Catherine died in circumstances which gave rise to suspicions that her mother had poisoned her. Guilty or not guilty, Marguerite now inherited the Saint-André fortune. By a deed of gift, signed on 4 July 1564, she made over the entire estate, including Vallery, to the prince de Condé. Condé accepted the gift – or perhaps we should say the bribe – but he did not fulfil his half of the presumed contract. He was at that moment caught up in an affair with a demoiselle d'honneur of Catherine de Medici named Isabelle de Limeuil. Isabelle was a Catholic and managed to entice her lover so far from his Huguenot persuasions that he led the troops against the Protestants at Le Havre.

The price which Isabelle paid for the conversion of Condé resulted in her having to quit a public audience by the queen mother and give birth to a son in the ante-room. Her indiscretion was punished by imprisonment in a convent, but a year later she regained her freedom and made straight for Vallery, where Condé was calmly living. Her arrival coincided with that of the Amiral de Coligny who had come to win back Condé to the Protestant cause. The affair ended like the last scene of a Mozart opera. As René Planchenault puts it, 'the time for one to tire of his beautiful mistress, for the other to mourn the loss of her beautiful château, and for the third to paint cuckold's horns on the portrait of her defective seductor', the comedy for the enactment of which Vallery had been the theatre as well as one of the stakes, was to end, according to the excellent rules of the game, by three marriages. The prince de Condé married Mlle de Longueville; the maréchale, Geoffroy de Caumont; and the former maid of honour, the rich banker Scipio Sardini. Vallery remained in the possession of the prince de Condé and became once more the rallying point for the leaders of the Huguenot party.

The Wars of Religion

By the beginning of the sixteenth century the fortunes of the Catholic Church had reached a low ebb. A long period of schism, with rival popes at Avignon and Rome, had discredited the papacy. The private lives of some who held that office did nothing to enhance their reputation. The great days of scholasticism were over; intellectually, the Church was exhausted; its inspiration had dried up and its structures had become brittle. Worst of all, in its attempt to assert its temporal power over Europe, the Church had betrayed its spiritual commission and lost its soul in secular engagement. It was rich, it was powerful, it was corrupt. The clergy were, for the most part, no longer shepherds of their flocks. 'If they sought the cure of souls', wrote Imbart de la Tour, 'it was not to feed the sheep but to fleece them.'

In 1430, Dom Toussaint du Plessis records, Jean de Brion, bishop of Meaux, had tried to reform the cathedral chapter, stating that 'no honest woman would have dared set foot in the cathedral close'. A successor of his, Guillaume Briçonnet, tried to restore the ancient discipline of the Church, but had to admit that 'throughout the whole extent of his diocese, there could scarcely be found fourteen priests capable of teaching the people or administering the sacraments'. Such a Church was in no condition to withstand the onslaught of the new teachings of Luther and Calvin. The only response of which it was capable was one of savage persecution.

What was true of France was true of Burgundy. In 1534, Jacques Hurault, bishop of Autun, was bemoaning the corruption and incompetence of his clergy in a pastoral letter.

I do not know by what misfortune we have reached the point at which the most indolent and the most unworthy are the only ones who aspire to a profession so honourable . . . The ignorance of many of those who are charged with the sacred ministry and are responsible for the instruction of the people is so notorious that if you were to put into their hands a simple summary of doctrine and good rule, they are capable neither of sensing nor of understanding what their actions or their feelings ought to be in matters human or divine.

His words were not heeded.

The Church, incapable of reforming itself, fell victim to a Reformation which was to shatter its unity. In spite of persecution the number of those who followed Luther or Calvin steadily increased, especially among the artisan classes. There were, it is true, various attempts at establishing peace and a measure of toleration. In 1562 the mayor of Autun, named Jacques Bretagne, boldly put the case for the Protestants before Charles IX.

Your most humble subjects recommend that it should be permitted to those who cannot in all conscience partake in the ceremonies of the Church of Rome, that they may assemble publicly, in all modesty, in a temple or in some place separately, either private or public, in broad daylight, to receive instruction in the Word of God, to offer prayer and supplication in the language intelligible by the people for the remission of the sins of the Church, for the queen your mother, for our lords and princes of the Blood and for the needs of your subjects.

He carried a third of the chapter of Autun Cathedral with him. But the situation was already beyond repair. The rallying of the Catholic party in Burgundy owed much to the activities of Gaspard de Saulx, comte de Tavanes.

In 1522 Gaspard de Saulx had entered the service of François I as a page at the age of thirteen. Three years later he won his spurs at the battle of Pavia; he was with Montluc at the victory of Cerisoles, and at the battle of Renty he so distinguished himself that Henri II took the collar of Saint-Michel off his own neck and placed it around that of Gaspard, saying: 'Vous êtes un lion qu'il faut enchaîner.'

Gaspard was a passionate supporter of the Catholic party and he set himself, in his own words, 'to impose strength and unity on the movement for the resistance to heresy, by choosing always good Catholics to command the garrisons or to administer the towns'. While fighting the Huguenots with all the forces which he could muster, he was busy founding the Confrerie du Saint-Esprit at Dijon, the Association des Catholiques de l'Auxois at Semur, the Fraternité des Catholiques at Chalon-sur-Saône. When, in 1568, the Edict of Longjumeau confirmed the Edict of Amboise in conferring certain rights upon the Huguenots, Tavanes wrote to Catherine de Medici: 'To conceal nothing from you, everything cries out against peace, against the king and against yourself.'

Such attitudes only caused an escalation in the conflict. In April 1569 a German Protestant prince, the Herzog von Zweibrücken, invaded France. The Huguenot Amiral de Coligny, with an army of 8,000, marched on Beaune and threatened Dijon. The comte de Cossé-Brissac was sent to confront them, but on 27 June 1570 he was defeated at Arnay-le-Duc. The devastations caused by both sides reduced parts of Burgundy to a pitiable condition. Auxerre was described as being 'like a new Jerusalem, which only wanted a Jeremiah to weep over its misfortunes'. The abbeys of Cluny, Cîteaux and La Ferté were sacked; the vineyards of Volnay, Pommard and Meursault were destroyed and some 400 villages were burnt. A member of the parlement de Dijon, Vintimille, asked whether 'in the presence of so many battles, assaults, destructions of towns and villages and the loss of so many great men, the world was not reaching its catastrophe'.

On 26 August 1572, the culminating act of Catholic perfidy was performed – the massacre of St Bartholomew. By this time Gaspard de Tavanes had been replaced as governor by the more moderate Léonor de Chabot, comte de Charny. He was supported by Pierre Jeannin, a lawyer from Autun. Antoine de Vienne, comte de Commarin, brought orders from Paris that the massacre was to be repeated at Dijon. Pierre Jeannin, to his eternal credit, quoted the law of the Emperor Theodosius which forbade local governors to execute commands of an extraordinary nature and which were against the forms of justice, within thirty days. Chabot-Charny placed the principal Huguenot leaders under protective arrest. The massacre did not take place. In the reading room of the Archives de la Côte d'Or is a large inscription: 'Pierre Jeannin empêcha par sa sagesse que la ville de Dijon n'éprouvât les horreurs de la St Barthélemy en Aoust, 1572.'

One of the principal victims of the massacre of St Bartholomew was the Amiral de Coligny. Coligny and Tavanes were the protagonists of their respective parties. Each is associated with a Burgundian château of the first importance – Coligny with Tanlay and Saulx-Tavanes with Sully.

The Château de Sully

'A *Grand Seigneur*', wrote Cardinal Bernis, 'was once a man of illustrious birth, who possessed large estates and the great offices of the Crown. Master of his own region, he was not ashamed to reside there. He had influence with the king, but he seldom went to Court.'

Just such a person was Gaspard de Saulx, whose father had purchased the estate of Sully in 1515. It had belonged, during the fifteenth century, to the family of Montaigu, but in 1470 the last of the family was killed at the siege of Buxy and left only an illegitimate daughter, Jeanne. Louis XI proceeded to legitimize her. She married Hugues de Rabutin and from them were descended not only Roger de Bussy-Rabutin, but Madame de Sévigné and St Jeanne de Chantal, a consequence of his action which Louis XI could hardly have foreseen.

The Rabutin family owned Sully until they sold it to Jean de Saulx. By the time that Gaspard succeeded his father, he was the heir to an immense estate. 'The Château de Sully', writes Robert Forster, 'was the centre of a chain of twenty-four domains and seigneuries, comprising over forty villages and extending from Autun north-eastward through the Dijon plain almost to Langres.'

It was not an easy position to maintain. Gaspard put his finger on the central issue when he said: 'Wealthy gentlemen with three sons should place two in the army and middling nobles only one. The rest should enter either the Church or the Law, and only the eldest should have children. Marry few daughters, for that is the ruin of a noble house.' Owing to the law of *partage* the younger children had a right to a share of one third of the inheritance, and dowries were generally exorbitant. The family fortunes had constantly to be increased in order to compensate for this loss to the estate at each generation. We have seen, at the Château de Brandon, how this right – the Custom of Burgundy – could have a disintegrating effect.

Claude de Saulx, grandson of Gaspard, repaired the family fortunes by his marriage with Françoise de Brulart, daughter of the premier président du parlement de Dijon. She brought him not only the considerable dowry of 120,000 livres, but a large share of the business acumen of her family. Gaspard had bluntly repudiated the idea that such families were unworthy of the *noblesse d'épée*. 'How stupid is the opinion of brutes that presidents and councillors are not gentlemen.'

Françoise kept the most careful accounts, which have happily survived, even noting such minute items as 'thread to mend the coat of Monseigneur'. If later generations of Saulx-Tavanes would have ordered a new coat, it was partly thanks to Françoise de Brulart.

Their sense of thrift, however, did not extend to the size of their family. Eleven of their offspring survived the perils of childhood. The problem was dealt with in a way of which Gaspard would have approved. Three of their four daughters became nuns and, luckily, their only married daughter had no children. Two of their sons died unmarried and in the end they had to provide for only two cadet branches.

It was against a background of family finance such as this that we must set the rebuilding of the châteaux of Le Pailly and Sully. In 1563, profiting from the Peace of Amboise for a little leisure, Gaspard de Saulx started to rebuild the Château du Pailly, some 10 kilometres south-east of Langres. He retained the irregularities and some of the defensive features of the original *château fort*, but he reclothed the façades of the court in a rich Renaissance style and recast the apartments 'tous voutés à la forme d'Italie'. The building has been attributed, but without evidence, to Nicolas Ribonnier, an architect of Langres.

Ten years later Gaspard began rebuilding the Château de Sully, near Autun, but he died in the summer of that year, 'n'ayant fait que tracer le bâtiment de Sully', according to his son. It was left to his widow to put the plan into execution. The Maréchale Françoise specified that she wanted 'to make the second house [Sully] equal in value and estimation as that of Le Pailly' in order that her two sons could be equally provided for.

The first building – 'le chastel, maison forte et forteresse de

Sully' – determined the dimensions of the second. It also prescribed its most distinctive feature, the four square towers set obliquely at the four corners of the moat.

Three of the outward-facing façades have been subsequently rebuilt; judging by an early water-colour they were originally of a more rough and irregular design. Only the entrance front, in the style of the late Renaissance, gives any hint of the magnificence that is to follow. For it is only within the security of the quadrangle that the especial glory of Sully is revealed.

The architecture is both simple and dignified, with a rusticated lower storey supporting a *piano nobile* above, proportioned to an Ionic order of coupled pilasters. The windows are mostly round-arched, those of the upper storey retaining the mullion and double transoms of the windows on the entrance front. But the architect has made a subtle use of the rustication. It is so designed as to form, as it were, pilasters corresponding with those above so that there is a marked vertical accent throughout, which contributes much to the general effect. In its pristine state the court was enriched with mural paintings, with allegorical figures in the niches. When Madame de Sévigné described Sully as 'the Fontainebleau of Burgundy' she must have been thinking of this courtyard.

It attracted also the superlative praise of Bussy-Rabutin. In a letter to Madame de Sévigné, dated 2 September 1678, he describes a visit to Jacques de Saulx-Tavanes. 'Nous entrâmes dans la cour de Sully', he wrote, 'qui est la plus belle cour de château en France, sept carosses à six chevaux à la suite les uns des autres.' Since all had come a considerable distance and from different directions, their simultaneous arrival 'showed how punctual we were for the rendezvous'. It is surprising to learn that eleven guests should have been too large a number to accommodate in so capacious a house. 'Since Tavanes was unable to sleep so many, Monsieur d'Epinac took us off in the evenings – M. and Mme de Toulongeon, the Abbé Bonneau, my daughter and myself, to sleep at Epinac.'

It is difficult, in this peaceful courtyard, to recapture the spirit of the sixteenth century; to think that the man who planned it was one of the chief perpetrators of the massacre of St Bartholomew and ran round Paris shouting 'Bleed them! Bleed them! Doctors say bleeding is just as good in August as in May!'

The first victim of the massacre was Gaspard de Coligny. He and his two brothers were the most redoubtable figures in the Huguenot party, and the youngest, François, seigneur d'Andelot, began the rebuilding of the Château de Tanlay, near Tonnerre.

Having lost their father in 1522 when they were still in their infancy, the Coligny brothers were brought up by their uncle, the Connétable Anne de Montmorency. He took a close interest in their education and upbringing and demanded of their tutor, Nicolas Bérault, that he should be 'adverted faithfully of everything that manifested itself in them, both good and bad'. It was he who decided that Gaspard and François should have a military career and that Odet should go into the Church. Odet, 'being lazy by nature and a great lover of his leisure, was delighted to find so respectable a pretext for escaping the fatigues of warfare'. With this somewhat negative vocation he received Holy Orders and in 1533 was made a cardinal at the age of sixteen, archbishop of Toulouse at seventeen and évêque-comte de Beauvais and thus one of the Twelve Peers of France at eighteen.

The three young men received an excellent classical education in the new humanist tradition, which, although not in itself anti-Catholic, often paved the way to Protestantism. François d'Andelot was the first to be converted. In 1556, after the campaign in Parma, he was made a prisoner and detained in Milan. This gave him leisure to read and whatever he read convinced him of the errors of Rome.

In 1552 Odet was still sufficiently in communion with the Holy See to be appointed Grand Inquisitor. It was not until 1562 that he joined the Huguenots. But he retained the bishopric of Beauvais, with its enormous revenues, while only using the title of count. On 1 December 1564 he married Isabelle d'Hauteville, but he continued to wear his scarlet soutane at Court and Isabelle was known, unofficially, as Madame la Cardinale.

In May, 1557, Gaspard de Coligny was included in the list drawn up by Theodore Beza of those 'whom we think not enemies of our cause'. But it was not until August 1560 that Gaspard de Coligny spoke out openly as a Protestant. There was no reason to doubt his sincerity, but it is always difficult to judge the element of political ambition in such a conversion. Brantôme sums it up thus: 'Certain people have implied that he had more ambition than religion and that his actions tended more to the former than to the latter. Now I cannot tell what he might have thought in his heart of hearts, but the zeal and devotion which he has always shown towards his religion is something all would attest.'

The Château de Tanlay

François d'Andelot, the youngest of the three Coligny brothers, was the builder of the first part of the château that we see today. He inherited it from his mother, Louise de Montmorency. The Connétable Anne de Montmorency was the owner of Ecouen and Chantilly, two of the most magnificent houses of France. Ecouen abounded in works of art but also in the sumptuous and libertine luxury of a *grand seigneur*. The stained glass windows at Ecouen, wrote Michelet, were guilty of 'a shocking immodesty that would have made Rabelais blush'.

The architect Jean Bullant had designed Ecouen during the last years of the reign of François I, and also the Petit Château at Chantilly. But there are no real grounds for attributing Tanlay to Bullant. Charles Porée proposes the less well-known name of Bertrand de Cazenove, an architect from Champagne and a Huguenot. Between 1561 and 1567 he is known to have been working elsewhere for d'Andelot. He may have furnished the designs for Tanlay.

D'Andelot decided to rebuild the old château in the new style, beginning with the north-west tower and the two blocks which run south and east from it. These have been incorporated into the new building carried out between 1643 and 1648 by the architect Pierre Le Muet for the rich financier Michel Particelli. It is impossible to say to what extent Le Muet retained the architecture of his predecessor and to what extent he superimposed his own. There are, however, elements in the style which could date from d'Andelot. Domes, for instance, which here replace the more typical *poivrières*, had already appeared at Assier, built for Galliot de Genouillac between 1524 and 1535. The two staircase towers, also, which occupy the inward angles of the Cour d'Honneur, might have been inspired by those at Meudon, which bore the dates 1539 and 1540 respectively, or, even more probably, by a similar one in the courtyard of Chantilly, dating from the reconstructions of Pierre Chambiges, which were started in 1535. But it is no longer possible to distinguish, from the outside, the buildings of d'Andelot from the vast and sumptuous ensemble of Pierre Le Muet.

'This massive great château', wrote Montégut, 'creates the impression of a fat Burgundian dowager, robust of form, who has in attendance the most elegant of pages.' The young page is, of course, the gatehouse, originally known as the 'portail neuf', but now more often as the 'Petit Château'. Although it is built in the style of a grotto, the gatehouse served a defensive purpose and was slotted for a drawbridge.

It forms a transition between a medieval gatehouse and a triumphal arch. Louis Hautecoeur accepts the tradition that d'Andelot built only the lower storey, with its fantastic, vermiculated rustications, and that it was his daughter, Anne de Coligny, who married the comte de Charny, who built the upper parts between 1610 and 1630. But however it was built, it remains a delightful example of late Renaissance architecture. As Hautecoeur says: 'The balance between the rustication below and the rich ornament above, the solidity of the volumes, the happy contrast between the plain and the decorated surfaces, make this little château, the name of whose architect is regrettably unknown, one of the great works of this period.'

It is difficult to account for the positioning of the new gatehouse. One would have expected it to be in line with the west wing of the entrance court – which was that rebuilt by d'Andelot – so as to leave the prospect of the château proper unimpeded. Instead it is placed well to the east of the west wing and encroaches seriously upon the outer, or Green, Court, which has consequently no symmetry. The entrance to the vast Cour des Communs, which ought to face the entrance to the château, is set awkwardly to one side.

If it is difficult accurately to discern the hand of d'Andelot in the architecture of Tanlay, at least the fresco in the so-called Tour de la Ligue definitely dates from his time. The artist, who must have been of the school of Primaticcio, has made use of the inside of the dome for a vast composition of figures, some naked, some clothed, some 'armed at all pieces'. Various conjectures have been put forward as to the precise symbolism of these figures, but the most convincing is that of Marguerite Christol, writing in 1956, who sees clearly behind the mural a 'hymn' by Ronsard celebrating Henri II.

Ronsard was a friend of the Coligny family in general and of the Cardinal de Châtillon in particular:

> Mon Odet, mon prélat, mon Seigneur, mon confort,
> Mon renom, mon honneur, ma gloire, mon support;
> Ma Muse, mon Phoebus qui fait ma plume écrire,
> Qui anime ma langue et réveille ma lyre.

It was not unlikely that d'Andelot should turn to the author of those words in search of inspiration. The characterization of Ronsard's hymn can be fitted with great ease over the figures of the fresco.

The scene is Olympus and in the centre is Henri II as Jupiter, looking down upon the personalities of his Court. Juno, with her peacock, represents Catherine de Medici. She is in the nude, but, unlike the others, turns her back upon the artist. No such delicacy attends Diane de Poitiers as Venus. To the right of Juno is Mercury. Mercury was the ambassador and plenipotentiary of the gods, but his character was not entirely admirable. He was the god also of thieves, pickpockets and dishonest persons and was in many ways dishonest himself. But Ronsard suggests nothing uncomplimentary:

> C'est ce grand demi-dieu, Cardinal de Lorraine,
> Qui, bien aimé de toi, en ta France ramène
> Les antiques vertus.

It must be remembered that the Coligny brothers and the Lorraines had started out as the best of friends. The final rupture was yet to come.

Next to Mercury is Minerva, naked but wearing a plumed helmet and holding a lance. Minerva was first and foremost goddess of wisdom and the liberal arts. She is here depicted as Marguerite de France, sister of Henri II and duchesse de Savoie. Next to her are the other two Coligny brothers: Gaspard as Neptune, described by Ronsard as 'Fidèle serviteur de votre grand'Majesté' – a point which d'Andelot was only too anxious to underline; and beside him Odet, Cardinal de Chatillon, 'l'Hercule chrétien' – a title which he was soon to forgo in the eyes of the Catholics.

More difficult to interpret is the figure of Janus, crowned and two-faced, female towards the left and male holding a key towards the right. It is suggested that this represents the Crown of France, but Marguerite Christol does not think that Janus is meant to be presenting a smiling face towards the Catholics and a stern frown towards the Protestants. That is contrary to the whole tenor of the hymn. But the fresco is incomplete. In 1562, with the massacre of Vassy, the Wars of Religion took a turn for the worse. The three Coligny brothers were all to fall victims. Odet and d'Andelot were almost certainly poisoned: Gaspard was the first victim of the massacre of St Bartholomew. The Guise brothers were also to fall by the hands of assassins.

There were, in fact, atrocities on both sides. Arthur Young, writing with the detachment of the eighteenth century after a visit to Blois, stated that 'the character of the period and of the men that figured in it were alike disgusting. Bigotry and ambition, equally dark, insidious and bloody, allow no feelings of regret. The parties could hardly have been better employed than in cutting one another's throats.'

Bibliography

The Chapelle de Bouton

H. David: 'La Chapelle de Bouton', in *Congrès Archéologique de France*, 91, Dijon, 1928.

Pagny-le-Château

H. Baudot: 'De l'Ancien Château de Pagny', in *Mémoires de la Commission des Antiquaires de la Côte d'Or*, 1835.

H. David: 'La Chapelle du Château de Pagny', in *Bulletin Monumental*, Vol. 87, 1928.

L. Marcel: *Le Cardinal de Givry*, 1926.

Montigny-sur-Aube

Y. Christ: 'La plus belle Chapelle Renaissance', in *Connaissance des Arts*, 1959.

Saint-Michel de Dijon

J. Vallery-Radot: 'L'Eglise Saint-Michel de Dijon', in *Congrès Archéologique de France*, 91, Dijon, 1928.

Hugues Sambin

H. David: *De Sluter à Sambin*, 1932.

B. Prost: 'Hugues Sambin', in *Gazette des Beaux Arts*, 1892.

Ligny-le-Châtel and Cravant

J. Vallery-Radot: in *Congrès Archéologique de France*, 116, Auxerre, 1958.

Saint-Pierre d'Auxerre

J. Vallery-Radot: 'L'Eglise Saint-Pierre d'Auxerre', in *Congrès Archéologique de France*, 116, Auxerre, 1958.

The Château d'Ancy-le-Franc

P. du Colombier: 'Le 6e livre retrouvé de Serlio', in *Gazette des Beaux Arts*, 1934.

J. Guillaume: 'Serlio est-il l'architecte d'Ancy-le-Franc?', in *Revue des Arts*, No. 5, 1969.

L. Hautecoeur: 'Château d'Ancy-le-Franc', in *Congrès Archéologique de France*, 91, Dijon, 1928.

The Château de Jours-les-Baigneux

P. Gras and P. Quarré: 'Le Château de Jours', in *Mémoires de la Commission des Antiquités de la Côte d'Or*, Vol. XXVI, 1963.

E. Nesle: *Voyage d'un Touriste dans l'Arrondissement de Châtillon-sur-Seine*, 1860.

The Château de Vallery

P. du Colombier: 'L'Enigme de Vallery', in *Humanisme et Renaissance*, 1937.

R. Planchenault: 'Les Châteaux de Vallery', in *Bulletin Monumental*, Vol. 121, 1963.

L. Romier: *La Carrière d'un Favori: Jacques d'Albon de Saint-André, Maréchal de France*, 1909.

The Wars of Religion

A. Kleinclausz: *Histoire de Bourgogne*, 1909.

J. Desbordes: *Meaux*, 1971.

The Château du Pailly

P. Vitry: 'Le Chateau du Pailly', in *Congrès Archéologique de France*, 91, Dijon, 1928.

The Château de Sully

D. Grivot: *Le Château de Sully*, s.d.

R. Forster: *The House of Saulx-Tavanes*, 1971.

The Château de Tanlay

M. Christol: 'La Fresque du Château de Tanlay', in *Bulletin de la Société de l'Histoire du Protestantisme*, 1956.

L. Crété: *Coligny*, 1985.

L. Hautecoeur: 'Château de Tanlay', in *Congrès Archéologique de France*, Vol. 116, Auxerre, 1958.

C. Oulmont: 'Le Château Historique de Tanlay', in *Révue Art et Industrie*, 1932.

J. Shimitzu: *Conflict of Loyalties: Politics and Religion in the Career of Gaspard de Coligny, Admiral of France*, 1970.

THE SEVENTEENTH CENTURY

To the sixteenth century – 'le Siècle Détraqué' – succeeded that which was to be known as the 'Grand Siècle', the century of Henri IV, of Richelieu and of Louis XIV. Of these three, the first had by far the hardest task.

'It was not France', wrote Etienne Pasquier, 'that emerged from the forty years of conflict, but the carcass of France.' To the proud monarchy of the first Valois had succeeded a king 'with his shirt in tatters and his doublet out at the elbows'. But Henri IV was endowed with those qualities which the French most admire. He was made to be king and with his great minister Maximilien de Béthune, duc de Sully, he set about the rebuilding of France.

It was their policy to encourage the landowner to live upon his land. 'It has been from time immemorial the honour of the gentlemen of France', said Henri IV, 'to live in the country, and only to go to the towns to do their service to the king.' If they were to live in the country, it was understood that they should be properly housed. 'His Majesty', wrote Guillaume Girard, 'urged the greater part of the most wealthy members of the nobility to plan the erection of fine houses.' The seventeenth century witnessed a great programme of building and a strong development of the *vie de château*. What was true of France in general was true of Burgundy in particular; one of the first to be built in the new century was the Château de Cormatin, some 13 kilometres north of Cluny.

The Château de Cormatin

'This estate, known *ci-devant* by the title of *Marquisat d'Huxelles et Baronnie de Cormatin* . . . combines, by the beauty and elegance of the building and by the delights of its accommodation, all that a *Grand Seigneur* and a very rich family could desire.' So runs the notice for the sale of the property issued on 28 July 1808.

The area in the middle of which the château stands contains nine *hectares* [some 22 acres]; the plantations and the gardens are superb and they are bordered by a fine river *très poissonneuse* on the banks of which is a terrace with an avenue of limes longer than that of Les Feuillants in Paris. The so-called *Chambre Henri IV* and the rooms designated as *Appartements Dorés* are as rich as His Imperial Majesty's at Fontainebleau.

The climate is extremely favourable and the proof of it is that the Tulip Trees, the Catalpa, etc., which have grown from seeds which the present owner, Monsieur Desoteux-Cormatin, brought back from America twenty years ago, have grown superbly.

The Château d'Uxelles, just half a league from Cormatin, formed the focal point of the view to the north; 'The great age of the castle and its situation combine to form a prospect which is extremely picturesque.'

The Château de Cormatin is the scene of one of the most important restorations of our time. Nothing could demonstrate more clearly the need to see a building in its original setting before we judge it.

Perhaps the most significant recovery is the moat. Carefully filled in by the owners of the château in the nineteenth century, it was carefully dug out again by the present owners in 1987. The original retaining wall or *contrescarpe* was revealed and the water allowed to return to its natural level.

The first thing which this achieves is the restoration of the original proportions of the façade, for the level of the water is considerably lower than that of the ground. The château can now be seen to stand upon a solid base above which the two main storeys, of equal height, are no longer top-heavy. Secondly, the very broad moat – in some places it is 78 feet across – offers a complete reflection of the façades, which are thereby doubled; the composition becomes vertical rather than horizontal.

The destructions of the nineteenth century, however, were on too large a scale for a total restitution to be possible. The original building was ranged between four pavilions round three sides of a quadrangle; the façades were all in the same style, the roofs were symmetrical and all covered in the same Anjou slate. But in 1815 the south wing was turned into a cotton mill and the walls were so weakened that they collapsed. In the subsequent restoration the south-west pavilion was reduced in height and roofed in brown, Burgundian tiles; although newer it looks older, as if the north wing had been added to a building more in the vernacular style. A complete restoration of Cormatin would require the reinstatement of the south wing and the re-roofing of the whole in the blue-grey tiles of the north wing. We would then see a chateau of the most imposing dimensions – something on the scale of Ancy-le-Franc or Sully.

The architecture of the courtyard is of a rough masonry dressed with string courses and quoins in stone of a rich ochre colour. The façades are of an extreme simplicity which emphasizes by contrast the rather elaborate porches, with coupled columns set against a heavily rusticated arch supporting a broken pediment. Presumably the south range offered a similar façade. There was originally a low screen of some sort enclosing the Cour d'Honneur which would have had an entrance pavilion that was perhaps even more elaborate than the porches, in the style made popular by the du Cerceau family.

It is not known who was the architect of Cormatin, but certain drawings – of mantelpieces and a fountain – now in the RIBA library are signed by Jacques Gentilhâtre and bear inscriptions such as 'courmatin a monsieur le marquis du xelles' (sic). Gentilhâtre clearly belonged to the circle of the younger du Cerceau brothers and their cousin Salomon de Brosse. He had worked at Montceaux and at Fontainebleau with Rémy Collin; in 1614 he was at Chalon-sur-Saône and Saint-Gengoux. He was therefore in the neighbourhood of Cormatin when it was first started, which suggests that he was furnishing designs rather than recording existing features.

The outward façades are nobler than those of the courtyard and built of a fine white freestone. The north front is the only outward façade to have survived unaltered. It has a great dignity conferred by its size and a great charm derived from its simplicity. It is built 'in the French pavilion way'; that is to say, that each element in the façade has its own roof – the central *corps de logis*, the massive corner pavilions and the slender inward towers with their little conical roofs *en poivrière*.

This articulation of the façade reflects the basic formula on which the interior is planned, the *appartement*, made up of an ante-room, a bedroom, an oratory, a study and a *garderobe*. Each pavilion contains such an *appartement* with the oratory, opening out of the bedroom, in the little tower.

It is possible that even the furniture of the apartments has influenced the façades. It is at once apparent to anyone approaching the château by the main entrance that the windows in the large pavilion to the right of the courtyard are not placed symmetrically, but to the left of centre. Since the façades are in all other respects symmetrical, some reason for this departure must be sought. This disposition of the windows, however, makes sense when seen from the inside, for the large four-poster bed of the marquise d'Uxelles occupies the place, traditional in the early seventeenth century, in the corner of the room. Had the windows been opened as the symmetry of the façade requires, it would not have left space for the bed. This same off-centre arrangement of the windows occurs also at the Château de Rosny, which is on the Seine a little downstream of Mantes-la-Jolie. This was started in 1595 by the duc de Sully.

Another example of the way in which the interior disposition can control the façade is to be seen on the entrance front, on the courtyard side of the north wing. A central feature is provided by the close grouping of the windows and doorway. This grouping is required by the presence behind them of a remarkable staircase. It was built in about 1610 and is one of the earliest and one of the largest examples of an open cage staircase. Four huge piers of masonry rise from the basement to the attic – a height of 75.5 feet – and act as newels between which, on each storey, four great arches, like rising bridges, carry the flights of steps. To this bold and dramatic design the varied colours of the local stone provide the only decoration.

The two apartments of the marquis and marquise d'Uxelles have survived unaltered from their original condition and provide an astonishing and almost unique example of the *style Louis XIII*. They were decorated between 1625 and 1628 by a team of artists who are known to have worked for Marie de'Medici at the Luxembourg.

Richly sculptured, richly painted and richly gilded, these rooms are of a sumptuosity which is almost overwhelming. Two different approaches to panelling can be distinguished; one known as *de hauteur*, which treats the whole wall as a flat, decorative unit, and another known as *d'appui*, where the wall is divided into two distinct storeys by a cornice.

Of the first sort is the ante-room or Salle du Roi in the apartment of the marquise. It takes its name from the portrait over the mantelpiece of Louis XIII on horseback; he stayed here in 1629. The way that he sits his charger recalls the saying of Pluvinel: 'The king on foot is king of his subjects: the king mounted is king of kings.' The ceiling is in the French manner of the times with exposed beams – *poutres apparentes* – with all surfaces delicately painted.

A similar ceiling, in which the dominant colour is the lapis-lazuli blue made fashionable by the famous Salon Bleu of the marquise de Rambouillet, covers the bedroom next door, but the walls here were destined for tapestries.

The rooms of the marquis d'Uxelles are more Italian in flavour. The ceilings in particular are *à caissons* – deeply recessed and heavily framed compartments. Here, too, the panelling is *d'appui*, and the horizontal division of the walls is put to a good use. In the richest of all the rooms, the Cabinet de Sainte-Cecile, the upper range of panelling is recessed above the cornice. Below the cornice the panelling is artfully contrived to provide doors behind which is installed a chest of drawers. The decoration of this room is so complete and so demanding that it would be difficult to place any furniture against it.

On 26 August 1705, Madame de Sévigné's cousin, the marquis de Coulanges, visited Cormatin. His description is so vivid that it deserves to be quoted at length. The party came from Cluny and the impressive silhouette of the Château d'Uxelles acted as a landmark.

At last we took the road to Cormatin, guided by the Château d'Uxelles. But what a beautiful château is Cormatin, Madame! You have never told me about it. What? Three large wings and four great pavilions with towers built out on corbels which struck me as masterpieces. Hungry as I was, I began at once to go all over this fine château while our great Cardinal [de Bouillon], while waiting for us, got between two sheets in a very good and beautiful bed in your own apartment.

Coulanges was particularly struck by the beds:

I was very content with the one in which I slept, of red damask with panels of embroidery, in a lovely room beyond the chapel, enriched with panelling with the emblems of du Blé and Phélypeaux [the family names of the marquis and marquise] . . . Never have I slept in a better bed nor between sheets so well conditioned. One can now reach this room through a large salon, newly panelled, which gives evidence of the great pains taken by the Maréchal, as do also the fruit garden and the espaliers which he had planted and the expense which he went to in shoring up the sides of the moat in order to set them up again. I am sure that it will be most attractive when the river Grosne is free to flow into it. I looked with extreme pleasure and attention at the picture of Henri IV which is at the end of the gallery.

There is a tradition, supported by Peigne, that Henri IV was once a guest at Cormatin.

It was in Burgundy, at the battle of Fontaine-Française, that Henri IV dealt the final blow to the ultra Catholic League, which continued to reject him even after his conversion to Catholicism and his coronation – a ceremony which had to take place at Chartres because Reims, the traditional place of coronation, was still in the hands of the league.

This party was now under the leadership of Charles de Lorraine, duc de Mayenne, who did not scruple to ally himself with the king of Spain against his own countrymen. Thus it was that at the beginning of the year 1595 Don Ferdinand de Velasco was in Franche-Comté with an army 15,000 strong with a view to joining forces with Mayenne to secure Burgundy for the league.

On 4 June Henri IV arrived at Dijon, where triumphal arches had been erected for his reception. On the same day Mayenne joined up with Velasco at Gray, some 50 kilometres north-east of Dijon. Henri IV had only some 500 cavalry with which to oppose this army and was rallying supporters wherever he could. 'Fervacques, à cheval!' he wrote to the comte de Grancey, 'j'ai besoin de ton bras. Je suis Henri.'

On the morning of 5 June the king, 'dressed in a doublet of white fustian that was out at both elbows', was observed at the Sainte-Chapelle 'praying to God with an inconceivable ardour'.

Henri, with his diminutive troop, attacked with a ferocity which unnerved their opponents, who could not believe that there were not considerable reinforcements behind him. He was always to be found where the fighting was fiercest and risked his life a dozen times. By the end of the day Mayenne and the Spaniards were in full flight and the cause of the league was lost. Henri retired for a well-earned rest to the Château de Fontaine-Française, then a feudal fortress. Here he was harangued by an alderman named Lebury. Uncertain of the outcome of the battle, Lebury had prepared two addresses. In the fluster of the moment he began to deliver to Henri the oration intended for Mayenne. On realizing his mistake the poor man broke off with a horrified 'Ah! Pardon, Sire!' to which the king merely replied, 'The intention was good, but my cousin Mayenne is now a long way off.' That night he wrote to his sister: 'On other occasions I have fought for glory, but this time I was fighting for my life.'

One of the many Burgundians who fought by the side of the king and who was particularly commended for his courage was Christophe de Rabutin, baron de Chantal, whose wife was later to become a saint. Her granddaughter was Madame de Sévigné; his nephew was Roger de Bussy-Rabutin. The two families form a nexus of relationships and owned between them some of the most interesting châteaux in Burgundy.

Bourbilly and Monthelon

When the ultra Catholic League was formed, Bénigne Frémyot, président du parlement de Bourgogne, 'won over a dozen, both of counsellors, lawyers and registrars, and, abandoning his house and fortune, took them to Flavigny and Semur in order, he said, that there should be one place in Burgundy which administers justice in the name of the king. What he did was not just for a few months, but for several years while the Wars of Religion lasted, regardless of his own impoverishment.'

He had, for some reason, left his youngest son André in the care of his brother at Dijon and the directors of the league took him as a hostage, threatening Frémyot that if he did not join them they would send him the head of his child. He replied 'that he would be happy to sacrifice to God so beloved a child in so good a cause, and that it would be better for the son to die innocent than for the father to become guilty of treachery, sinning against God and his king'. In the end the boy was released for a stiff ransom.

In 1585 Frémyot was so overcome by the news of the murder of Henri III that his hair turned white, but he persisted in his loyalty to the legitimate succession, in the hope that once Henri IV had embraced the Catholic faith and had been crowned king, 'he would find in this corner of Burgundy a faithful troop'. In 1595, after the coronation at Chartres, Frémyot returned in triumph to Dijon. The king wished to reward him with the gift of the archbishopric of Bourges, but, having been married, he could not be ordained. The young André, however, took Holy Orders and the archbishopric was conferred upon him.

Three years earlier Frémyot's daughter Jeanne had married Christophe de Rabutin, baron de Chantal, whose father made over to him their *château et maison forte* at Bourbilly and went to live in the more modest residence of Monthelon, near Autun.

Bourbilly today is a handsome reconstruction of a château of the
fifteenth century, restored by the comte de Franqueville. It is built
upon the old foundations and may well resemble the house which
belonged in turn to Jeanne de Chantal and to her granddaughter
Madame de Sévigné, who describes a visit here in one of her letters.
On 16 October 1673 she came to stay 'dans le vieux château de mes
pères'. 'This was the scene of their triumphs. I found my beautiful
meadows, my little river, my magnificent trees and my beautiful mill
just where I had left them.'

Monmerque, who edited her letters, found here in 1862 a
farmhouse contrived within the ruins: 'The towers have been
demolished, the staircases which they housed replaced by wooden
steps; a few rooms retained their ancient chimneypieces, and the
chapel – which is used as a stable – has a fine Gothic window.'

In 1821 it was described in slightly more detail by the baron
Walckenaer. It was completely in ruins.

One of the principal façades had just been pulled down; the vast rooms in
the main lodging which had been preserved were now converted into barns.
Nothing remained of their antique magnificence but the curiously wrought
mantelpieces and the half effaced paintings on the walls, among which
could still be distinguished the Arms of the Rabutin family, who by their
alliances were related to the first dynasty of the dukes of Burgundy and the
royal family of Denmark. One portrait alone had survived all these
destructions: it was of the pious Chantal.

Born on 23 January 1572, she was canonized a saint on 16 July 1767.

At Bourbilly Jeanne de Chantal came face to face with the facts of
life. The château was dilapidated and the estate encumbered with
debts. Her first reaction to the prospect of so uphill a task was one of
repugnance: 'il lui fâchait extrêmement de sacrifier sa liberté
innocente'. But she set herself to restoring the family fortunes. Years
later, when her daughter, the comtesse de Toulongeon, found herself
in much the same position, her mother wrote to her: 'Apply yourself
with care to the government of your house,' she insisted; 'if I had not
had this courage, at the beginning of my married life, we would never
have had enough to live on, for our income was less than yours and
we were 15,000 écus in debt.'

As mistress of the household she acquitted herself well. One of the
hallmarks of the good *châtelaine* is the ability to gain and retain the
esteem of her domestics. 'It was a great proof of her prudence and

gentle conduct', wrote her biographer, the Mère de Chaugy, 'that in the eight years of her marriage and the nine years of her widowhood she made only two changes among her menservants and maidservants . . . her virtue caused them both to love and fear her. In short her household was the home of peace, honour, civility and Christian piety and of an innocent and noble joy.'

It was in this early experience of the management of her household that she discovered those gifts of administration which later enabled her to found and rule the convent of the Visitation.

It is difficult to say whether or not we may detect a budding saint in the life of the young *châtelaine*, but there are several anecdotes which illuminate her character. She certainly possessed the Christian virtue of compassion. Her husband, who was every inch a Rabutin, liked to make others feel the weight of his authority. 'Sometimes', wrote the Mère de Chaugy, 'he would throw peasants into the prison of his château, which was most unhealthy because of the damp; when it was for an offence which she judged slight, when everyone in the building had retired, she would take the prisoner out of the cell and put him in a bed, and very early the next day, so as not to offend her husband, she put him back in his prison.'

This was the easier because the baron de Chantal liked to lie in late. She, of course, had to be up early to give her orders for the day. 'When it began to be late', she would tell her nuns of the Visitation, 'I would go into the bedroom, making enough noise to wake him, so that we could start the Mass in the chapel . . . I went and pulled the curtains, telling him that it was late, that he must get up; that the chaplain was robed and about to start the Mass; finally I took a candle and held it below his eyes and so tormented him that I dragged him out of his sleep and out of his bed.'

We must set this picture, however, against a background of tender and even passionate affection. After only eight years of married life her husband was killed in a shooting accident. He was taken to the nearest house in the village where he was soon joined by his wife. 'Lord, take everything that I have in the world,' she prayed, 'my parents, my possessions, my children – but leave me my dear husband whom you have given me.' Christophe de Chantal died nine days later, leaving Jeanne a widow with six children.

The first identifiable step on the route to sanctity was the conviction that she needed a spiritual director; the second was her discovery of such a director in the bishop of Geneva, François de Sales, who, like herself, was later to be canonized. But first for a short time she had another director.

On the death of her husband, her father-in-law, Guy de Rabutin, insisted on her leaving Bourbilly and coming to live with him at Monthelon, threatening, if she refused, to marry again and dis-inherit her children.

Monthelon, some 6 kilometres west of Autun, is hardly a château, but rather a *ferme fortifiée*. Seen from the east, where the river Selle passes through its meadows, its façade is dominated by its two towers, which give it both strength and distinction. But apart from them, all is irregular; the windows are disposed without the least regard to symmetry.

Seen from the west it is architecturally more interesting; there is a conscious design. Its elements are quickly listed. There is a central block with an open gallery beneath the roof – a design typical of some of the farmhouses and *maisons de vigneron* in Burgundy. Beneath this, twin front doors, approached by eight steps of rough-hewn masonry set between symmetrically placed windows, each divided vertically by a stone mullion, form a conscious composition. But that is as far as the design goes. This grouping is not related to the gallery above.

Over the double doors is the only suggestion of nobility in the form of a panel with the coat of arms, in high relief, of Rabutin-Chantal. But what really distinguishes this side of the house is the chapel which proclaims its presence only by its little belfry – an octagonal spire growing out of a rather squat pyramid upheld by a timber arcade.

The coming of François de Sales was a great relief to the household at Monthelon. The domestic staff would say: 'The first director that Madame had made her pray three times a day, and it was a nuisance to all of us; but Monseigneur de Genève makes her pray at all hours of the day and that does not inconvenience anyone.'

Life at Monthelon was difficult enough already. The old baron was entirely under the domination of one of his domestics. Nothing could happen in the household without her approval and even Jeanne, who was technically the *châtelaine*, 'would not have dared to give a messenger a glass of wine without her authority'. The situation was a severe test of Jeanne's Christian virtues, but, according to the Mère de Chaugy, 'in order to react in accordance with the gospel, she took every occasion to render good services to her from whom she received such ill services. This saintly woman even made herself schoolteacher and servant to the children of this woman, teaching them to read, combing their hair and dressing them with her own hands.'

During this time Jeanne was under the constant spiritual direction of François de Sales. It is clear that a deep and tender affection united the hearts of the two future saints. Probably only those who have experienced true Christian love – who can understand the command of St Peter: 'See that ye love one another with a pure heart fervently' – can penetrate the relationship of François and Jeanne. As he put it himself: 'Cette affection est blanche plus que la neige, pure plus que le soleil.' So confident was he of the purity of his affection that he could take it with him to the altar. 'Such is my ardour, it seems, for your advancement in the most holy, divine love, that when I celebrated this morning I began by offering you; it was as if I held you up in my arms as one would a little child.'

On 1 March 1610, Jeanne left Monthelon to take up her position at the convent of the Visitation. A large crowd had assembled to bid her farewell, including the poor of the neighbourhood, who had benefited from her constant charity and generosity, 'crying out aloud and forming so lamentable a cortège that it drew tears from the most impervious . . . but what was most touching and pitiable of all was the poor father-in-law who came to say goodbye with so many tears that he nearly fainted'. At last the coach moved off on the road to Autun. A fortnight later she left Burgundy for Annecy.

Two months later Henri IV was murdered by the fanatic Ravaillac. The new king, Louis XIII, was a boy of nine and the country was ruled by his mother, Marie de' Médici. In 1617 he took over the reins forcibly, driving his mother into exile, but from about 1624 the Cardinal Richelieu became the real ruler of France. One of the many lucrative offices which he held was the abbacy of Cluny.

Cluny then was in a fairly lamentable spiritual condition and Richelieu determined on an immediate reform, but in doing so he destroyed it as an institution. There was at that time a limited revival of monastic life centred on the houses of Saint-Vannes and Saint-Maur, near Paris. The monks were bound to a strict rule – *l'étroite observance*. Richelieu imported some of these to Cluny and gave them full authority over the existing hierarchy. In 1634 Cluny was joined to the order of Saint-Maur with the title of Congrégation de Saint-Bernard. It had lost its very name and as a spiritual order it had ceased to exist.

Its temporal power was also destroyed. A royal edict had decreed that all *châteaux forts* not belonging to the Crown were to be dismantled. Cluny had originally relied for its military protection upon the Château de Lourdon, a little north of Cluny itself and on the eastern slopes of the Charollais hills, near Lournan. As recently as 1631 the Cardinal de Guise, abbot of Cluny, had restored Lourdon, which had suffered at the hands of the Huguenots, and had added a magnificent tennis court for his own use. Richelieu decreed the demolition of the castle. Today the ruins of Lourdon, distinguished by tall piers of masonry surviving from the tennis court, symbolize the ruin of Cluny, for the château was, as the historian Lorain puts it, 'son dernier souvenir d'indépendance'.

Richelieu, however, was more concerned with the government of France than with the spiritual state of Cluny. In 1629 he accompanied Louis XIII to Grenoble to make war on the Spaniards in Mantua. Their route took them through Burgundy, passing through Sainte-Seine, Dijon, Beaune, Chalon, Tournus and Macon. Everywhere the king was received with loyal enthusiasm. But in the same year the central government announced the imposition of a tax on wine. The parlement of Burgundy refused to accept it. On 27 February 1630, a riot started in Dijon. It was led by a colourful personality known as 'Machat' and took as its marching song a popular refrain called *Lanturelu*, which has given its name to the rebellion. In the course of it a painting of Louis XIII was publicly burnt.

The reprisals were immediate and severe. The military governor, the marquis de Mirebeau, arrested most of the rioters and there were many executions. The city was deprived of its privileges, the ramparts were dismantled, the Tour Saint-Nicolas was reduced to half its height, the king made his solemn entry 'comme dans une ville conquise', and the Dijonnais were left in no doubt as to who was their master.

The scene was set for a trial of strength between the central administration and the local privileges of Burgundy – and the result was a foregone conclusion. What chance had a local provincial aristocracy against the absolutism of Louis XIV? That story, however, belongs more properly to the history of Dijon.

The reign of Louis XIV

The reign of Louis XIV was not a great period for the historian of the French château. The necessity of being seen at Versailles drew the noblemen of France away from their estates; to be ordered to live on them was regarded as a punishment and used as such by the king. Generally speaking the *vie de château* was at a low ebb.

But there are nearly always exceptions to general rules and the history of Burgundy offers many notable examples of a great château being loved and lived in. Two of these were the result of banishment from the Court – Mademoiselle de Montpensier at Saint-Fargeau and Bussy-Rabutin at Bussy-Rabutin. A third was a voluntary exile, that of Louvois's widow at Ancy-le-Franc.

On 29 October 1694, Philippe-Emmanuel, marquis de Coulanges, wrote to his cousin, the marquise de Sévigné, extolling 'a life in the country where all is liberty, all is enjoyment; a life which Madame de Louvois savours so much that she would no longer dream that there is such a place in the world as Fontainebleau or Versailles'. It would be perhaps more true to say that Ancy-le-Franc was her Fontainebleau and that she found more satisfaction in being hostess in her own palace than guest in the palace of the king.

Coulanges's letter is one of the classics of French epistolary art and could rank with those of Madame de Sévigné, to whom it was addressed.

When the weather is fine we are at Ancy-le-Franc; whenever it is foul we retreat to Tonnerre. Everywhere we go we keep Court. Thank God, we are adored. When the weather invites us, we make long expeditions in order to appreciate the extent of this 'State'; and when our curiosity leads us to enquire the name of the first village: 'To whom does it belong?' we get the answer: 'C'est à Madame.' 'To whom, then, belongs that one which I see a little further off?' 'It belongs to Madame.' 'But over there I see another.' 'It belongs to Madame.' 'And these forests?' 'They belong to Madame.' 'See this great, long plain.' 'It belongs to Madame.' 'But I see a fine château.' 'It is Nicei, which belongs to Madame, a very considerable estate which was the property of the counts of that name.' 'What is this other château on the top of the hill?' 'That is Pacy, which belongs to Madame. It came through her Mandelot inheritance, through her great-grandfather.' In one word, Madame, *tout est à Madame en ce pays*; I have never seen a property so vast nor so well consolidated.

Madame de Louvois loved her life in the country because she knew how to make herself beloved by the country people. Everywhere she went she was showered with presents.

There is nothing which they do not offer to Madame in token of the conscious joy that they feel to live under her dominion. All the villagers run before her with flutes and drums; one offers her cakes, another chestnuts, another nuts, while pigs, calves, sheep, turkeys, partridges, all the birds of the air and all the fishes of the stream await her at the château. There, Madame, you have a little description of the greatness of Madame, for she is known by no other name round here; and in the villages and everywhere that we went there were cries of 'Vive Madame!' which were unforgettable.

Epoisses

There hangs at Epoisses a ground plan of the *çi-devant* château drawn in 1794 when the revolutionary authorities decreed the demolition of one half of the building. It is a document of considerable interest. It shows the full extent of the 'château within a château' which was once so typical a design. The outer *enceinte* contains a vast area at the eastern end of which are clustered the buildings of what looks like a village and its church. In fact Saint-Symphorien was originally a collegiate church and many of the houses shown on the plan were those of the canons. It was only in the seventeenth century that this became the parish church.

It is not clear from the plan what purpose most of the buildings served, but we know that there was a 'hospital' and there were lodgings affected for the use of *retrayants*, that is to say, those villagers who belonged to the *seigneurie* and had the right to retreat here in times of danger. The obligations of feudality were, at least in theory, reciprocal. In return for the right of sanctuary within the *basse cour*, the villagers had the duty of mounting guard and maintaining the fortifications.

Another outstanding building in this ensemble was the *colombier* or dovecot, the visible symbol of another feudal right – the *droit de colombage*. A landowner was allowed one pair of pigeons per hectare (2.5 acres) of land. The size of the dovecot therefore announced the importance of the estate. At Epoisses there was accommodation for 3,000 birds.

Within the western area of the outer fortification is shown the château proper, encompassed by a moat. It is roughly circular in outline and set about by seven great towers, six of them square and one octagonal. On the inside of the encircling wall are ranged the seigneurial lodgings. Since this plan was associated with the order to destroy one half of the buildings, it offers a detailed drawing of the portion to be demolished, which was the south side of the courtyard. The lodgings on the north side, which are those which survive today, are only outlined. Among the buildings destroyed was what looks like a magnificent Grande Salle with a central arcade and vaulted ceiling.

The buildings which remain stretch from gatehouse to gatehouse, a pleasing medley of styles represented chiefly in the decoration of the windows. There is not much about the façade to suggest the richness of the interior.

The state rooms date for the most part from the seventeenth century when it was still acceptable to leave the beams and struts of the ceiling visible and to make of them one of the main decorative features of the apartment. Later ages preferred to conceal the structural skeleton above a plaster ceiling.

But the chief decoration of the rooms comes from the large and varied collection of paintings. In the vestibule the walls are virtually panelled with portraits. At Bussy-Rabutin there is a similar series of European personalities, which are, perforce, largely spurious. The spelling of their names is something special. Mary Queen of Scots comes through as 'La Reine de Cose' (d'Ecosse), Montmorency is spelt 'Monmoransi' and Buckingham 'Boucquincan'. As he is described as *comte* in the painting – or the original from which it was copied – it can be dated before 1623 when Buckingham was made a duke. The rather similar portrait of him at Bussy-Rabutin gives him that title.

There are two extremely fine bedrooms, both in a wonderful state of preservation. The first is the Chambre du Roi, once slept in by Henri IV, and the second, the Chambre Sévigné, a room with another impressive ceiling of *poutres apparentes* and the most delightful tapestries in *verdure* where the famous marquise is reputed to have slept on her many visits to Epoisses.

Writing to her daughter from here on Wednesday, 25 October 1673, she was delighted to find her cousins the Toulongeons, Madame de Chastellux and the marquis de Bonneval all staying with the Guitauts. 'This house is of an astonishing size and beauty,' she wrote; 'M. de Guitaut takes much pleasure in the fitting out of his house and he is spending a lot of money on it . . . I am sorry for those who cannot give themselves this pleasure. We talked for ever, the Master of the House and myself; that is to say that I had the merit of knowing how to be a good listener.'

Guillaume de Guitaut, marquis d'Epoisses, had come into the possession of the château through his wife, Madeleine d'Arquien. Her early death could have deprived him of his rights, for, according to Burgundian law, a wife could not leave her property to her husband. For that reason she left Epoisses to the prince de Condé with the request that he should return it a year later to her husband. As Guitaut had been a great supporter of Condé during the Fronde and, when that episode was over, had successfully negotiated Condé's reconciliation with the king, she could die confident that her wishes would be carried out.

Before the Guitauts, Epoisses had been through many distinguished owners. The marquisate had been created by Louis XIII in favour of Louis d'Anssienville. He had married Claude de Saulx-Tavanes and was thus connected with the builders of Sully. During the wars of the league the Maréchal de Tavanes commanded the armies of the king; those of the league were commanded by the duc de Nemours, whose family had previously owned Epoisses.

Jacques de Savoie, duc de Nemours, was one of the outstanding figures at the Court of Henri II. A cultivated humanist and a bigoted Catholic, distinguished for his gallantry, both in the face of the enemy and in his relations with the opposite sex, he found his place not only in the history but the fiction of France. Madame de La Fayette made him the hero of her celebrated novel *La Princesse de Clèves*.

Madame de La Fayette was a close friend of Madame de Sévigné – perhaps her closest friend. Shortly before her death she wrote to Madame de Sévigné: 'Croyez, ma très chère, que vous êtes la personne du monde que j'ai le plus véritablement aimée.' After her death, the marquise wrote to Madame de Guitaut at Epoisses a letter in which she reveals some of the depth of her own religion. 'For our consolation, God granted her a quite particular grace . . . she made her confession at Corpus Christi with a carefulness and a consciousness which could only have come from Him and received Our Lord in the same manner.'

Madame de Sévigné

Madame de Sévigné was to make one of the most important con-
tributions to the literature of the Grand Siècle. 'It was not until
after Richelieu and after the Fronde', writes Sainte-Beuve,

under the Queen Mother and Mazarin, that all of a sudden, out of the
middle of the fêtes of Saint-Mandé and Vaux-le-Vicomte, out of the salons
of the Hôtel de Rambouillet and the ante-rooms of the young king, there
emerged, as if by miracle, three great wits, three minds of genius, gifted in
different ways but all three possessing a taste that was both pure and naïf, of
a perfect simplicity and of a happy fecundity, nourished on their native
grace and delicacy and destined to set the scene for a brilliant and glorious
age in which none were to surpass them – Molière, La Fontaine and
Madame de Sévigné.

Of these only the last can be claimed by Burgundy. Born in 1626,
Marie de Rabutin-Chantal was first cousin to Bussy-Rabutin and
granddaughter to St Jeanne de Chantal, from whom she inherited
the Château de Bourbilly. Bourbilly was a fief of the Château
d'Epoisses, and it was here, rather than in her own house, that she
would stay for choice when the management of her estates required
her presence in Burgundy.

There is a portrait of her at Epoisses; it is somewhat stylized and it
is a little difficult to see in it the same character as that portrayed by
Robert Nanteuil in the Musée Carnavalet, which was Madame de
Sévigné's house in Paris. This shows the face of a plump and pleasing
person with eyes set widely apart – Bussy described them as 'small
and sparkling' – and there is a smile playing about her lips. She was a
woman who owed more to her complexion, 'le plus beau teint du
monde', than to her features.

But the best portrait of her comes, not from the brush of a painter,
but from the pen of a writer – Madame de La Fayette. Her real
charm, it seems, existed only in a direct relationship to her powers as
a conversationalist. 'Your complexion', writes her friend, 'has a
beauty and a flower which insist that you are only twenty' (she was
in fact thirty-three at the time):

Your mouth, your teeth, your hair are incomparable; but I do not need to
say such things to you; your mirror will tell you as much, but since it does
not amuse you to talk to it, it cannot tell you how attractive you are when

you are speaking, and that is what I want to tell you. Know, therefore, Madame, if by chance you do not know already, that your wit adorns and beautifies your person, that there is no one in the world so charming as you are when you are engaged in animated conversation where all constraint is banished. The brilliance of your wit lends such a lustre to your complexion and to your eyes that, although it would seem that wit appeals only to the ear, yet it is certain that yours dazzles the eye and that when one is listening to you, one no longer notices that there is something lacking in the regularity of your features and one assigns to you the most perfect beauty in the world . . . Your presence increases pleasure and pleasures increase your beauty when you are surrounded by them; in fact joy is the true condition of your heart and nothing could run more counter to your nature than sorrow.

No doubt because of her charm she seems to have been adulated wherever she went. One of the earliest glimpses that we have of her comes from the Abbé Arnauld, describing a meeting in 1657. 'It is as if I could see her still now,' he writes, 'just as she appeared the first time I had the honour of seeing her, arriving deep in the back of her coach, sitting between her son and her daughter, all three just as the poets represent Latona with the young Apollo and the young Diana on either side, so radiant was the charm both of the mother and of the children.'

Marie de Rabutin-Chantal had lost her own father before her first birthday and her mother before she was seven. She was brought up by an uncle, Christophe de Coulanges, abbot of Livry, who saw to it that she received a sound classical education. Married at eighteen to the marquis de Sévigné, she was widowed seven years later when her husband was killed in a duel, leaving her with two children, Charles and Françoise-Marguerite, later to be comtesse de Grignan and the one consuming passion of her mother's life.

'Love me always, dear daughter,' she wrote on 31 May 1671: 'your friendship is my whole experience; as I said to you the other day, it is all my joy and all my sadness. I admit that the rest of my life is filled with shadows and sorrows when I reflect that so much of it will be passed in separation from you.'

Her friend Pomponne puts it in almost epigrammatical form. 'It appears that Madame de Sévigné passionately loves Madame de Grignan. Do you want to know the other side of the coin? It is that she loves her passionately!'

It was this, more than anything, which caused her to write the thousands of letters for which she is so justly celebrated. But behind her brilliant skill as a writer there lay this aptitude, it seems no less brilliant, for conversation. Such a gift was all-important in the society in which she lived. 'We need all sorts of people to be able to talk on all sorts of subjects in our conversation', wrote Mademoiselle de Montpensier, 'which, to your taste and to mine, is the greatest pleasure in life.'

Today conversation is almost a lost art, though the French are still better at it than the English. It flourishes best in a society in which all the members move at ease and have nothing better to do than to get to know each other; it requires a life of leisure. Even as early as 1829 Sainte-Beuve could write: 'We can only with difficulty today, accustomed as we are to positive occupations, form any true picture of that life of leisure and of talk.'

But conversation requires the presence of the other party. In the event of lengthy separation, the art of conversation becomes perforce the art of letter-writing. With Madame de Sévigné three factors combined to make her mistress of the art: her brilliance in conversation, her passionate affection for her daughter and the long periods during which she was separated from her.

Françoise-Marguerite had married the comte de Grignan in 1669. A year later her husband was appointed lieutenant-general of Provence and in April he went off to take up his command. Françoise-Marguerite was pregnant and stayed behind with her mother until her first child, Marie-Blanche, was born. Leaving the baby in her mother's care, she set out to join her husband in February 1671.

Seldom, if ever, can there have been such an outpouring of maternal affection.

You make me feel all that it is possible to feel of tenderness, but if you ever think of me . . . be assured that I continually think of you: it is what religious men call a habit of thought; it is what we ought to feel for God if we did our duty. Nothing can distract me. I am always with you. I see this coach which travels always forward and will never come nearer to me; I am always on the high road; it seems that sometimes I am afraid of its overturning; the rains which fell these last three days threw me into despair; the Rhône [which she had to cross] filled me with the strangest fears. I have the map before my eyes; I know everywhere where you will sleep. Tonight

you are at Nevers and on Sunday you will be at Lyon where you will find
this letter.

Madame de Sévigné wrote as she spoke: that is, without
artifice. 'En vérité', she admitted, 'il faut bien un peu entre amis
laisser trotter les plumes: la mienne a toujours la bride sur le cou.'

The most vivid sensation evoked by the reading of her letters is
the feeling that you are there. You are there when she walks
round the gardens of the Abbaye de Livry, thinking only of
Françoise-Marguerite – 'at the end of that little dark alley which
you love, or that mossy seat on which I have sometimes seen you
lie, but, good God, where have I not seen you? There is no spot,
no place, neither in the house, nor in the church, nor in the
country round, nor in the garden, where I have not seen you.
There is nowhere that does not evoke some memory.'

You are there, on 20 June 1672, when she takes you on that
most devastating of all missions, to announce to a mother the
death of her son. It was Mademoiselle de Vertus, sister of the duc
de Montbazon, who broke the news to the duchesse de
Longueville.

Mademoiselle de Vertus had only to show herself; this precipitate return
was a clear sign of something ominous: in fact the moment she appeared:
'Ah! Mademoiselle, how is my brother?' [the Grand Condé]. Her
thoughts did not dare to venture further. 'Madame, he is recovering well
from his wounds.' 'There has been a battle! What of my son?' There was
no reply. 'Ah! Mademoiselle, my son, my dear child; answer me, is he
dead?' 'Madame, I can find no words with which to answer you.' 'Oh my
dear son! Did he die instantaneously? Did he not have a single moment?
Oh my God what a sacrifice.' And on that she fell on her bed; and all that
the keenest pain can do, both by convulsions, and by faintings, and by
mortal silence, and by suffocated cries and by bitter tears, by outbursts to
Heaven, and by the most tender and pitiable lamentations, she sustained
them all.

You are there, on less emotional occasions, as when she describes the
beauties of nature.

If you really want to know, in detail, what Spring is, come to me. What I
used to know was entirely superficial. I am studying it this year down to its
first little beginnings. What do you think is the colour of the trees this last

week? Answer me. You were going to say 'green'. Not at all; they are red. They are little buds, all ready to burst, which are really red; and when they each produce a little leaf and since this is unevenly, that makes the prettiest possible mixture of red and green.

Spontaneous as they were, however, these letters were not all written exclusively for the eyes of the recipients. They were clearly circulated among her friends. Madame de Coulanges recounts the arrival one morning of a lackey from Madame de Thianges. He had come to beg the loan to his mistress of the 'lettre du cheval de Madame de Sévigné et celle de la prairie'. They were duly despatched; 'Vos lettres font tout le bruit qu'elles méritent,' concluded Madame de Coulanges; 'il est certain qu'elles sont délicieuses, et vous êtes comme vos lettres.'

But the outlook of Madame de Sévigné was set firmly within the limitations of the class structure of her times. When, in 1685, there was a revolt in Brittany put down by the governor, the duc de Chaulnes (always *notre bon duc* to Madame de Sévigné), in a manner reminiscent of the Bloody Assizes, innocent men were being broken on the wheel or hanged on all sides. Madame de Sévigné calmly records: 'The mutineers from Rennes escaped long ago; the innocent will suffer for the guilty; but I find everything very good provided that the four thousand soldiers who are in Rennes do not prevent me from walking in my woods, which are of a wonderful height and beauty.'

But Madame de Sévigné has been judged by posterity not by her character but by her writings. The last word may be left to her cousin, Roger de Bussy-Rabutin. 'Nothing could be more beautiful', he wrote, 'than the letters of Madame de Sévigné. The pleasing, the playful and the serious in them are alike admirable. One would say that she was born for each of these qualities. She is natural, she has a noble facility of expression and sometimes an audacious negligence which is to be preferred to the precision of the academics.' Himself a member of the Académie française, he was well qualified to judge.

Bussy-Rabutin was an author of no mean standing, but his particular place in the history of Burgundy owes more to the remarkable decoration which he created in the château from which he took his name.

The Château de Bussy-Rabutin

At the foot of the Mont d'Auxois the river Oze is joined by the smaller stream of the Rabutin, which has carved out a little valley running from north-east to south-west. Half-way up this valley, and opposite the village of Bussy-le-Grand, a steep re-entrant opens towards the south; here, embowered by the trees of an ancient park, can be seen the cone-capped towers of one of Burgundy's most famous châteaux, named from its village and its valley, Bussy-Rabutin.

Raised on the foundations of a feudal fortress and still retaining something of its militant disposition, the buildings are ranged round three sides of a quadrangle set between four corner towers, offering to the south a sunny courtyard on which all the architectural contrivance has been concentrated. To right and left, the wings which join the main block to the towers belong to the early French Renaissance. The ground floor of each is devoted to an open cloister with the low arches known as *'en anse de panier'* ('like a basket handle') upholding a gallery lit by twelve closely set windows. The façades are rhythmed by pilasters and entablatures which recall, in the delicacy of their ornament, the Hôtel Pincé at Angers. These wings were in all probability built for Antoine de Chandio, who had fought in Italy under the Chevalier Bayard.

The garden front, which faces the north, is simple by comparison and cries out for some central feature. At first sight it appears to be symmetrical – a façade of seven windows between the towers. But the 'centre' is not central. The right-hand tower stands further from the main façade than the left-hand tower. A clever attempt has been made to mask this lack of symmetry. The windows form two groups of three to left and right of the central bay, but the windows on the right-hand side are set almost imperceptibly further apart than those upon the left.

This irregularity results from the medieval ground plan. The four towers do not mark the corners of an exact rectangle; the north-west tower is slightly further west than the south-west tower. Since the main architectural emphasis is on the south façade, this is strictly symmetrical; it follows that the north front could not be. It also follows that the north front cannot have been designed earlier than the south front.

This was built in 1649 by Roger de Bussy-Rabutin, whose

grandfather had purchased the château in 1602. It is an attractive example of provincial mannerist architecture which, in its use of broken pediments and oval niches, has certain affinities with Corbineau's frontispiece at Brissac. Together with the little galleries it forms the most delightful entrance court imaginable.

There is nothing about this remote and peaceful place to suggest its connection with one of the major literary scandals of the century. On 16 April 1665, Bussy-Rabutin was arrested and imprisoned in the Bastille, where he was to remain until 15 May in the following year, when he was released on medical grounds. In August he was given permission to retire to his estates in Burgundy, where he remained in exile until 1681. His offence was that of having written a short book entitled *Histoire Amoureuse des Gaules*. It was a series of tales, partly true and partly embroidered, about four noble ladies, the comtesse d'Olonne, the duchesse de Châtillon, the marquise de Sévigné and the marquise de Montglas. It dealt with their 'affairs', the complexity of which extended as far as certain members of the royal family – notably the prince de Condé, governor of Burgundy, who had no love for Bussy-Rabutin. It was almost certainly Condé who brought about his downfall.

As the result of the condemnation of its author, the *Histoire Amoureuse* acquired the reputation of being a somewhat salacious piece of scandal-mongering. It is much more than that. It is of a high literary quality as befitted a member of the Académie française.

It is probable that Bussy was telling the truth when, just before his arrest, he wrote to the duc de Saint-Aignan an *apologia* for his work.

Five years ago, not knowing how to amuse myself in the country where I was living, I justified the proverb that idleness is the mother of all the vices; for I set myself to write a Tale – or rather a satirical Romance – without any intention, believe me, of ill-using in any way those involved, but simply to provide myself with an occupation and, at the most, to show it to one or two good friends, to give them pleasure and to earn for myself a little praise for my skill in writing.

If Bussy imagined that his portraits would cause no offence he knew little of female psychology. Three years after the publication of the *Histoire Amoureuse*, Madame de Sévigné could still write: 'Do not deceive yourself, *Monsieur le comte*, I was outraged; it caused me whole nights of sleeplessness.'

Set thus in the context of the boredom of country life, the *Histoire Amoureuse* has much to teach us of the mentality of the Grand Siècle. The charmed circle of the aristocracy constituted a society small enough for everybody to know everybody and for the king to know quite a lot about nearly everybody. It was a military aristocracy, but in winter, when the men were not on campaign, it was forced back on its own resources for its entertainment. Such a society was naturally introspective; its members were interested in one another, and, being French, their interest was greatest when it concerned the affairs of the heart. The delicate perception of nuances in their complex interrelationships was the material of their conversation and the inspiration of their literary endeavours.

For Bussy-Rabutin, exile from the intimacies of such a society could have been a living death. Never to see again the Louvre, Saint-Germain, Saint-Cloud, Versailles or Fontainebleau; not to move at ease among the titled personalities who enjoyed the freedom of those palaces, was social extinction. In this remote re-entrant which encloses the Château de Bussy-Rabutin, shut off from the world and shut off from all but his provincial neighbours, he had to create an interior which would in some way compensate for his loss. He surrounded himself with paintings of the places from which he was excluded and of the people who represented the world from which he was ostracized.

It is one of the most astonishing and successful achievements and second only to the portrait gallery created by Jean Monier at the Château de Beauregard in the Loire Valley. Bussy himself describes it in a letter to Madame du Bouchet dated 24 August 1671.

I am so glad that your friend d'Hauterive found my house at Bussy to his liking. There are certain features which are highly diverting and not to be seen elsewhere. For example, I have a gallery in which are the portraits of all the kings of France from Hugues Capet to the king [Louis XIV] and beneath each an inscription which gives you all that you need to know of their actions. Opposite are statesmen and men of letters. To brighten all that up a bit, you find in another part the mistresses and good friends of our kings, starting with the beautiful Agnès, mistress of Charles VII.

All these were in the long gallery which joins the château proper with its chapel in the south-west tower. It is no longer exactly as Bussy described it. There are portraits of the dukes of Burgundy of which he makes no mention, and the series of kings has been continued up to Charles X by the comte de Sarcus, who purchased the château in 1835. There is also an interesting collection of portraits of the Rabutin family, including one of St Jeanne de Chantal and her son, Celse-Bénigne, the father of Madame de Sévigné, who was thus Bussy-Rabutin's first cousin.

Another interesting portrait claims to represent Sebastien, a bastard of Hugues I de Rabutin, in mortal combat with a wolf. This is a copy of the painting to the left of the mantelpiece in the great Salle de Bal at Fontainebleau. According to Bussy it was his ancestor who killed, in the Forêt de Milly, a savage wolf which was ravaging the countryside. According to Loret, however, (letters of 8 and 16 October 1655) the wolf was killed in the Forêt de Fontainebleau by the *Grand Louvetier*, Monsieur de Saint-Hérem.

At the same time that the portraits of the gallery were being collected and hung, another room was being created, described by Bussy in the same letter to Madame du Bouchet as 'a large ante-room . . . in which are the men illustrious in war, starting with the comte de Dunois'.

There are sixty portraits in all, beginning, not with Dunois, but with du Guesclin, 'prodige de valeur'. Their names resound like a roll-call of honour of the chivalry of France: La Tremoïlle, 'surnommé le Chevalier sans reproche'; Charles de Cossé, Maréchal de Brissac, 'un des plus honnêtes hommes et des plus grands capitaines'; Montluc, 'qui, de fort petit gentilhomme, s'éleva par son mérite extraordinaire à la dignité de Maréchal de France'; Henri de Lorraine, duc de Guise, 'appelé le Balafré . . . assassiné à Blois en 1588'; François de Bassompierre, 'un des plus galants de son siècle'. These and many others are complemented by such foreign warriors as the Emperor Charles V, William of Orange, Buckingham (spelt Bouquingan), Cromwell and Wallenstein. Turenne, we may note in passing, is allowed no other distinction than 'Souverain de Sedan par sa femme'. Bussy disliked Turenne.

Fourth from last, but assuredly not least, came Bussy himself, 'Maître de Camp, Général de la Cavalerie Légère de France'. It is a copy of the portrait by Claude Lefèvre in the Salle des Devises. At first sight it is the typical depiction of a *grand seigneur*, resplendent in the mixture of lace and armour-plating which expresses the dual role of courtier and soldier. With his upright bearing and slightly disdainful smile, he looks uncommonly pleased with himself. But behind the posturing there is more than a hint of wounded pride and shaken self-esteem.

For Bussy-Rabutin was a man who could have distinguished himself both as a courtier and as a soldier. He possessed the wit and the taste requisite in the one, and the courage and leadership expected of the other. But in both he failed. Despite his gallant behaviour at the battle of the Dunes, he was dismissed by Turenne, in a somewhat sarcastic letter to the king, as 'the best soldier in the army – at making lampoons'. He was not forgiven, but Turenne was right: Bussy never could control his caustic wit and never knew when he had gone too far. Shortly after the death of his first wife, he caused a scandal by the abduction of Madame de Miramion, a lady whom he erroneously supposed to return his volatile affections. That was in 1648 when he was thirty. Eleven years later he was still so far from maturity as to take part in a puerile act of blasphemy and *lèse-majesté* known as the 'débauche de Roissy', at which obscene versions of religious songs were sung, a future cardinal baptized a frog, and Bussy improvised verses on the love affair between Louis XIV and Marie Mancini. This earned him his first period of exile in Burgundy. Here he made amorous advances to his cousin, Madame de Sévigné, and took offence when she would not – or could not – lend him money.

As we look at his portrait we must imagine what were the feelings of this soldier *manqué* when he opened the letter from Madame de Sévigné dated 20 May 1667. 'Toute la cour est à l'armée, et toute l'armée est à la cour. Paris est un désert.' She knew what bitter longings this would stir in his heart, but she told him. 'It is painful for a man of courage to be at home when there is so much going on in Flanders. It is imprudent on my part to tread once more on ground so delicate.' She had the imprudence, however, to tread upon it.

A year later she twisted the knife in the wound. 'You have been once again the cause of sad and bitter affliction to me on seeing these three new marshals of France.' Had he not been in disgrace, Bussy might well have been one of them. 'Madame de Villars, on whom we called, made us think of the visits which might have been on similar occasions, if you had been willing.'

There was a sort of love–hate relationship between Bussy and Madame de Sévigné. On 4 December 1668, she wrote in radiant mood to announce her daughter's engagement to the comte de Grignan, ending with the words: 'Adieu, mon cher cousin . . . et que notre amitié soit désormais sans nuages.' In the following year she was upbraiding him again: 'You really are a man of extremes; is it not strange that you should be incapable of finding any middle ground between causing me the greatest offence and loving me more than your life?'

Madame de Sévigné never came to the Château de Bussy-Rabutin, but she left her mark on its history. There is a room formerly known as the 'Chambre Sévigné'. It was in fact Bussy's bedroom and it took its name from the portrait of the marquise. Bussy records that the pictures in this room were all of his family; some of these are now in the gallery. They were exchanged, probably by the comte de Sarcus, for the portraits of the royal mistresses – Agnès Sorel, Marie Touchet, Diane de Poitiers, Gabrielle d'Estrées, Anne de Pisseleu and Madame de Maintenon.

But the portraits which gave the room its name are those which form a triptych depicting Madame de Sévigné, her daughter Madame de Grignan, and Bussy's wife, Louise de Rouville, who played little or no part in her husband's life and came here as seldom as possible.

In this room Bussy was surrounded by his memories. 'I live here very comfortably,' he wrote; 'I do myself very well; every day I embellish my beautiful house. Here I have neither master nor mistress, for I have no ambition and I am not in love; I feel, what I would have thought impossible two years ago, that one can live without these two passions.'

In another letter he describes a typical day at the château: the writing of a few letters; a round of visits to the masons, carpenters and painters at work on his décor; dinner at midday. 'After dinner I sit with my family round me; with them I find more diversion than with a thousand visits in Paris.' Then he went out again to see his workmen; 'the day is passed pottering around.' One cannot help feeling that he was putting a brave face on an empty life, but it is clear that the decoration of his château was the one redeeming feature of his exile. In the south-west tower, which adjoins his bedroom, he created his masterpiece – the Grand Salon or Tour Dorée.

There is something perhaps deliberately theatrical about it – a rich and restless decoration, better suited to the architecture of some opera house. The figures in the upper range of portraits look down into the room as if from their private boxes in the grand tier – or, indeed, the royal box, for these are, with the exceptions of Richelieu and Mazarin, all members of the royal family.

Above this gallery the whole sumptuous crescendo reaches its climax in the magnificence of the painted ceiling. Round the outer perimeter are represented the four seasons, interspersed with military trophies on which the coat of arms of the Rabutin family is proudly blazoned. In the corners of the central square the coronet of a count alternates with that of a marquis – or rather a marquise – for the monogram beneath is that of Bussy's mistress, Isabelle-Cécile Hurault de Cheverny, marquise de Montglas. Her portrait also has the place of honour on Bussy's right above the doorway. That she had betrayed him when he was in the Bastille and abandoned him when he was in exile did not deter Bussy from giving her pride of place – 'not being angry enough to deprive her of it'.

The decoration of the Tour Dorée was the last of those referred to in Bussy's letter to Madame du Bouchet in 1671. His next embellishment was of a room on the ground floor known as the Salle des Devises. Having provided himself with portraits of the personalities of a society from which he was excluded, he now filled a room with reminders of the palaces from which he was banished. In no particular order we see among the royal houses Versailles, Marly and Saint-Cloud; Chambord, Vincennes and Villers-Cotterets; Saint-Germain and the Luxembourg together with such private palaces as Gaillon, Anet, Richelieu's Rueil, Colbert's Château de Sceaux and certain public buildings such as the Observatoire and Les Invalides.

The paintings, which must have been done from drawings or engravings, are of a deplorable mediocrity, but they are not without interest and can be dated with some accuracy. Sceaux, for instance, was built between 1673 and 1676; the façade shown of Saint-Cloud was not begun before 1677. The view of Versailles, taken from the entrance side, marks a particular moment in the development of the entrance courts by Le Vau. Bussy's artist shows the iron grille which enclosed the Cour Royale still running between two little dome-capped guardrooms which disappeared in 1672. This does not of course mean that the paintings could not have been done a year or two after these dates: it does mean that they cannot have been done before.

As early as 1667, in a letter to Mademoiselle d'Armentières, Bussy makes mention of certain *devises*, notably one concerning Madame de Montglas. The word '*devise*' is probably best translated 'motto', but in a sense elastic enough to include a sort of cryptic epigram which accompanies an emblem. A simple example, taken from the Salle des Devises, is a painting of a reed with the words 'Flector non frangor' ('I bend but I do not break').

It would be infinitely tedious to enter into the details of the hundreds of *devises* of this sort throughout the château. It was the fashion of the times to indulge in their invention, and a number of these were first conceived and worn by the participants in the famous *Carrousel* at the Tuileries in 1662. Behind many of those at Bussy can be detected the affronted vanity of an unsuccessful man.

We must not forget, however, that Bussy was a member of the Académie française; it is as an author that he takes his modest place in the halls of fame. Charles Perrault conferred upon Bussy the accolade of the literary critic with the words: 'We have among us an author of the same sort as Petronius, whose narratives have as much precision as those of that arbiter of elegance, but more polish.'

As a writer Bussy excelled in the art of the *portrait*, which stood high in the literary fashion of the day, ranging from the *Caractères* of La Bruyère to the *Galerie des Portraits* of Mademoiselle de Montpensier.

Mademoiselle de Montpensier – 'La Grande Mademoiselle' – the daughter of Gaston, duc d'Orléans, the rather troublesome brother of Louis XIII, provides another example of an exile from the Court being obliged to live on her estates and discovering a taste for country life and particularly for the delights of building and decorating a château. She enters the history of Burgundy as the owner of the Château de Saint-Fargeau.

The Château de Saint-Fargeau

When the last hereditary owners of Saint-Fargeau felt obliged to sell the property, one of the family, the well-known author Jean d'Ormesson, immortalized the château in his book *Au Plaisir de Dieu*. He concealed it under the name of Le Plessis-lez-Vaudreuil. It was an attempt, in his own words, 'to counter our own death with a sort of resurrection'. There are not many châteaux in France which have not passed, even frequently, through death and resurrection. Saint-Fargeau is no exception.

Jean d'Ormesson gives us his pen-protrait of the house he loved.

With its prodigious bulk, its formidable dimensions, its enormous round towers and its endless roofs of slate, Saint-Fargeau manages miraculously to be gigantic and to retain its gaiety. The smallest ray of sunshine lights up the immense pentagonal courtyard and gives it a festive air. With its park *à l'anglaise* and its lake dotted with islands, nothing could be more welcoming, more appealing than this huge monster, emerging from the obscurity of the past. With all its history and with all the bloodshed that goes with history, it is a place of peace and thankfulness where it was a pleasure to live.

It is difficult to imagine the little town of Saint-Fargeau as it used to be, but a mixture of luck and conservationism has preserved one of its former gatehouses, a pretty little building of fifteenth-century brickwork with a fine belfry. It is slotted for a drawbridge, from which we may infer the existence of a moat and a fortified *enceinte*. But for a town gate it is small and throws into contrasting relief the enormous size of the château. Another contrast is formed by the huge drums of the towers and the millions of tiny bricks of which they are built.

The château which we see today dates from the middle of the fifteenth century. On 5 February 1450, it was purchased by the richest man in France, Jacques Coeur. He was a business man and merchant well in advance of his times and amassed a wealth which is reflected in the size and magnificence of his house in Bourges. At Saint-Fargeau his name is still attached by tradition to the largest of the towers, which is so large that it contains a little inner courtyard, crossed by a timbered gallery, above which the inward slope of the roof rises like the wall of a gigantic well.

It is doubtful, however, if Jacques Coeur could have done much building here, for on 31 July of the following year he was arrested on the charge of having poisoned Agnès Sorel. As the result of his arrest his vast possessions were put into the hands of the king. The first trial was succeeded by a second which took the form of an enquiry into his accounts.

It was an appalling travesty of justice. He was allowed no counsel for the defence, and the president of the Commission of Enquiry was his sworn enemy, Antoine de Chabannes. Chabannes was as typical of his age as Jacques Coeur was untypical. He had fought under Joan of Arc, but when the war ended he continued to ravage the countryside with the infamous band of redundant soldiers known as *les écorcheurs*. He was captured, condemned to death, imprisoned in the Bastille, escaped, forced the son of Jacques Coeur to abandon Saint-Fargeau, was received back into the royal favour and ended his life as grand maître de France and comte de Dammartin. It was he who built the château in the form that we see it from the outside today. The west front still contains some windows surrounded by the beautiful mouldings of the fifteenth century.

Antoine de Chabannes died on Christmas Day 1488 at Saint-Fargeau. His son lived here until 1505, known to history only for his pious foundations. His daughter married the comte René d'Anjou; their daughter married François de Bourbon, duc de Montpensier; their daughter married Gaston, duc d'Orléans. *Their* daughter, Mademoiselle de Montpensier, inherited Saint-Fargeau and with her opens a new chapter in the life of the château.

One day towards the end of October 1652, Mademoiselle, as she was called in the language of the Court, made her first visit here. She was, in fact, in exile from the Court. During the Fronde she had actively supported the prince de Condé against the young Louis XIV and his minister Cardinal Mazarin. She had played, in the words of her biographer, Victoria Sackville-West, 'a pseudo-heroic part in the whole absurd, abortive affair . . . The Fronde and Mademoiselle were, in a way, made for one another.' Now she was paying the price for her escapade.

She arrived, she records in her memoirs, 'at two in the morning and had to enter on foot, the bridge being broken. I entered into an ancient mansion to which there were neither doors nor windows and grass knee-high in the courtyard. It filled me with horror. I was conducted into a wretched room with a prop-pole in the centre. I was so overcome with fear, horror and vexation that I burst into tears.' She went on to spend what remained of the night at the nearby Château de Dannery.

The next day things looked brighter. One of her men, La Guérinière, went back to Saint-Fargeau and returned with a more optimistic report: the house was good and strong and easy to escape from. It only needed putting in order.

Three days later Mademoiselle returned. 'I was conducted to an apartment which I had not seen and which I found more commodious. It had been done up for the duc de Bellegarde [governor of Burgundy] whom my father allowed to stay there.' She immediately started having ideas about where the doors and fireplaces ought to be and to make provision for an alcove. It was the beginning of a new outlet to her energies. During the Fronde she had played the Amazon: now she was to play at Dido rebuilding the walls of Carthage.

She had to have suitable accommodation for herself and for her visitors. The duchesse de Sully and the marquise de Laval came to call on her soon after her arrival. 'I was more ashamed than I can possibly say to have nowhere to lodge them in the house; every evening they had to go and sleep at the bailiff's.' The unfortunate bailiff was newly married and had purchased a new bed in honour of the occasion. Mademoiselle first borrowed it for herself and then expected it to be at the disposition of her more distinguished guests.

Early in that December Mademoiselle went to Blois to see her father. From Blois they went to Chambord for a few days, in the course of which Gaston tried to persuade her to change her residence. 'There was much talk of the ugliness of Saint-Fargeau and that I should find a more beautiful house nearer to Blois. It was said that Châteauneuf-sur-Loire was for sale.' On her way back she went to inspect Châteauneuf, but her preference was clearly for Saint-Fargeau. If it was ugly, the answer was to embellish it.

'I sent for an architect from Paris', she records, 'named Le Vau.' This was François, the younger brother of Louis Le Vau, the architect of Vincennes, Vaux-le-Vicomte and Versailles. It was in the same year that his elder brother received his first important commissions, from Mazarin at Vincennes and from the king at the Louvre. 'Assuredly that was not a waste of time,' wrote Mademoiselle, 'for the building work provided me with much diversion, and those who see Saint-Fargeau will find it magnificent and worthy of me. I could not have done anything more extensive for I was only doing up an old house which had, none the less, a certain grandeur, although it was the work of a private individual.' She clearly believed that the whole building was the work of Jacques Coeur, for she continues: 'He was at all events a Superintendent of Finance under Charles VII, but in those days these superintendents were not so magnificent as they are today.' She was obviously thinking of Nicholas Fouquet's palace at Vaux-le-Vicomte; 'I could have wished that they had been and that my house were as fine as theirs; I would not then have spent as much money as I did, which at 200,000 francs is a lot for me, but little enough for those gentlemen.'

François Le Vau is chiefly known for his unsuccessful design for the south front of the Louvre. He was responsible also for two dignified but not outstanding châteaux at Bercy and Sucy-en-Brie. At Saint-Fargeau he showed an originality which was the secret of his success.

An architect is often more resourceful when he is obliged to conform to the demands of an existing building than when he has a free hand. Le Vau respected the huge towers of the fifteenth-century edifice but brought them a little more *au goût du jour* by capping them with slender cupolas which are reminiscent – and surely intentionally – of Chambord. Towards the park he did little more than to regularize the fenestration. Within the courtyard he made his own creation, rebuilding entirely in his own style, but harmonizing his façades with the old by his use of brick and stone. He has placed his entrance pavilion very imaginatively in the south-east corner. It is in the form of a domed rotunda, opening by three arches towards the court and giving access by three doors to the Salle des Gardes, the chapel and the kitchens.

The work took six years. At the end of it Mademoiselle had a palace with seventy bedrooms. Furniture was brought from Blois, the Tuileries, the Luxembourg, and the Château d'Eu; paintings of the royal family were assembled, but pride of place was given her grandfather, the duc de Montpensier. 'He is the Master of the House,' she wrote, 'if he had not left it to me I would not own it.' Unfortunately her own apartment was destroyed by fire in 1752. It was never restored.

The supervision of the building gave her something creative to do and she revelled in it. 'I worked from morning till evening at this task and only left my rooms to come down for dinner or to the Mass. That winter was a bad one for being able to get about, but the moment it was fine I went on horseback, and when it froze I went on foot, to visit my workmen'.

First she made a *Mail*. It is the word from which we get the name 'The Mall' – a promenade shaded by trees. It required the extension of a terrace, 'which is most effective, for from this terrace one can see the château, the outskirts of the town, woods and vineyards, and a *prairie* with a river, which comes from the lake, flowing through. This landscape is not disagreeable.'

To be in charge of such operations was something new to her. 'How surprised I should have been, when I was at Court, if anyone had told me that I would acquire a knowledge of the price of bricks, of lime, of plaster, of cartage, of workmen's time sheets, in short of all the details of the building trade, and that every Saturday I would check the accounts. And yet I have been on the job for over a year.'

One thing led to another. 'It was during this time', she wrote, 'that I began to like reading, which I have greatly enjoyed ever since.' Reading led to writing and both provided an agreeable occupation. Contrary to her expectations, *la vie de château* was beginning to appeal to her.

There was a time when I should have found it difficult to imagine any form of diversion for a person who, like myself, was accustomed to living at Court with the rank to which my birth entitled me, when reduced to living in the country; for I had always thought that nothing could offer any amusement in a compulsory banishment, and that absence from Court must, for persons of high rank, represent complete isolation ... Nevertheless, since I came into retirement in my own house, I have found, with a quiet satisfaction, that in the recollection of the events in one's life, time passes agreeably enough.

It was this recollection of past events which led her into writing her memoirs – 'tout ce que j'ai pu remarquer depuis mon enfance jusqu'à cette heure'. The trouble was that she was almost illiterate and her spelling was largely phonetic; when she wanted to admit that she had been at fault – 'j'ai eu tort' – she wrote 'jay utor'. It did not embarrass her in the least. 'As I write very badly, I gave it to Préfontaine [her secretary] who made a fair copy.'

The finished product was summed up by Voltaire: 'Her memoirs are those of a woman absorbed in herself, rather than of a princess, witness of great events.' She was a collector of those literary miniatures in the painting of which the authors of the seventeenth century so often excelled – *les portraits* – and her memoirs might be described as an 'extended self-portrait'.

This portrait affords an interesting comparison with the paintings of her which have survived. They all agree in showing a large, heavy-featured face which is at its best dull and at its worst inane. The large canvas painted by Pierre Bourgignon, which hung over the mantelpiece in the Salle des Gardes at Saint-Fargeau, is an example of the latter. She is posing as an Amazon in a plumed helmet which is slightly absurd, and she exhibits with her left hand a portrait of her father, the weak and perfidious Gaston d'Orléans. She had something of the tomboy about her and she thoroughly enjoyed

Dijon. Rue des Forges. Façade by Hugues Sambin. Lithograph by Hubert Clerget.

Auxerre. Église St. Pierre. Lithograph by E. Sagot.

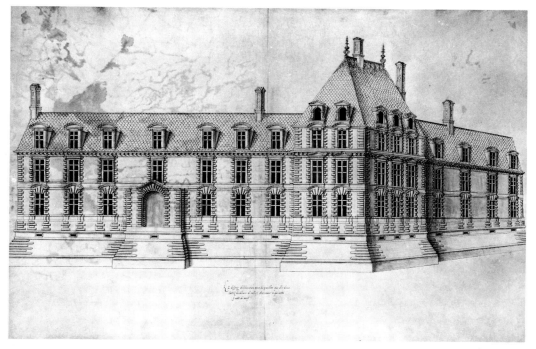

Château de Vallery. West and south fronts. Drawing by A. du Cerceau.

Château de Monthelon. Lithograph by E. Sagot.

Chateau de Bussy-Rabutin. Entrance Court.

Chateau de Bussy-Rabutin. La tour dorée.

Mlle. de Montpensier. Painting by
P. Bourgignon.

Vauban. Bust by Coysevox.

The Grand Condé. Bust by Coysevox.

Château de St. Fargeau. Drawing by V. Petit.

Dijon. Hôtel Legouz de Gerland. Façade on the rue Liegeard. Lithograph by Hubert Clerget.

Dijon. Place Royale, Palais des États and Sainte-Chapelle in 1688. Drawing by J-H. Mansart.

Buffon. Bust by Houdon.

Château de Vantoux. Entrance front.

Dijon. Château de Montmusard. Painting by J-B. Lallemand.

Château d'Arcelot. Garden front.

the opportunities offered by the Fronde for playing at warfare. No doubt the plumed helmet stands for this.

During the second Fronde, or 'Fronde des Princes', she actually entered Orléans by escalade, climbing up a ladder and being pushed through a hole in a door. She was greeted with shouts of joy, of 'Vive le Roi! et point de Mazarin!' She was then carried shoulder-high through the streets. 'My joy made me quite beside myself,' she admitted; 'everyone was kissing my hands and I was in fits of laughter at seeing myself in so entrancing a situation.'

Her chief interest to the prince de Condé was that she was immensely rich. With a little encouragement from him she raised and paid a regiment of her own. 'I must confess', she wrote, 'that I went a bit childish and rejoiced at the sound of the trumpets.'

From Orléans the princes' party was able to enter Paris while the king's army was waiting and watching on the north-east of the city. It was on this occasion that Mademoiselle performed the one action for which she is remembered in popular history – she ordered the cannons of the Bastille to be fired on the king's troops. It was probably the stupidest thing she ever did.

I went to the Bastille, which I had never seen before, and walked for some time on top of the towers and I had the cannons changed; they were all aimed towards the town; I had them turned towards the river and the faubourg to defend the bastion. I looked through a telescope and saw, on the heights of Charonne, a large crowd and even some coaches, from which I rightly judged that the king was there.

Further east, towards Bagnolet, the royal army was manoeuvring into position. She could see the generals deploying their cavalry. Turenne and La Ferté began to advance towards Paris; it was then that it happened – 'Two or three volleys were fired from the cannons of the Bastille, as I had ordered when I left it.' Mazarin, observing the action from a safe distance, remarked: 'Elle a tué son mari.' Since Mademoiselle was hoping to marry Louis XIV her efforts in fighting against him were somewhat counterproductive. She tried to exculpate herself, for Madame de Motteville records: 'She told me that it had not been done by her command.' In her own memoirs, however, she clearly admits responsibility.

Whether the king had any serious intention of marrying his cousin is far from certain, but a daughter of the house of Orléans, who was reputedly the richest woman in France, was clearly a matrimonial prize of the first importance. Charles II of England was among her suitors. It was in the natural order of things that such a marriage should be arranged for purely political reasons. There could have been no place for love in the choice of her husband. Perhaps because, deep down, she knew that this was the inevitable lot of royalty, she kept Cupid at bay.

'I do not know what sweet sayings are,' she admitted, 'for no one has ever dared address any to me, not on account of my birth, since some queens we know have heard them, but on account of my humour, which is known to be far removed from coquetry.'

But, as Bussy-Rabutin wrote to Mademoiselle de Scudéry, 'Love is an illness, like smallpox; the later you catch it, the worse you take it.' These words were only too tragically true of Mademoiselle. At the age of forty-three she fell hopelessly in love with the most unworthy object for anyone's affections – Antoine Nompar de Caumont, marquis de Puyguilhem, third son of an impoverished member of the provincial aristocracy of Gascony, the comte de Lauzun.

He was described by the marquis de la Fare as 'the most insolent little man ever seen for a hundred years', and by Saint-Simon, whose brother-in-law he became, as 'always pursuing some intrigue, envious, spiteful, bold and audacious in every way, loving very few, impertinent to the last degree with women'. His effrontery knew no bounds. Though not a person of the slightest consequence, he presumed to aspire to the position of Grand Maître and actually hid under Madame de Montespan's bed to overhear her conversation with Louis in which she advised the king not to grant him the post. That evening Puyguilhem escorted the royal mistress to the ballet and repeated verbatim the conversation which he had overheard. Summoned next day by the king to give an account of himself, he lost his temper and snapped his sword in two, swearing that he would not use it again in the service of a master who broke his word at the bidding of a whore. It was then that Louis performed what Saint-Simon called 'perhaps the finest action of his life' – he opened the window and threw his cane out of it, saying that he would have regretted having struck a gentleman. He sent him to the Bastille, but not for long.

Puyguilhem, who is more usually known by his later title of Lauzun, must have had some strong hold on Louis XIV that enabled him to survive such a disgrace. It was not long before he began to insinuate himself into the affections of Mademoiselle. In the course of the year 1670 she began to experience a new and strange form of agitation; finally she admitted to herself that the ambitious little Gascon 's'était glissé dans mon coeur'.

On 15 December in that year, Madame de Sévigné wrote one of her most famous letters to the marquis de Coulanges, then at Lyon.

I am about to tell you the most astonishing thing, the most surprising, the most marvellous, the most miraculous, the most triumphant, the most bewildering, the most unheard of, the most singular, the most extraordinary, the most unbelievable, the most unexpected, the greatest, the smallest, the most unusual, the most common, the most dazzling, the most secret until today, the most brilliant, the most enviable; in short a thing whose parallel is only to be found in bygone centuries, and even this comparison is not exact; a thing which we cannot credit in Paris, so how can it be credited in Lyon? A thing which makes everybody cry Mercy on us! a thing which fills Mme de Rohan and Mme de Hauterive with delight; a thing, finally, which will take place on Sunday, when those who witness it will think their eyes have tricked them; a thing which will take place on Sunday and will perhaps not have taken place by Monday. I cannot bring myself to give it away; guess; I give you three guesses. Do you give it up? Well then, I must tell you: M. de Lauzun is going to marry, on Sunday, at the Louvre, guess who? I give you four guesses, I give you ten, I give you a hundred. Madame de Coulanges says, 'That's easy; it is Mme de la Vallière' – not a bit of it, Madame – 'Then it is Mlle de Retz?' Not a bit of it; how provincial you are. 'Ah!' you say,' how silly we are, it is Mlle Colbert.' – even less likely. – 'Then it must assuredly be Mlle de Créqui?' No, you have not got it. So in the last resort I must tell you: M. de Lauzun is marrying on Sunday, at the Louvre, with the king's consent, Mademoiselle, Mademoiselle de . . . Mademoiselle . . . guess the name; he is marrying Mademoiselle, my faith! by my faith! my sworn faith! Mademoiselle, La Grande Mademoiselle, daughter of the late Monsieur, granddaughter of Henri IV, Mademoiselle d'Eu, Mademoiselle des Dombes, Mademoiselle de Montpensier, Mademoiselle d'Orléans, Mademoiselle, first cousin to the king, Mademoiselle destined to a throne, Mademoiselle, the only match in France worthy of Monsieur.

The king's consent to such a match was too good to be true, and there were those who advised Mademoiselle to lose no time in making the step irrevocable. She delayed three days and those three days were fatal. The queen was outraged and told her that she had far better not marry but leave her fortune to the king's second son, the duc d'Anjou. The duc d'Orleáns flew into a rage; Louvois protested; the prince de Condé and Maréchal de Villars begged Louis to reconsider his decision. Their counsel prevailed. The royal permission was withdrawn. Lauzun discovered that Madame de Montespan had advised against the marriage. In a furious row he went to the extreme of calling her 'bougresse de putain'. They were not words to be addressed to the reigning mistress of Louis XIV. Lauzun spent the next ten years in the fortress of Pignerol. On his return it was rumoured that he had secretly married Mademoiselle. The truth may never be known, but she certainly heaped gifts upon him and in 1681 presented him with the dukedom and the Château de Saint-Fargeau.

Mademoiselle de Montpensier and Bussy-Rabutin were rather rare examples of exiles from the Court who discovered the delights of country life in general and of the building and embellishment of a château in particular. There were, of course, other reasons why other people lived on their estates and either rebuilt or redecorated their châteaux *au goût du jour*. One of the most successful of these adaptations was the work of one of the most distinguished Burgundians of the century – the Château de Bazoches, by the Maréchal de Vauban.

Vauban and the Château de Bazoches

'You are right to esteem Monsieur de Vauban as highly as you do,' wrote Boileau to his friend Brosselle on 26 May 1684: 'in my opinion he is one of the men of our century of the most outstanding merit and to say in a word what I think of him, I think there is more than one Marshal of France who, on seeing him, would not blush to be a Marshal of France.' It was not until 1703 that the dignity of marshal was finally conferred upon Vauban, and he took his elevation with a becoming humility.

In some ways he was 'kicked upstairs'. In his eagerness to capture Kehl in the same year he appealed to the king to authorize him. He received the reply: 'Cet emploi est audessous de votre dignité.' One cannot avoid the feeling that he regretted his former freedom, for Vauban seems to have been a person who enjoyed taking deliberate risks. At the siege of Maastricht, the marquis de Sourches relates, he boldly undertook a reconnaissance 'en apparence impossible', after which, to avoid a long detour, he went by night straight through the enemy lines.

Saint-Simon has left one of his brilliant little pen-portraits of the man.

Vauban, whose name was Le Prestre, was, at best, a *petit gentilhomme* of Burgundy, but perhaps the most honourable and the most virtuous man of his century and, while he had the highest reputation as the man most skilled in the art of siegecraft and fortification, remained the most simple, the most genuine and the most modest of men. He was of medium height, thick-set and with the bearing of a soldier, but with an outward appearance that was boorish and coarse, not to say brutal and ferocious. He was nothing of the sort; no man was ever more meek, more obliging, more civil, more respectful, but without any artificiality; protective to the point of miserliness of the lives of his men, and possessing a valour that took everything upon himself and gave the credit for everything to others.

His contribution to the military successes of the reign was prodigious. In the first place his undertakings were on a colossal scale. At Longwy the operation involved the shifting of 640,000 cubic metres of earth and the erection of 120,000 cubic metres of masonry. It was this capacity to 'think big' which contributed so much to the Grand Siècle. 'We do not live in a reign', wrote Colbert, 'which is content with little things. With due regard to proportion, it is impossible to imagine anything which can be too great.' Without the financial backing of Colbert, Vauban might never have been able to realize his genius.

The fortification of Lille was the first great work of Vauban and perhaps the most important – 'sa fille aînée dans la fortification', as he called it himself.

It was in September 1667 that Louis determined on Lille as the key fortress to the north-east defences of his realm. The Chevalier de Clerville was still chief engineer and produced a plan which did not meet with the royal approval. Vauban was given his chance and he set himself to the task with energy – 'il travaille avec la dernière application', wrote the governor of Lille, the marquis d'Humières.

In plan, Vauban's design for the citadel had the geometrical precision of a snowflake – one five-pointed star superimposed upon another and circumscribed within a ten-pointed star. In section the three 'stars' are seen as three levels, each overtopping the one in front. Each point to each star was elongated, forming a projection the shape of a bishop's mitre, and the cross-fire made possible by the superimposition of these projections was devastating. The long, sloping parapets enabled the infantry to use their muskets in almost complete safety and to move with ease and under cover from one position to another. The effect upon morale which such a system must have produced was not the least of its virtues. But Vauban's intimate understanding of the principles of defence made him master also of the possible methods of attack.

Of all military manoeuvres, the siege of a town was the one which appealed most strongly to Louis XIV. There was an element of the spectacular about it and he saw to it that the subjects were fully recorded by his artists. 'I have told your son to send a painter', wrote Louis to Colbert on 11 June 1673, 'car je crois qu'il y aura quelque chose de beau à voir.'

On 6 June of that year Louis attacked Maastricht with an army of 25,000. The town was strongly garrisoned under Jacques de Fariaux; he was 'a brave man with a good record' and his hopes were high, but he reckoned without Vauban. With a task force of 20,000 peasant labourers he proceeded to dig his way towards the fortress. The process is described by Christopher Duffy:

Parallel gave way to zig-zag saps, zig-zags to a further parallel and so on until the French were close enough to take the hornwork and ravelin of the Tongres Gate by battering and assault.

The siege parallels had the simplicity of genius . . . the first of the parallels was dug just out of effective cannon range . . . as further parallels were dug closer to the fortress, so they offered to the besiegers secure sites for their batteries, a defence against sorties and start lines and supports for assaults. In other words Vauban assailed the fortress with a marching fortress of his own and stole for the siege attack the tactical advantage which had hitherto been the preserve of the defence.

The success was immediate. Fariaux reported from his side that 'from the first day they had lost hope' and admitted that 'he who conducted the trench work must have been the craftiest man in the world'. From the other side Louis recorded in his memoirs that 'the way in which we conducted the trenches prevented the defenders from doing anything against us, for we advanced towards the fortress in broad and spacious lines, almost as if we were drawn up for a field battle. Neither the governor nor his officers had ever seen anything like it.'

On 1 July Fariaux capitulated. Madame de Sévigné wrote at once to Bussy-Rabutin: 'What do you think of the conquest of Maastricht? All the glory goes to the king.' That was the comment of a courtier. The true merit of Louis XIV was to have recognized the ability of Vauban and to have provided him with all the facilities which he needed in order to make full use of it.

In 1675 Louis XIV paid Vauban a 'gratification' of 60,000 livres for his success at Maastricht and this enabled him to purchase the Château de Bazoches.

Situated on the north-west extremity of the Morvan and overlooking the wide expanse of country bounded to the north by the distant silhouette of Vézelay, Bazoches dominated the obscure corner of Burgundy where the obscure family of Le Prestre was seated. Their own little fief of Champignolles and their own little Château de Vauban lay, socially speaking, beneath the shadow of Bazoches. To move from Vauban to Bazoches was a transition from farmhouse to fortress, with all which that implied in terms of feudal prestige. Nothing could symbolize more aptly the brilliant career of Sębastien Le Prestre than the contrast between these two châteaux.

The Château de Vauban is the residence of a gentleman farmer; the house itself, a plain but pleasing building with a brown roof *à la mansarde*, is almost dwarfed by its magnificent barns and outbuildings. Here is the typical establishment of Saint-Simon's 'petit gentilhomme de Bourgogne'. From the high ground on which Vauban stands there is a magnificent view up the valley of the Cure and northward to Vézelay. On the eastern slopes of the valley can be seen the cone-capped towers of Bazoches rising above the trees by which they are embowered.

There had been here since at least 1170 a *place forte* of some importance, guarding as it did the old Roman road from Autun to Sens. By the seventeenth century it had become the most important château in the district. It is built in the form of a triangle of which the eastern apex has been cut off, thus creating a fourth, short side to the quadrangle. To the north, a massive square projection, the original donjon or keep, breaks the symmetry of the design, while across the courtyard an entrance pavilion interrupts the skyline with its tall pyramid of roof. The four angles are marked by corner towers, but the north-west tower, taller than its companions and encircled by a *chemin de ronde*, stands sentinel to the whole and provides a look-out tower over the open sweep of country to the west. The whole forms an impressive compendium of towers, roofs and pavilions, built throughout in the typical Burgundian vernacular, with brown tiled roofs and quoins of local stone.

Such was the castle which Vauban purchased and adapted to his own particular use. To the south he built new stables, capable of housing some sixty horses. They form a charming set of façades in seventeenth-century architecture of the greatest simplicity, but dignified by its dormers. The stables surround on three sides a deep *abreuvoir* in which tired horses could be watered. The stables and the *abreuvoir* together evoke the continual arrival and departure of couriers, for Vauban had to keep in touch with the frontier garrisons where work was in progress.

For it was here at Bazoches that most of the drawings and designs for his fortifications were prepared. The west range of the château was rebuilt by Vauban to contain a vast gallery in which his draughtsmen could work. Here also were made the models of the completed designs which were to be offered to the approval of the king. For, as with the fountains and statues of Versailles, Louis XIV always insisted on a three-dimensional model before he would accept a design.

Beneath the windows of this gallery was laid out a *jardin français* to which, of course, is attached the name of Le Nôtre. It is indeed probable that Le Nôtre should have furnished designs for one of the most distinguished men of his time.

On the east front Vauban opened a new entrance archway which was made at the expense of half the chapel. It is embellished with a simple frontispiece of rusticated stone. Otherwise he contented himself with the insertion of a large number of french windows with, as so often in Burgundy, special attention to the design of the dormers. The façades both outside and within the courtyard are unpretentious and homely. There is nothing about them to suggest the splendour in which he housed himself and his family. The private apartments are in the north wing and the marshal's bedroom, which occupies the whole first floor of the old keep, is truly magnificent. The bed itself, a capacious *lit à la duchesse*, is upholstered with canopy, curtains and counterpane incorporating panels of *petit point* set in a bold pattern of interlacing scrolls of dark brown velvet.

Connected with this by a narrow passage contrived within the thickness of the wall, a little private study occupies the corner tower. It is a five-sided room with deep-set windows and a coved ceiling painted with birds. It is small enough to be warm in winter, but insulated by the great thickness of the walls from the heat of summer. Here the marshal could work on his reflective writings which he called his 'oisivetés', and here, no doubt, he meditated on his final treatise which was to bring him to disgrace – *La Dîme Royale*.

For this little room reflects another side to Vauban's character. It was noted by Saint-Simon that he was 'protective to the point of miserliness of the lives of his men'. A century later Lazare Carnot, owner of the Château de la Rochepot, made the same point in a eulogy of Vauban pronounced before the Academy of Dijon. 'Vauban's principal care', he said, 'was always the preservation of his men. This kindness of heart, so characteristic of him, impregnated all his maxims and ideas.'

It was Vauban's concern for people which led him into this other side of his career – as a thinker and writer on sociology and politics. In 1706 he retired from active service in the army and devoted himself to the protection of twelve volumes of *Mémoires sur Différents Sujets*, which remained unpublished, dividing his time between the Château de Bazoches and his house in the rue St Vincent, almost in the shadow of the Louvre.

His writings were to prove his downfall. His ideas have a curiously modern ring about them; they were clearly out of tune with the presuppositions of the Grand Siècle. 'It is not so much by the extent of a State or by the revenues of the king that his greatness is to be judged, but by the number of his subjects who are well united and well contented.' Those were not words calculated to please Louis XIV

But Vauban was not one to confine himself to generalities. He was prepared to spell out his doctrines. First he proposed conditions for a new, properly recruited and well-trained army in which he seemed to anticipate Napoleon's principle: 'la carrière ouverte aux talents'. If the ordinary soldier could not have 'a marshal's baton in his cartridge case', at least the rank of officer should be open to any who were worthy of it; 'Dieu se moque de nos distinctions et loge le bon esprit où il lui plaît' ('God laughs at the distinctions which we make and distributes good sense wherever he chooses').

But at a deeper level Vauban saw that the real weakness of the *ancien régime* was in the intolerable burden of taxation which it laid upon the class that was least able to bear it.

France was in fact on the verge of bankruptcy. On 16 October 1706, Chamillart, contrôleur général des finances, wrote to the king in despair. His statement of accounts showed 32 million livres 'mangés d'avance', and some 73 million still owing for the years 1704–6, the years when Marlborough had won his victories; there were only 51 million in the royal coffers and his budget required the spending of 214 million. The duc de Vendôme declared that such an emergency required the calling of a States General. It was not summoned until 1788. The poverty of the poor was daily increasing; they were 'only skin and bone, reduced to hunger and thirst, to beggary and to death'.

None of this escaped Vauban. 'The kingdom is exhausted,' he wrote; 'it has reached a degree of weakness which puts it in danger of succumbing.'

Moved only by loyalty, integrity and common sense, he set himself to solve the financial problems of his country in a book entitled *La Dîme Royale*. It was addressed to the king.

I feel myself in honour bound to make representation to your Majesty that it appears to me that not enough consideration is given in France to the humbler classes; that too low a value has been set upon them; but they are the most ruined and miserable section of the population. It is, however, the section most worthy of consideration by its size and by the real and effective service which it pays.

The details of the proposed reforms lie beyond the scope of this book, but the comment of Puyzieux is perhaps the most significant. 'Votre projet est trop beau pour avoir bon succès; il trouverait dans son application de terribles obstacles, tant par sa nouveauté que pour d'autres raisons que vous avez prévu mieux que moi'. ('Your plan is too beautiful to succeed; in being put into action it would encounter terrible obstacles, as much for its novelty as for other reasons which you have foreseen better than I have'.

In February 1707, it was officially noted that 'there was on sale in Paris a book entitled *Projet d'une Dîme Royale*. Perhaps unwisely it was published without the permission and *privilège* of the king. On 22 March, d'Argenson gave orders for the seizure of the books 'malintentionnés et pernicieux' by Vauban.

On the following day Vauban was taken seriously ill. It is clear that he had this publication on his conscience, for he sent copies to his confessor and to the Père Labat for their frank opinion on the morality of the proposals. He never received their answers, for on 30 March he died.

It is difficult to say what would have happened if Vauban had not died at the critical moment. According to Saint-Simon, Louis gave the *Dîme Royale* a very cold reception and Vauban died 'a few months later, refusing to see anyone, consumed with anguish and depression'. According to Dangeau the king was deeply distressed at the marshal's death and said: 'I have lost a man wholly devoted to myself and to the State.' There was, however, no state funeral, no *oraison funèbre*, to honour his departure; when Fontenelle pronounced his *éloge* a few weeks later, he made no mention of the *Dîme Royale*.

What would have most likely led Vauban into trouble was his implied criticism of the Church. He saw clearly the fatal consequences of the Revocation of the Edict of Nantes and the misery to which France had been reduced, and he proposed the re-establishment of the Edict. Vauban was conventionally Catholic, but he suggested in his *mémoire* that if the Pope objected he could be told that the question was 'a temporal matter and purely political, in which the health of the State was at stake'.

Saint-Simon was more outspoken:

The Revocation of the Edict of Nantes, without the slightest pretext and without the least necessity . . . which depopulated one quarter of the realm, which ruined its commerce and weakened it in all its parts, which gave it over for so long to pillage, both public and endorsed, by the Dragoons, which authorized the tortures and executions in which thousands of people of both sexes died, which ruined so many . . . which lost our manufacture to other countries and caused them to flourish and abound at our expense.

The truth of this is clearly illustrated by the history of Burgundy. Colbert had gone to great lengths to establish manufactures of linen and serge, 'à la façon de Londres', and the cultivation of flax and hemp. He saw in this the only means by which 'the people can be raised out of their misery'. Conservatives in Burgundy had opposed such innovation in a land traditionally divided between agriculture and viticulture, but Colbert's persistence had won the day. But those who took to the new manufactures were almost invariably Calvinists. The Revocation put an end at one stroke to Colbert's work. In particular Beaune and Paray-le-Monial were to suffer acutely. At Beaune the manufacture of broadcloth, employing some 2,000 people, came abruptly to an end. At Paray the linen mills closed and the business was taken out of France.

But the loss was not merely financial; the horrors of the persecution, as Saint-Simon perceived, had lent a moral strength to the enemies of France, who viewed with righteous indignation the spectacle of 'a prodigious number of people proscribed, naked, fugitive, wandering, innocent of any crime, seeking asylum far from their native land; which sent men who were noble, rich, elderly, men often highly esteemed for their piety, their learning, their virtue; men of ease, frail and delicate, to the galleys under the lash, only too effective, of the officer in charge of convicts – and all because of their religion and nothing else'. Almost worse in his eyes were the forced, and therefore hypocritical conversions; 'from torture to abjuration and from abjuration to receiving Communion, there was often only a period of twenty-four hours'. Vauban made the same point about Languedoc – 'pays pavé de nouveaux convertis, qui sont Catholiques comme je suis mahométain'.

How different was the attitude of another eminent Burgundian of his day, Jacques-Bénigne Bossuet, bishop of Meaux. 'Let us publish abroad this miracle of our times; let us indulge in an outpouring of the heart over the piety of Louis; let us raise our applause to the very heavens themselves; let us say to this new Constantine, to this new Theodosius, to this new Marcion: "this is the worthy achievement of your reign; this is its true character; through you heresy is no more; God alone has made this marvel!"' These words were spoken in the *oraison funèbre* for Michel Le Tellier, Chancellor of France and father of the great Louvois. It was he who had signed the famous Revocation.

It is always difficult to know how much to believe Saint-Simon, but here he is not far from the truth: it is even more difficult to know how to handle the panegyric. It was an accepted form of oratory in seventeenth-century France: it is not in England today. It demands a conscious effort of transposition to appreciate the *oraisons funèbres* of Bossuet.

Bossuet

If we compare the Bossuet of the *oraisons funèbres* with the Bossuet of perhaps his greatest work, *L'Exposition de la Doctrine Catholique*, we can almost see two different men. In the former, one principle seems to have been inviolate: *De mortuis nihil nisi bonum*. No praise could be too lavish, no superlative too extreme, no panegyric too preposterous to serve his purpose. Of the Queen Marie-Thérèse, wife of Louis XIV, he claimed:

She was in fact without reproach before God and before men; there was no part of her life from her childhood till her death that was not proof against the attacks of slander; and a glory so pure, a reputation so beautiful, is like a precious perfume which rejoices both Heaven and earth . . . It was God's will that she should be raised by her august birth to an august marriage, in order that we might see her honoured above all the women of her century for having been beloved, esteemed and, alas too soon, mourned by the greatest of all men.

If she did not quite qualify in Bossuet's eyes for immaculate conception and bodily assumption, she repented at once of any peccadilloes of which she was guilty. 'Voyez comme elle frappe cette poitrine innocente, comme elle se reproche les moindres pêchés, comme elle s'abaisse cette tête auguste devant laquelle s'incline l'univers!' Hyperbole of that sort may easily appear ridiculous and even offensive to modern ears: those of the seventeenth century were more attuned to it.

In his other writings, Bossuet shows himself eminently reasonable. His purple passage about the Edict of Nantes must be seen alongside his actual treatment, as a diocesan bishop, of members of the Reformed Church. To him they were 'frères séparés' and his method always was 'to win the heart and to convert the soul'. The *Exposition de la Doctrine Catholique*, the book which had been the means of converting the great Turenne, was in tune with these gentle principles and it had an impressive record of success. In 1677, eight years before the Revocation, Arnauld could claim that there had been 30,000 conversions to Catholicism in five years.

On 21 August 1670, Bossuet was appointed tutor to the son and heir of Louis XIV, a boy of nine. He was known to the Court as the Grand Dauphin, though it may be questioned whether anyone was ever called 'great' with less justification.

Bossuet's broad intellect and profound learning enabled him to create a syllabus which matched the high destiny of a future king of France. Since the Grand Dauphin died before his father that destiny was never achieved and Bossuet's formation of the young prince was never put to the ultimate test; but to all appearances it failed. For a teacher requires more than a syllabus; he requires an understanding of the juvenile mind and an ability to relate to the young. Men of broad intellect and profound learning do not necessarily possess these qualities. It is possible that Bossuet did not. It is also possible that the dauphin was, as Saint-Simon claimed, radically incapable of receiving instruction. Certainly he does not appear on the pages of history as a shining example of a well-educated man. If we allow for Saint-Simon's capacity for exaggeration and personal dislikes, we still find someone whom the duchesse d'Orléans (Liselotte von der Pfalz) described as being content to spend a whole day lying on a sofa, tapping his feet with his cane.

Bossuet, however, was not unaware of the apparent failure of his efforts. On 6 July 1677, he wrote: 'Everything is so little established that the least influence of the world can overthrow all. I would dearly love to see something more solidly founded, but perhaps God will do it without me.'

Bossuet may not have been cast for the role of tutor to the dauphin: he was more effective as spiritual director to the king. In this he showed both integrity and courage. He even tried to persuade Louis to give up Madame de Montespan. 'I do not require, Sire,' he wrote, 'that you should extinguish instantaneously so violent a flame; that would be to ask of you the impossible; but, Sire, try, little by little to diminish it; beware of entertaining it.' Those were brave words. They take us a long way from the obsequious flatteries of the *oraisons funèbres*.

The *oraisons* were not, however, wholly devoted to flattery. Bossuet showed himself the master of his art in his ability to conjure up a dramatic occasion or to present a striking comparison. His *oraison funèbre* for Henriette d'Angleterre, duchesse d'Orléans, known to the court as Madame, had, according to Voltaire, 'the greatest and most rare success, that of succeeding in reducing the court to tears. He was obliged to pause after the words: "O nuit désastreuse! O nuit effroyable, où retentit tout à coup, comme un éclat de tonnerre, cette étonnante nouvelle: Madame se meurt, Madame est morte.' The audience broke into sobs and the voice of the orator was interrupted by their sighs and tears.'

In another memorable passage, on the death of the Grand Condé, he compared the man of war to the man of peace.

Always great, both in action and in repose, he appeared at Chantilly as he appeared at the head of his troops. Whether he was embellishing this magnificent and delectable mansion, or whether he was provisioning a camp in the middle of enemy territory and fortifying a position, whether he was marching with an army through places of peril, or whether he was conducting his friends through these superb alleys to the sound of so many fountains, which were never silent by day or by night, he was always the same man, and his glory followed him everywhere.

The Grand Condé

On 11 September 1686, Louis de Bourbon, prince de Condé, died at Fontainebleau. On receiving the news, Louis XIV said: 'I have just lost the greatest man in my kingdom.' He was probably right, and it was generous of him to say so, for during the seven years of the 'Princes' Fronde', Condé had been in armed revolt against him.

Condé is chiefly known to history as a brilliant military commander. At the age of twenty-two, when he was still duc d'Enghien, he won the startling victory of Rocroy. It was only four days after the infant Louis XIV had come to the throne, and it was an auspicious introduction to the new reign. He seems to have been born to command. Bossuet tells how, on the night of the battle, 'which he had to pass in the presence of the enemy, like a vigilant captain he was the last to retire to rest – but never did he rest more peacefully. On the eve of so great a day . . . he is untroubled, so completely is he in his natural element; it is well known that the next day, at the hour agreed, this second Alexander had to be awakened from a profound sleep.'

The portraits of him at Chantilly do not do him justice. Both David Teniers le Jeune and Juste Egmont show a face on which one would not trouble to bestow a second glance. He has rather a long nose and that is about all. But Coysevox gives us a very different picture, both in his bronze bust in the library and in the medallion struck to mark his funeral. The face is unforgettable; here we can see, in Bossuet's words, 'un Prince du sang qui portait la victoire dans ses yeux' – a face that could have put a new spirit into the troops before

Rocroy. There is something farouche about his blazing eyes and wild, unkempt appearance. He had, as Primi Visconti observed, 'l'air d'un brigand'.

Madame de Motteville gives a thumbnail sketch in which she does not descend to flattery:

He was not handsome; his face was an ugly shape. His eyes were a vivid blue and in his expression was a look of pride. His nose was aquiline, his mouth most displeasing because it was too large and the teeth too prominent, but in his whole countenance there was something great and proud, something of the eagle.

Condé's life, as Bossuet underlines, divided into two parts – that of a great master of the art of war and that of a great promoter of the arts of peace. To some observers the change from captain to courtier was seen as something unworthy. The Venetian ambassador Foscarini wrote of him: 'Just as in former days he was incompatible with the court, haughty with the great and insatiable for the flattery of his familiars, so now he had become the servile partisan of ministers, courteous, easy, agreeable to all alike.' Madame de Motteville also observed that he was 'tout à fait changé', but she insists that he was 'as great in his humility and meekness as he had been in his victories'.

By his lineage, Condé was the last of the great feudal magnates. The blood of the Connétable de Bourbon and of Montmorency, always as ready to bear arms against their sovereign as for him, flowed in his veins. With the rise of Louis XIV he recognized the coming of a new era, but instead of allowing himself to be domesticated at Versailles, he kept his own court at Chantilly, where he surrounded himself with men of letters and showed himself a valiant patron of the arts.

He had his father to thank for an excellent education. He was brought up at Bourges, where he lived in the magnificent medieval house of Jacques Coeur. He went to the Jesuit Collège Sainte-Marie, where he followed the same curriculum as the other boys, but insulated from them by a gilded balustrade. At the age of sixteen he replaced his father as governor of Burgundy. He applied himself with great diligence to the task and after only a year's experience, was able to receive Louis XIV in his province. The Secretary of State de Noyers recorded: 'His conduct was full of prudence, wit and grace. I could not wish for anything more important than the preservation of this young prince.'

At a slightly later age he indulged in the debauchery of his contemporaries to such an extent that his father wrote to him: 'It would be better to knife yourself than to continue the life you are living.' But with the debauchery came an introduction to the world of letters which centred on the Hôtel de Rambouillet. Foundations were being laid on which he was later to build the chief creation of his life, the cultural circle of Chantilly.

The two sides of Condé's nature were reflected in the fabric of the Château de Chantilly. He had inherited through his mother the great sixteenth-century castle of the Montmorencys. Outwardly it was still a fortress, standing in a wide moat and set about with seven massive towers; but already the Connétable Anne de Montmorency had added the Petit Château to the south – a building in Renaissance style of a purely domestic nature. War and peace were already juxtaposed in the architecture and Chantilly was never more magnificent than when the Petit Château could be seen backed and overtopped by the pinnacles and pointed roofs and gables of the older building. Condé made no significant alteration to its outward appearance, but inside he filled the rooms with pictures and tapestries and created a library of 10,000 books. The Great Château has been twice rebuilt since his day, but something of Condé's creation can still be seen in the lay-out of the park by Le Nôtre, with its gargantuan flights of steps and its glittering expanses of water.

In many ways Chantilly under the Grand Condé resembled Rabelais's *Abbey of Thelema*, a temple for free-thinkers. Rabelais had placed over the doors of his 'Abbey' the motto *Faict que voudras*, 'Do what you will'. His abbey was a club and the condition for membership was a lust for living. All lived for pleasure, but their pleasures were those of men who thirsted after knowledge as keenly as they thirsted after wine; 'so nobly were they instructed that there was not a man or woman amongst them who could not read and write, sing, play musical instruments, speak five or six languages and compose in them both verse and prose.'

The picture of Condé's household and way of life is not dissimilar. 'Chantilly', wrote Saint-Simon, 'était ses délices.' He describes how the great commander would review his gardens, followed by a bevy of secretaries armed with pen and paper ready to take down on the spot the ideas which occurred to him for the elaboration of the lay-out. They were turned into realities by Le Nôtre.

All the great names of the Grand Siècle occur in the annals of Chantilly, for Condé understood men of letters. Bishop Burnett declared that 'there was not in France a better judge of wit or knowledge'. Madame de Sévigné, Madame de La Fayette, La Bruyère, Racine, Molière, Boileau, La Fontaine – all were here and with all of them Condé loved to argue and frequently became so carried away that he lost his temper. 'Il aime extrêmement la dispute', wrote La Fontaine, 'et n'a jamais plus d'esprit que quand il a tort.' Boileau once extricated himself from such a predicament by saying: 'I always agree with your Highness, especially when you are in the wrong.'

Condé was particularly interested in the theatre and he supported Racine with the same spirit with which he had supported Corneille. He was delighted with Molière and stood by him when *Tartuffe* was banned by the authorities of the Church. This says nothing about Condé's attitude to religion, for *Tartuffe* was aimed at religious hypocrisy and not at true religion.

Although for many years Condé was not a practising Christian he always enjoyed religious controversies. The son of a devout Catholic and the grandson of a fighter for the Protestant cause, he was equally accessible to men of both persuasions. As the duc d'Aumâle, the last châtelain of Chantilly, wrote, 'Il lui plaisait que sa maison fût un terrain neutre.' He was a great friend of Bossuet, who introduced Fénelon to the delights of Chantilly, and the two could be seen arguing beneath the shade of the Allée de Philosophes.

With anyone unworthy of his mettle Condé could be devastating. In 1668, when the controversy over Port Royal was at its height, the publishing of a translation of the New Testament was condemned by La Feuillade, archbishop of Embrun. Condé went straight into the attack: 'Admit frankly that you condemned it without reading it. You don't understand a word of Greek; how can you have judged it?' The archbishop, unable to answer the accusation, made a shabby attempt to shift the ground: 'It is not for worldly men to talk of the affairs of the Church' was all he could say. Condé moved in for the kill. 'Good; it is not for us to judge such matters, but it is all right for you to get involved in court intrigues and jostle for positions in embassies, and we find no cause for criticism. I tell you, however, that as long as you mind our business I think we are at least entitled to talk of yours.'

On 18 August 1683, the Abbé Malebranche was invited to pass two or three days as the guest of Condé who was reading with great interest his book *Recherche de la Vérité*. 'Monsieur le Prince has a lively mind,' he recorded, 'penetrating and clear-sighted, and he is, I think, steadfast in the truth once he has accepted it, but he wants to see clearly.'

Above all, Condé was always grateful to the Jesuits for the education which he had received from them at Bourges. It was a Jesuit and an old schoolfriend, Agard de Champs, who finally converted him. On Easter Day, 1685, Condé received Communion in the chapel at Chantilly, a thing he had not done, according to the marquis de Sourches, for at least seventeen years. He died not only reconciled to the Church but to the king.

In April 1671, after eleven years of coldness towards his cousin, Louis XIV accepted his invitation to visit Chantilly, where he was most splendidly entertained. Louis then took Condé back into his service. He was there at the famous crossing of the Rhine, where he was wounded; he was responsible for the victory of Seneffe and for the campaign in Alsace in the course of which his old friend Turenne was killed. That was his last campaign. When he replaced his sword in its scabbard it was never to be drawn again.

Shortly afterwards he was received at Saint-Germain by Louis, who awaited him at the top of the Grand Staircase. Condé, who was suffering from gout, apologized for his slowness in mounting, but received the answer: 'My cousin; when one is so loaded with laurels it is impossible to walk fast.'

Condé, for his part, made atonement for the years of the Fronde by commissioning a large painting for the Galerie des Batailles at Chantilly by Lecomte. It was to be entitled *Le Repentir*. Condé is seen declining the fanfares of Fame, while at his feet Clio, the muse of history, tears out the offending pages from her register.

Bibliography

Marquise de Sévigné: *Lettres de Mme de Sévigné, de sa Famille et de ses Amis*, 14 vols, 1862–6.

The Château de Cormatin
Letter of the marquis de Coulanges to the marquise d'Uxelles, 16 August 1705: in *Lettres de Mme de Sévigné*, Vol. X.
A. de Gaigneron: 'Profession de Châtelaine', in *Connaissance des Arts*, 1982.
R. Coope: 'Jacques Gentilhâtre', in *Catalogue of the Drawings of the RIBA*, 1972.

Bourbilly and Monthelon
Baron Walkenaer: *Mémoire Touchant la Vie et les Ecrits de Marie de Rabutin-Chantal, marquise de Sévigné*, 1856.
H. Bremond: *Sainte-Chantal*, 1912.
Mère de Chaugy: *Mémoires sur la vie et les vertus de Sainte Jeanne-Françoise Frémyor de Chantal*, 1874.

The Château de Bussy-Rabutin
M. Dumolin: *Le Château de Bussy-Rabutin*, 1933.
Comte de Bussy-Rabutin: *Histoire Amoureuse des Gaules*, 1967.

The Château de Saint-Fargeau
Baron Chaillou des Barres: *Les Châteaux d'Ancy-le-Franc, Saint-Fargeau, Chastellux et Tanley*, 1845.
A. Bourgeois: *Saint-Fargeau*, 1978.
G. Souffert: *Saint-Fargeau et Ancy-le-Franc*, 1978.
Mlle de Montpensier: *Mémoires de Mademoiselle, duchesse de Montpensier*, 1859.
V. Sackville-West: *Daughter of France: La Grande Mademoiselle*, 1959.

Bossuet
V. Giraud: *Bossuet*, 1930.

Vauban
Sir R. Blomfield: *Sebastien Le Prestre de Vauban*, 1938.
A. Rébelliau: *Vauban*, 1962.

C. Duffy: *The Fortress in the Age of Vauban and Frederick the Great*, 1985.

Condé
G. Montgrédien: *Le Grand Condé*, 1959.

DIJON

Apart from a short period during the Fronde, when the Grand Condé was replaced first by the duc de Vendôme and then by the duc d'Epernon, the princes of the house of Bourbon-Condé were governors of Burgundy from 1631 until the Revolution. It was during these two centuries that Dijon expanded from being a fortified frontier town in the medieval manner and became the city of private palaces and impressive public buildings which it has since remained.

The former reflected the prestige of the local authority; the latter, as often as not, the power of the king. The two were held in more or less uneasy tension. The local authority was represented by the premier président: the power of the king by the intendant. In practical terms this meant that the intendant was the agent of Colbert.

Colbert had a particular interest in Burgundy, for his Château and marquisate of Seignelay were in the vicinity of Auxerre. His collaborator at Dijon was Claude Bouchu, who was intendant from 1654 to 1683. Bouchu shared Colbert's capacity for work and was said never to retire until four in the morning. The Président Brulart detested him and tried to blacken his reputation, calling him 'a man in whose hands the simplest matters become exceedingly difficult'. Together, the two represented the rival claims of a centralized monarchy and provincial aristocracy.

The architecture of Dijon bears the imprint of this provincial society. Like all such societies it was a mixture of men of real quality and ability together with a wide penumbra of genteel nonentities.

A census taken towards the end of the seventeenth century enables us to see a diagram of the population of Dijon – 'La liste des officiers privilégiés et exempts de taille et de logement des gens de guerre'. In all a total of 643 hearths ('feux') were of families exempt from these burdens. Of these the parliamentary families accounted for 168 and the Chancelry only another 28. Of the remainder the greater part were themselves a burden on the 3,688 families of Dijon which were outside the circle of privilege.

'It is quite astonishing', wrote Gaston Rupnel, 'this complex multitude, this deliberately complicated hierarchy, this multiple administration which seems to have had no other purpose than to maintain this parasite superfluity of useless *fonctionnaires*.'

Above all their functions carried with them the titles necessary to membership of the respectable classes, and offices were bought simply because they conferred status. Pierre Taisand records unashamedly how he wrote to Bossuet begging the bishop to obtain for him 'any one of the titles which would procure exemption for me . . . the slightest of qualities, the least of commissions would serve me at the City Chamber'. After two years of obsequious solicitation, Taisand obtained the charge of trésorier général. He had put his foot on the first rung of the social ladder.

At the top of the ladder were the members of the old Burgundian aristocracy – names like de Vienne, de Beauffremont, de Tavanes and de Dinteville. These had provided a *noblesse de fonction* under the ducal administration. They intermarried with the great parliamentary families – the Bossuets, the Brularts, the Bouhiers. But already the parliamentarians were becoming an aristocracy in the real sense of the word. For the word 'aristocracy' needs to be defined. In its literal meaning of 'the rule of the best' it would fit well over the magistrates of Dijon. They did rule and they were often men of the highest quality and education. In two centuries they turned Dijon from a fortified frontier town into a cultural centre second only to Paris. But in the sense that the word 'aristocracy' was used at Versailles, which was only concerned with the number of centuries for which a family had been ennobled, the parliamentarians were middle class – 'les bourgeois du Parlement', as the Grande Condé was wont to call them.

Foisset, in his biography of the Président des Brosses, sees them as 'l'avant garde des classes moyennes', but who, during the sixteenth and seventeenth centuries, were steadily taking over the functions of the old nobility. Foisset draws attention to the rule whereby 'if, for example, a marquis happened to be a président or a conseiller, parliamentary custom required him to suppress his hereditary title – l'homme de qualité disparaîssait derrière le magistrat'.

Like all artistocracies, they had their distinctive robes which they wore on their ceremonial occasions. 'It was a grand and beautiful spectacle', wrote Charles Oursel,

their *Messe Rouge* when the whole corps of the magistrature, before the reopening of their audiences, came solemnly to invoke *celui qui juge les justices*. As for me, when I recall the three mitred bishops in the little chapel of the Palais, with the abbot of Cîteaux in cape and rochet next to them, and then, at the steps of the altar, the Premier Président Brulart – the Mathieu Molé of Burgundy – surrounded by the nine présidents in their ermine mantles and with their *mortiers* on their heads, the chevaliers d'honneur with their swords by their sides and their blue ribbands on their chests, and the sixty-four councillors in their red robes, not counting the five conseillers-clercs in full ecclesiastical robes, I wonder if, in Paris itself, the magistrature of the eighteenth century knew any such imposing ceremony.

These families, and especially those closely concerned with the administration of the city, built themselves private houses, or *hôtels particuliers*, which are the finest ornaments to Dijon.

The hôtels particuliers

The great houses of the aristocracy are not grouped together in some smart *quartier*, but stand neighbours to the more humble dwellings in nearly every street. 'Who has not felt at Dijon', wrote Chabeuf in his *Monuments et Souvenirs*, 'this close and continual contact between the noble and the common, between art and the populace?' This juxtaposition arose from a reluctance, before 1678, to build outside the line of the old fortifications. It meant that the builder of some imposing *hôtel particulier* was obliged to buy up a number of the poorer houses and demolish them. The process often involved a site restriction which entailed some irregularity in the building. This is particularly evident in the plan of the Hôtel de Vogüé.

The Hôtel de Vogüé

One of the finest of these houses to be built after the Wars of Religion was one of the first – the Hôtel de Vogüé in the rue de la Chouette, close to the apse of Notre-Dame. Of the two wings which enclose the entrance court, the western one is cut away obliquely in such a manner as to make symmetry impossible. The architect has wisely not attempted it.

Etienne Bouhier, conseiller de parlement from 1607 to 1635, was certainly the builder and allegedly the designer of this miniature palace. It was asserted by his grandson and biographer that he possessed 'the most exquisite taste in architecture' and that in his latter years he built the Grand Hôpital de Dijon 'from the designs, which I have seen, traced with his own hand'. His grandson also credits him with the authorship of his own hôtel.

If this was the work of an inspired amateur, it was an amateur inspired by a passion for the minutest details of Renaissance decoration. His pediments offer a variety and an elaboration which is worthy of du Cerceau, but, unlike du Cerceau, he uses his delicately chiselled ornament to offset large areas of smooth, undecorated wall.

This contrast is particularly effective in his treatment of the entrance arch, heavily pedimented and rusticated and slightly reminiscent of some of the designs by Jacques Gentilhâtre, which is set in an otherwise blank wall of masonry.

Throughout the house the ornament has been thoughtfully and skilfully disposed. The pediments on the ground floor are triangular and fairly plain; those of the first floor are segmental and rather ornate. The dormer windows, set against a colourful Burgundian roof, are ornate and triangular. The three façades which look inwards on to the courtyard are composed of two storeys each of three windows; the rhythm of each façade is created by the placing of a pediment over the central window and a straight lintel over those on either side. The whole has a classical dignity and repose created by logical lay-out, perfect proportion and exquisite execution which is quietly but deeply satisfying.

But the designer also understood the charm of the unexpected. Two delightful little doorways, roofed with quarter domes, cut across the inwards angles of the court. Symmetry required that there should be two, but that on the left-hand side is a dummy.

The right-hand doorway gives access to the foot of a fine staircase. Although the doorway is in a corner of the courtyard it is in the centre of the main block of the house. This is a further result of the site restriction already noted, which is clearly shown on the ground plan. In order to allow room for entrance into the garden area, which also contained the stables and coach house, the garden front has had to be pushed eastward of the central axis of the entrance court. The skill with which this eccentric plan has been combined with two symmetrical façades suggests the work of an architect of experience, rather than of a gifted amateur.

It is difficult, also, to believe that the inner face of the entrance screen is the creation of an amateur. The visitor who penetrates the courtyard passes through a triple arched screen which presents towards the house a *tour de force* of Renaissance architecture.

The three arches are contained within a Corinthian order. The central arch, slightly larger than those which flank it, forms the entrance and breaks forward enough to permit the use of free-standing columns; those to either side are flat pilasters. The frieze and cornice are of an intricacy of design which is only equalled by the precision of its execution. In both the side arches the spandrels are filled with figures of women who act as side-supporters to the monogram of Etienne Bouhier and his two wives – BMG: Bouhier, Massol and Giroud.

Etienne had two sons, both of them, somewhat confusingly, called Jean. The younger Jean inherited the hôtel and continued with the interior decoration in the style of Louis XIV. In particular he added the library – 'véritable sanctuaire du travail' – which was the subject of the most evocative description by the comte Melchior de Vogüé, written in 1861.

'Everything', he wrote, 'invites the visitor to study the past, from the serried ranks of dusty in-folios to the broad armchairs upholstered in red morocco, set in majestic order round the marquetry table, all in the silence of a peaceful retreat.' It was no doubt from these dusty in-folios comte Melchior made his own study of the past and formed his own picture of the cultural life of Dijon a generation or two before his time.

The last of the Bouhiers, heiress alike to their name and to their distinction of character, assembled in these apartments an élite society which included the best minds of the province; her Salon had a reputation of which the memory is preserved in the literary traditions of the Burgundian capital. My great-grandfather came to pass here such leisure as was left him by the king's service and the sittings of the Etats de Languedoc; here he rejoined his brother, Jacques-Joseph-François de Vogüé, the fourth bishop of Dijon, 'plus musicien qu'ecclésiastique', who also succeeded two of the Bouhiers on the episcopal throne of the new diocese.

All this luxury of good quality recalls the existence, both wide-ranging and intelligent, of the family who lived here for two centuries. Is it not the home of a race which personified, in a France which no longer exists, the spirit of the provinces? This spirit, bred of pride of race and rigorous education, which knew how to combine careful concern for public affairs with a literary culture and a taste for the arts and sciences – of this spirit, which our age no longer wishes to understand, there remain only the monuments which it created and upon which it left its mark.

Another early example of the new creation of private palaces is the Hôtel Bouchu in the rue Monge – now the Conservatoire de Musique. It occupies the site of a far older building, the Hôtel de Molesmes, some traces of which may be seen in the lower parts of the walls. The main façade stands back behind an entrance screen, recessed between two narrow wings. One of the dormers on the north side bears the inscription: 'le 2 septembre 1643 la dernière pierre a été posée'.

The Président Bouchu who was the builder had invited the architect Le Muet to design his hôtel. Le Muet was the architect also of most of the Château de Tanlay. It is difficult to see any resemblance between the two buildings. Here at the Hôtel Bouchu, he has relied almost entirely upon quoins, marking the corners and framing the windows, to achieve his decoration, which is somewhat severe. It must be remembered that the elegant balustrade and urns which now crown the entrance screen were added only in 1782.

During the Fronde, Bouchu took the part of the prince de Condé. His son was to become, as we have seen, Colbert's intendant in Dijon.

Another fine example of an *hôtel particulier* is the Hôtel Legouz de Gerland. It had been built during the sixteenth century by the family Chissey-Varange, to which we owe the three delightful little projecting towers or oriels which overlook the rue Liégeard. Eugène Fyot, who has so carefully established the documentation for these houses, puts forward the rather fanciful suggestion that these three turrets were inspired by the family coat of arms: 'd'azur à trois tours d'or maçonnées de sable'.

In 1586 Guillaume Legouz became avocat général to the parlement. He supported the league, but finally had to accept Henri IV as king. His grandson, Pierre Legouz-Morin, became the owner of this hôtel. On 5 February 1672 he put in an application to the Chambre de Ville to bring forward the façade of his house 'and also to construct a cabinet in the form of a corbel at the extremity of my house, the same height as the three other older ones . . . which will serve as an embellishment to the town as well as to the street'.

Pierre's son Charles married Constance, daughter of Jean-Baptiste de Cirey, seigneur de Gerland. Their son, Bénigne, was a great lover of the arts and travelled in Italy and England. He gave Dijon its Jardin Botanique and its Academy with a Cabinet d'Histoire Naturelle. Together with François Devosge he established the Ecole des Beaux Arts.

Charles Le Gouz de Gerland made considerable additions to his house, building the spacious courtyard on the west side, towards the rue de Vauban. With its elegant, arcaded hemicycle surmounted by a balustrade and urns and its handsome *porte cochère* 'pour faciliter l'évolution des carosses', it set a new style which was to reach its zenith in the building of the Hôtel Bouhier de Lantenay in the eighteenth century.

It was one of the Bouhier family, Jean, 'Ingénieur du Roi à Dijon', who presided, 'like a great surveyor under whose directions this new Dijon is being built', over the great campaign of improvement which was to bring Dijon some of the dignity and regularity of the Grand Siècle.

Thanks to the prudent administration of Colbert the city had been relieved of the burden of debt which had accumulated during the time of troubles. A period of security and prosperity ensued which was reflected immediately in the architecture of the town.

The public buildings

The sixteenth century, with its wars of religion, had not been a time propitious for building. In 1667 the Cistercian monk Dom Meglinger wrote: 'Nearly all the buildings are of wood and the interstices between the beams are simply filled with wattle and covered with plaster and clay; at first sight one might think them to be of stone if the rendering, attacked by the elements, did not lay bare the woodwork.' Such building was, of course, at great risk from fire. By the end of the seventeenth century all new buildings had to be of stone.

It was not, however, until the year 1678, with the annexation of

Franche Comté, that the city of Dijon, hitherto exposed to all the dangers of being capital to a frontier province, shook off the paraphernalia of defence and became the large and lovely city that it is. In 1684, Pierre Taisand noted: 'Dijon is being built efficiently and well; and if all those embellishments which have been begun during the last two or three years are brought to completion, it will soon be one of the most agreeable cities of France.' The ramparts were converted into boulevards and 'offered to the citizens the advantage of being able to take the air beneath the shade of lime trees which form a vault overhead; they were planted under the Mayors Labotte and Baudinet'.

The campaign started modestly with a decision taken on 27 June 1678, to pave the streets and a survey was undertaken of the encroachments made by the porches, stairways, outbuildings and other projections made by the householders. These were obliged to pull them down, receiving compensation only when the constructions had been made 'à bon titre'. The new *pavé* was welcomed as 'une très grande commodité aux habitants et un embellissement à la dite ville'.

A strict control was to be exercised over any new building which fronted the street. Previously each had built 'only considering his own interest and to the prejudice of that of the public', with the result that the façades were 'fort défectueuses et irrégulières'. Henceforth the design of any new building had to be approved by the authorities and all façades on the streets were to be built of freestone.

Next it was decided to create a *place* in front of the old Palais des Ducs, now known as the Logis du Roi, 'in order to make the access to it more easy and more beautiful'. Two commissioners, Jean Clamonnet and Jean Millot, architects of Dijon, were appointed and those houses, courts, or gardens which they judged it necessary to demolish were subjected to compulsory purchase. Martin de Noinville was commissioned to design the *place* and Jacques Hugot, 'Ingénieur Ordinaire du Roi', was entrusted with its construction. Noinville designed the great semicircular arcade which we see today; Hugot ensured that none of the houses behind it exceeded the height of the balustrade. The Place Royale, as it was now called, was completed in 1692.

The design was to include an equestrian statue of Louis XIV, which was ordered from Le Hongre, one of the many sculptors engaged on the decoration of the gardens of Versailles. In 1690 the statue was cast in bronze. It weighed 47,000 pounds. Its transport from Paris had never been properly thought out. It got as far as Brosse in the neighbourhood of Auxerre where it stuck in the mud and here it remained for the next twenty-six years. In 1720, five years after the death of Louis XIV, Pierre Morin, an engineer employed in the Ponts et Chaussées, undertook to complete the removal at a cost of 30,000 livres. Twenty yoke of oxen were required for the task. It was not until 1725 that the statue was finally set up in the Place Royale.

One might detect a certain lack of enthusiasm on the part of the authorities. Perhaps there is no apter symbol for their attitude towards the royal presence in Dijon than this colossal bronze figure, bogged down in a field by the borders of Burgundy and with nobody motivated to do anything about it.

In 1682 it was decided to rebuild the south side of the palace in the style of Versailles. Daniel Gittard, an architect in the service of the Prince de Condé, designed the immense Salle des Etats which enclosed the Cour d'Honneur on the west. Gittard died in 1686 and was replaced by the 'Premier Architecte du Roi', Jules Hardouin-Mansart, and his son-in-law Robert de Cotte. These were the authors of the final enlargement of Versailles. There can be little doubt that the proud porticoes and triumphant trophies of the new building were an assertion of dynastic power. Just as, in the thirteenth century, the Capetian monarchy had marked its presence by the construction of the great Gothic cathedrals, so Louis XIV left the imprint of his regime upon Dijon by the architecture of the Logis du Roi.

An engraving by François Devosges done in 1775 shows the Salle des Etats in all its splendour, with the floor at different levels to express the difference between the three Orders, a high rostrum and canopy for the governor and the walls hung with tapestries representing the arms of Condé.

'There is no spectacle more majestic', wrote Courtépée, 'than the opening session of this august assembly.' After a sumptuous ceremony in the Sainte-Chapelle they all processed in their silk and velvet robes to the Salle des Etats. 'The governor is placed in an armchair of blue velvet, powdered with golden fleurs-de-lis, placed beneath a canopy which upholds a portrait of the king. The premier président and the intendant are at his right hand; the officers of the

Bureau des Finances at his left; a little lower down are the secrétaires en Chef des Etats and the trésorier général.'

The senior officer of the Bureau des Finances opened the session with an exposition of the 'letters of convocation'. The governor then rose to assure the Estates that he would convey to the king an account of their fidelity and zeal. The premier président harangued them on the subject of justice; the intendant gave an account of the royal demands upon the province. 'Enfin l'Evèque d'Autun termine le séance par un discours en faveur des peuples dont il expose les besoins et les intérêts.' The Estates met once every three years.

The palace as it was after the building of the Salle des Etats is shown in a drawing by Mansart made in 1688. The statue of Louis XIV is seen to be facing a wing which projected southwards from the main block; it was known as the Aisle de Rocroi in honour of the Grand Condé's famous victory. A similar pavilion answered it to the east, near the Sainte-Chapelle. Midway between these pavilions a monumental gateway, with a portico reflecting that on Mansart's wing, gave access to the Cour d'Honneur or Grande Cour. The gateway served a double function in the symmetry of the whole; it balanced Mansart's portico towards the hemicycle, and it provided a central feature between the two pavilions.

To the east of this block was the Cour des Remises, enclosed on the north side by the Galerie de Bellegarde, mounted upon an open arcade and flanked by two external staircases, one of which survives. The Galerie de Bellegarde connected the ducal lodgings with a large, turreted pavilion; it was known as the Tour de Bar because the duc de Bar had been kept a prisoner here in 1431. The Tour de Bar connected with the Sainte-Chapelle and its ground floor accommodated the chapter house. From the Tour de Bar a wing projected southwards. It contained the kitchens, built by Philippe le Bon. This remarkable building has an octagonal vault with a central aperture for a *louvre*, not unlike those openings contrived in churches for the hoisting of bells. The wings ended in a pavilion symmetrical with that of the Aisle de Rocroi.

On the other side of the palace, to the west of the new Salle des Etats, Mansart's drawing shows a small courtyard, later to become the Cour de Flore. It is bounded to the south by the rue de Condé (now the rue de la Liberté) and to the north by the rue Notre-Dame. It was this area which was next to be developed. In June 1731, Jacques Gabriel, contrôleur des bâtiments du roi, was invited to

Dijon to take charge of the operation. He abolished the external stairways to the Salle des Etats, which formed a considerable obstruction to the Place Royale, and he built another, very beautiful internal staircase in his new wing fronting the rue de Condé.

At the far side of the courtyard was the south front of the old Ducal Palace. This was a fine if somewhat featureless façade covered by a roof, so tall as to include three storeys of dormer windows, above which projected the lofty Tour de la Terrasse. It had been built between 1450 and 1455 by Jean Poncelet for Philippe le Bon. This block contained the Grande Salle, today the Salle des Gardes, where the monuments of the dukes are exhibited.

It was not, however, destined to remain thus. Mansart, in the same year produced another drawing with the inscription: 'Le Logis du Roi comme on le voudrait faire'. It is essentially what we see today, but it took a hundred years before it was achieved.

During the eighteenth century a long series of projects for the completion of the ensemble was held under consideration, but lack of enthusiasm and lack of financial resources led to each in turn being rejected. First the designs of Pierre le Mousseux were turned down on account of 'l'immensité des plans et des dépences'. Then, in 1771, the architect Le Jolivet produced a sumptuous proposal. For the façade fronting the rue Notre-Dame he designed a grand portico with the figures of the four great dukes on the inclined planes of the pediment dominated by a statue of Louis XV above its apex. In his memorandum, Le Jolivet explained that in his design the three orders, Doric, Ionic and Corinthian, were used to represent the three Orders of the States General – the Tiers Etat, the Clergy and the Nobility. His project was turned down as 'trop fastueux'.

In 1776 the authorities agreed to a far simpler design by the architects Gauthey and Dumorey, which is in all important respects the building which we see today.

Finally, in 1781, it was decided to implement the full design of Mansart for a wing answering the Salle des Etats on the eastern side of the forecourt. This was to lodge more commodiously the Académie de Peinture et de Sculpture and François Devosges designed allegorical figures for the two arts to decorate the pediment.

By the time the building was finished the Revolution had started. No sooner was the Palais des Etats completed than the Etats themselves were abolished by the decree of 10 July 1790. The whole ornamental scheme with its heraldry and its allegories of royalty became 'décorations odieux aux Français'. Le Jolivet immediately produced a design for replacing a head of Louis XIV with a 'tête de Citoyen'. It did not save him from the guillotine.

The history of the Palais des Etats at this period spotlights an argument of the greatest importance. Were statues and paintings and buildings which represented the *ci-devant* tyranny to be destroyed as offensive to republican eyes or were they to be treasured as works of art?

To begin with, the former argument prevailed. The equestrian figure of Louis XIV which had taken so long to reach its destination was overthrown and the bronze sent to Le Creusot where it was melted down and provided six cannons for the Revolutionary army.

On 27 July 1790, the Directoire du Département decided to confine its hostility to heraldic achievements. François Devosges was given the task of replacing them with something more suitable, such as the allegories of Justice, Prudence and Philosophy which may still be seen today.

The prince de Condé, having emigrated and set himself at the head of a royalist army with the avowed intention of reconquering the throne of France for the house of Bourbon, was now a figure of particular detestation and his emblems and armorials were all obliterated by an order dated 21 December 1792.

But in the following year a new policy was outlined. On 11 January 1793 the Minister of the Interior, 'recognizing that the fine arts are children of liberty even more than they are of despotism', expressed a fear that by destroying all the symbols of feudalism they might be destroying works of art 'which form part of the glory of the name of France, and would cast a shadow over the brilliance of our success in the arts'. The authorities of the département de la Côte d'Or agreed to preserve its monuments. Dijon therefore has largely survived in the form in which the eighteenth century left it, and with its buildings it retains its memories of those who built them.

They were a remarkable breed of men, the parliamentarians of Dijon, numbering among their élite society names distinguished not only in jurisprudence but in the world of science, letters and the arts; names like Jean Bouhier, seventh generation in his family to be Président of the High Court and member of the Académie française, whose library contained 35,000 books and some 2,000 manuscripts. He made translations of Homer, Virgil, Ovid and Cicero and could discourse as pertinently on ancient marbles as on the essays of

Montaigne. Equally erudite was the Président Charles de Brosses, collector of manuscript versions of Sallust and another of *Letters from Italy*, which are as entertaining as they are instructive; these interests, however, did not distract him from his profession and he remained firm to his principle: 'Il faut être magistrat avant d'être homme de lettres.'

This was not always the case. Jean-Baptiste Jeannin de Chamblanc, whose *hôtel particulier* hides its *porte cochère* in the rue Jeannin, abandoned his legal career in order to concentrate on his scientific interests. He formed a vast and varied collection of birds and mammals, minerals, machines that were both pneumatic and electric, optical instruments, microscopes and lenses. The Abbé Sièyes wrote: 'Dijon has, in the *Cabinet Jeannin* alone, as it were a little museum, like an encyclopaedia in three dimensions and alive.'

Much more serious as a scientist was Guyton de Morveau, appointed avocat général in 1762. In his hôtel in the Place Bossuet he installed a laboratory, in which he conducted experiments, of which Arthur Young declared that he possessed a number and a variety of apparatus such as he has never seen anywhere else. His book on chemistry was applauded throughout Europe. Guyton was the friend and colleague of the greatest Burgundian scientist of his age, Georges-Louis Leclerc, comte de Buffon.

Buffon

The Hôtel de Buffon consists of two buildings at right angles to each other, of which the older dates back to the middle of the sixteenth century, as may be seen from the decoration of its dormers. 'Apart from its undeniable historic interest', runs the report of the Commission des Antiquités, 'it offers an example of classical architecture whose lines harmonize most happily with those of the other private hôtels in the rue de Buffon, which make this street one of the most characteristic urban areas and one of the most evocative of Old Dijon.'

The Hôtel de Buffon is not far from the Collège des Godrans, a Jesuit foundation at which Georges-Louis Leclerc, later comte de Buffon, received his education. His precocity, especially in mathematics, first astonished and then disquieted his teachers. The rector went so far as to consult the Président de Brosses. The président, however, had more perspicacity than the rector. 'Leave him alone', he said; 'he will go far.'

Georges-Louis's father was the next to be disconcerted; he had destined his son to the magistrature. His uncle, Jean Nadault, showed more understanding and encouraged his young nephew. When Georges-Louis's father protested, 'You are robbing the family of a président of the High Court', Nadault answered: 'What does that matter if I add one more glory to France?'

Georges-Louis would doubtless have made a good magistrate. Condorcet attributed to him 'a constitution which gave him the power for long and sustained work, a zeal which enabled him to digest, without distaste and almost without boredom, the minutest details, a character in which could be detected none of those qualities which detract from success'. These, however, were destined to be used not for the minutiae of the law but for the vast, immeasurable field of science.

For this prodigious undertaking he seems to have been destined by Providence. 'None of the qualities of a man of science were lacking in him', wrote Emile Faguet:

neither the taste for observation nor the patience to observe; nor the hard work, enormous, continuous and patient; nor the sense of order; nor the lucidity; nor the ability to be dispassionate and open-minded; nor the scientific imagination – that is to say, the power to make generalizations and to form hypotheses, and hypotheses as working conveniences which are always of a provisional nature and destined always to be abandoned; nor the power to create systems; nor the mistrust of systems when they try to pass as unshakeable dogmas and blind the human reason which has produced them.

When Georges-Louis was still a boy, his father had bought the position of conseiller au parlement de Dijon and the Hôtel Quentin to go with it. He also purchased the domain of Montbard; the château was in ruins, but it carried with it the title of comte de Buffon. By this name Georges-Louis is usually known.

There is a portrait of him at the age of fifty-four by Drouais, one of the more penetrating artists of the eighteenth century. It shows him as the *grand seigneur* in embroidered waistcoat and powdered wig. The picture recalls the words of David Hume: 'He looks more like a marshal of France than a man of letters.' But behind the rather heavy features there is a strength and a seriousness not always to be found in marshals. In the two busts by Houdon, as well as in Drouais's painting, the lips are slightly parted. It is the expression of a man who ponders deeply, but has not yet reached a decision.

David Hume reminds us that Buffon was not only a great scientist but a great writer. Much of his text was in the first place drafted by the Abbé Vexon, but this was usually worked over and rephrased by Buffon himself in his own, more readable style. As he dictated nearly all his work to a secretary, his style lends itself somewhat naturally to being read aloud.

Above all he excelled in the art of evocative description which reveals the closeness of his observation. A good example is his passage on the red kite – a bird happily still common in this part of Burgundy and noted for the extreme beauty of its flight. Buffon writes:

One cannot but admire the manner in which he accomplishes it; his long narrow wings seem to be motionless; it is the tail which appears to direct his every movement, and it is never still. He rises without effort, sinks as if sliding down an inclined plane; he seems more to swim than to fly; he gains speed, slows up, stops and remains hanging on the air, fixed in the same place for hours on end without one's detecting the slightest movement of his wings.

Buffon was lucky both in his wife and in his friends. In 1752, when he was forty-five, he married Françoise de Saint-Belin-Malain, who was twenty. 'Her enthusiasm for his talent', wrote Condorcet, 'eclipsed in the eyes of Madame de Buffon the inequality of age, and he had the good fortune to inspire in her a passion that was at once tender, constant, cloudless and undiluted; each new work of her husband, each new palm added to his glory, was a source of renewed rejoicing in her.'

We know less about Buffon's affection for his wife, but he was certainly a man who understood the art of friendship; perhaps he knew no greater pleasure than the prospect of a visit from the Président Charles de Brosses. 'How deliciously exciting is the prospect of having you here all to myself at Montbard for three of four days. I seem to have a hundred thousand things to say to you, and as many sentiments to express . . . I will think every day of your coming to Montbard. If you give me two days' notice I will send horses. Leaving Dijon at five or six in the morning you could be here

for dinner and we will dine at our ease and my joy will be complete.'
His chef Guenot was reputedly one of the best cooks in France.

His house at Montbard, Number 1, Place Buffon, still stands. It
was described in an enthusiastic account of a visit to Montbard by
Hérault de Séchelles in 1785. 'With what palpitations of joy was I
seized when I first perceived in the distance the Tour de Montbard,
with the terraces and gardens which surrounds it! With eager eyes I
sought out the château; they could not be too eager to see the
dwelling of the famous man with whom I was going to talk. One
cannot distinguish the château until one is before it, but instead of a
'château' you are to imagine yourself entering a house in Paris.'
There were twelve separate *appartements* but the building lacked
regularity, he complained, 'and although this defect must make it
more commodious than beautiful, it is nevertheless not devoid of
beauty'.

From the house they proceeded to a tour of the gardens, which
were cast into thirteen terraces, climbing the steep slope of the hill
beneath the old castle. From the summit 'one discovers an immense
panorama, with magnificent views, prairies across which the rivers
cut, vineyards and sunny, cultivated slopes, and the whole of
Montbard'. He was shown an aviary in which Buffon kept birds from
foreign parts which he was studying, and a part of an old moat in
which he had kept lions and bears.

But the real object of Séchelles's visit was to see the Cabinet de
Travail in the old Tour de Saint-Louis, the scene of so many of
Buffon's labours. He was astonished at the simplicity of the room.
Beneath its high, Gothic vault was placed 'a bad wooden desk and an
armchair. That was all! Not a book, not a sheet of paper. But do you
not find something impressive about this nudity? One clothes it with
the beautiful writings of Buffon, with the magnificence of his style
and the admiration which it inspires.'

In fact this room was unheated and used only in high summer.
There was another room, panelled and almost papered with pictures
of his birds. It was here that Rousseau went down on his knees to kiss
the threshold of the great man's study. Buffon, however, had no such
admiration for Rousseau. 'Je l'aimais assez', he said, 'mais lorsque
j'ai vu ses *Confessions* je cessai de l'estimer. Son âme m'a revolté.'

Hérault de Séchelles had an almost exaggerated admiration for
Buffon. At a merely social level, however, people sometimes found
him a bore. To Madame du Deffand his conversation was 'of an

unbearable monotony; what he knows he knows, but he concerns himself only with animals; one has to partake of the animal to be devoted to such an occupation'.

The salons of an élite society were no place for such a man; it was in the deep silences of the countryside that he was most truly himself. 'I have often passed the entire day in the forest,' he wrote, 'where one is obliged to listen with attention in order to pick up the distant sound of the horn and the voices of men and hounds.'

Although possessed of a large fortune, Buffon was not averse to using his scientific knowledge to his own financial gain. In 1767 he was writing his *Histoire Naturelle des Minéraux* and occupied in making experiments with heat, and in particular with the action of fire on iron. He finally succeeded in making 'from our worst mines in Burgundy an iron as fine as that from Sweden or Spain'. This was the year of the foundation of the Forges de Buffon, where he gave employment to some 400 workmen, for whom he was obliged to build accommodation. 'This forge is situated at a distance of one league from Montbard', wrote Gabriel Jars, inspecteur des forges of Burgundy:

and a quarter of a league from the village of Buffon a little downstream of the confluence of the two rivers of the Brenne and the Armançon, the first coming from Montbard and the second from Semur. Monsieur de Buffon has managed to profit from the advantage of these two rivers so that he is never short of water; he recognized the necessity arising from the lack of declivity of these rivers and what he could not obtain from their fall he has gained from their volume.

It remains one of the most interesting architectural ensembles. Beside the forge proper is a vast quadrangle of buildings of differing height and size according to their function; low, single-storey dwellings for the workmen, larger, more distinguished houses for the maître de forge and the steward, vast halls for the storing of iron and fuel, a long range of buildings for the stables and a small chapel.

Buffon's views on religion are not easy to collate. Hérault de Séchelles claimed Buffon's own authority for saying that on principle he always respected religion because the people – and by that he meant the common people – had need of one. But the dogmas of a Church which had not yet seriously doubted that the act of Creation was accomplished in six days were bound to be in conflict with his ever-increasing realization of the immeasurable antiquity of the universe.

In 1749 Buffon's *Histoire Naturelle* was attacked by the Jansenists for setting man at the top of the same ladder as that of the animal kingdom. This, they claimed, was inconsistent with the words of Genesis, 'words which give us our finest titles to nobility and which remove us as far from the animals as they bring us close to God'. Buffon gave the doctors of the Sorbonne his assurance that he 'had no intention of contradicting the text of Scripture' and classed his hypothesis on the formation of planets as 'une pure supposition philosophique'.

Buffon has been accused by the intellectuals of hypocrisy, but his religion was not really inconsistent with his thought. It was typical of him to regard materialism as a temporary phase in the development of thought – one of those hypotheses which would serve their purpose for a while and would be ultimately discarded. The materialist's conception of the nature of man did not account for what was noblest in man, for, paradoxically, 'humanism', which in theory exalts Man as 'the measure of all things', tends to reduce the human to the level of the animal. Buffon saw another dimension in Man: 'Animals are in certain respects the products of earth,' he wrote; 'Man is always the creation of Heaven.' Those words were not spoken to pacify the doctors of the Sorbonne, for, unlike them, Buffon saw no necessary divergence between science and religion. 'Chaque nouveau pas que nous faisons dans la nature', he wrote, 'nous rapproche du Créateur.'

On 15 April 1788, Buffon died in the arms of Madame Necker, whom he believed, *in extremis*, to be his confessor, Ignace. His last words were those of a true Christian: 'Je déclare que je meurs dans la religion où je suis né, et j'atteste publiquement que je crois en Jésus Christ, descendu du Ciel pour le salut des hommes.'

If Buffon lends the distinction of his name to Montbard, that of another eminent scientist of the eighteenth century, Gaspard Monge, is chiefly associated with Beaune. Professor of mathematics at Mezières and a member of the Académie des Sciences at Dijon, Monge was the author of an important treatise on the founding of steel and another on the making of cannons. From 1792 to 1793 he was Ministre de la Marine, but his real interest was in education. He founded the Ecole Polytechnique with the encouragement of Napoleon. When Napoleon became emperor the pupils of the

Polytechnique refused to congratulate him. Monge defended them by saying: 'We had a lot of trouble turning them into republicans; give them time to become imperialists. Besides, you must let me tell you that you have been rather quick in changing yourself.'

The central square in Beaune, overlooked by the fourteenth-century belfry with its corona bristling with pinnacles, is named after Monge.

Beaune and the Côte d'Or

Situated at the heart of the Côte d'Or, the city of Beaune is one of the most interesting and charming in all Burgundy. 'It has none of those antique ruins,' wrote Arnoux in 1728, 'or cold relics which the air consumes and which time will reduce to ashes; it glories only in its good wines which give each year to the citizens of Beaune their renewed riches. Nevertheless it was, a century ago, a fortified town; it is still surrounded by a deep moat which is supplied with water by the river Bourgeoise which springs from a source half a mile distant at the foot of one of the hills.'

For the same hills which provided the inhabitants with their wines, furnished them also with a natural supply of little streams 'clair comme du cristal fondu'. The purity of the water contributed to the quality of the bread – 'le plus léger et le meilleur de toute la France'. The cattle also were neither so large nor so fat as those of England, but the flavour of the meat was more delicate; the game was delicious – a quality which Arnoux attributes to the abundance of thyme and marjoram in the pastures; their wine was the best in all the world, not only for its gastronomic value, but for its health-giving properties. 'The gout and disease are banished from these walls.' It was the wines of Romanée Saint-Vivant which had been prescribed for Louis XIV to restore him after his operation for the fistula. It was no less a man than Louis Pasteur who stated: 'Le vin est la plus saine et la plus hygiénique des boissons.'

With the decline in monasticism in the course of the sixteenth century, the vineyards began to pass into the hands of the citizens of Dijon. In 1621 Pierre Monnyot acquired the Clos de Bèze from the chapter of Langres. In the following year Jean Bouhier, son of the builder of the Hôtel de Vogüé, purchased the Clos de la Perriere at Fixin from the abbey of Cîteaux. In 1625 Jacques Venot, conseiller à la Chambre des Comptes, bought from the abbey of Saint-Vivant the little part of their vineyard which was to become the Romanée-Conti.

In 1760 it was purchased by the prince de Conti, from whom it takes its name. 'The prince used to make gifts of it to those whom he honoured by his kindness,' wrote a certain Monsieur de Cussy; 'In 1782 he gave some to Monseigneur de Juigné, archbishop of Paris. It was through his generosity that we were lucky enough to make the acquaintance of this precious wine – qui est tout à la fois du velours et du satin.'

During the Revolution the vineyard was confiscated and a report made to the Commissioners:

We cannot conceal the fact that the wine of the Romanée-Conti is the most excellent of all those of the Côte d'Or and even of all the vineyards of the French Republic. Its colour, brilliant but mellow, its scent and its flavour charm all the senses. This wine, if well cared for and well conditioned, arriving at its eighth or tenth year, continues to improve in quality. It is the balm of the aged, the feeble and the infirm and would give new life to the dying.

It is, of course, its situation which gives it this perfection – the most advantageous position for the fruit to attain the most perfect maturity. 'Plus élevé a l'occident qu'à l'orient, elle présente son sein aux premiers rayons du soleil, ce qui les procure les impulsions de la plus douce chaleur du jour.' The quality of a wine depends largely upon the quality of the soil, the orientation of the vineyard, the skill of the vigneron and, of course, the weather.

It is interesting to see how the Church was constantly called upon to put its spiritual authority at the service of the vigneron. François de Dinteville, bishop of Auxerre, made a somewhat original approach to the problem of frost. 'Ce noble Pontiffe', wrote Rabelais, 'aimait le bon vin.' To protect the vines from the late frosts he set about reordering the calendar of the Church, concentrating the *fêtes* of those saints who were supposed to concern themselves with frost, into the season immediately following Christmas, 'giving them licence', continues Rabelais, 'to freeze then and to freeze as hard as they liked, for frost at that time of the year could do no damage but is clearly profitable for budding'.

Spring was one of the most anxious moments for the vignerons, for a late frost followed by a clear sun could scorch the buds 'as if', wrote Arnoux in 1728, 'the fire had passed over them'. To avoid this, the peasants, then as always superstitious, would go on cold, still nights into the churches and ring the bells with all their might, 'supposing either that God might take note of this work of piety, or that the agitation which they caused in the air might somehow warm the air or change the direction of the wind. For whatever reason, they ring the bells during this season in such a manner that it is impossible to sleep.' The clergy felt it appropriate to read the Passion according to St John, but they did not give their services free. 'They take collections at all the presses when the wine is being made, and each vigneron is obliged to give them a certain quantity of wine.'

By the end of the eighteenth century the vineyards were all under lay ownership and the familiar titles of the Côte d'Or were fully established.

The Côte d'Or stretches for some 60 kilometres between Santenay and Marsanny, just short of Dijon. It begins with the great names of Chassagne-Montrachet and Puligny-Montrachet which share between them the greatest of all Burgundian whites; Le Montrachet, of which Alexandre Dumas said that it should be drunk in the posture of prayer – on one's knees and with head uncovered. A little further north is Meursault. In the eighteenth century, Cardinal Bernis – Madame de Pompadour's beloved 'petit abbé' – always celebrated Mass with a choice Meursault because, as he explained, 'he did not wish to grimace when confronting his Lord'. Volnay, of a delicate colour known as *oeil de perdrix*, Pommard, Beaune and Aloxe-Corton produce some of the best red wines of the Côte de Beaune and Corton-Charlemagne yields a white wine which, at its best, is second only to Montrachet.

The Côte de Nuits begins with its greatest names, those of the Vosne-Romanée. As the great historian of Burgundy, Courtépée, wrote in 1777, 'there are no common wines in Vosne'. Besides the Romanée-Conti, the names of La Tâche, Richebourg and Grands-Echezaux are names of magic to anyone who has been privileged to sample them.

A little further along the road is the Clos de Vougeòt, surrounding the palatial buildings of the abbots of Cîteaux. One must picture Colonel Bisson, in the days of the Revolution, making his troops salute the vineyard as they marched past. The name of the place is Clos *de* Vougeot, but the wine drops the particle and becomes Clos Vougeot.

Next comes Chambolle-Musigny, another red of great distinction, among which the names of two *premiers crus*, 'Les Amoureuses' and 'Les Charmes', seem to speak for themselves. The last of the great names is Chambertin, coupled with that of Clos de Bèze. It was Napoleon's favourite wine. He took a supply of it with him to Russia and after the fall of Moscow drank it in the Kremlin.

In 1878 the Côte d'Or was attacked by phylloxera, a burrowing louse which breeds at an incredible speed. It came from America and from America came also the remedy, for American stocks are immune against its attacks. The red Pinot Noir and the white Chardonnay could be grafted upon American stocks, thus enabling the replantation of the vineyards. But in many areas there are today no vines grown where once they were plentiful. The Côte d'Or used to extend to the very gates of Dijon.

The parliamentary châteaux

The beautiful town houses of the patricians have made Dijon one of the most distinguished and fascinating of provincial cities. Many of the greatest of these *hôtels particuliers* were the creation of the seventeenth century. It was the great age of town life. The country, so often and so lately devastated by war, offered no rival attractions except to the owners of great châteaux. 'Nous sommes ici dans un pays perdu', wrote Pierre Taisand in 1680; 'our only intercourse is with wolves.' In those days the cities offered refuge from the horrors of the country, not vice versa.

'Beati qui habitant urbes', 'Happy are those who inhabit the cities', wrote Genreau in 1662 in his eulogy of Dijon: 'In my dread of the disorders [of rural life] I contemplated the beauty of Dijon with its police, its justice, with its devotion to the wealth and well-being of its churches, so well decorated and so well served; I thought of the pleasant conversation, of the civility, the honour, the charity' – and he ends in a lyrical outburst: 'Dijon, que je te chéris! Dijon, que tu es aimable! Dijon, que Dieu te bénisse!'

In the eighteenth century, however, there was a movement back to the land. The parliamentary families, secure in their wealth and in their civic status, began to want to seat themselves in the country. The necessary complement to the study of these *hôtels particuliers* is that of the little ring of châteaux, some of them quite small but all of them beautiful, built or rebuilt usually in an easy proximity to Dijon.

Albert Colombet, who has made a special study of this movement, paints the picture for us.

Thus, when the first sun of summer began to raise the green corn, when the hay perfumed the meadows and when the first fruits were beginning to ripen in the orchards, the Palais was deserted, the austere town houses were abandoned, our patricians dispersed themselves throughout Burgundy and opened their windows to the smell of summer. They were all lovers of country life, and also it was their opportunity for overseeing the cultivation of their estates. Their lands provided the basis for their power.

Colombet made the significant discovery that among all the transactions concerning the purchase of property towards the end of the eighteenth century there is not a single record of the sale of land by one of these families. They wanted to buy land and they wanted to hold on to it. Not infrequently those who sold were members of the old aristocracy. In 1785 Verchère d'Arcelot bought the estate of Magny-Saint-Médard from the prince de Beauffremont.

The interest of these families in the running of their estates is revealed even in their most official correspondence. The Premier Président Legouz de Saint-Seine, writing to Filsjean de Talmay on serious matters, could not forbear from commenting on the weather and its consequences for agriculture, in June bemoaning the heavy rain and 'meadows lost in the water and vines which have hardly fared better' and in July rejoicing over a 'very fine spell which will prosper the hay-making and repair some of the damage done by the floods'.

Bénigne Legouz de Saint-Seine was to be the last premier président before the Revolution. Between the years 1771 and 1789 he can be seen quietly consolidating the estates on the banks of the Vingeanne – Sainte-Seine l'Eglise, Saint-Seine la Tour, Saint-Seine les Halles – from which he took his title 'as if', comments Colombet, 'his ambition was to become a feudal lord'.

On 31 July 1777, Saint-Seine was elected premier président, a position which made him *ex officio* proprietor of the Château de Vantoux in much the same way that the Prime Minister in England is *ex officio* proprietor of Chequers.

The Château de Vantoux

No chateau in Burgundy is more directly connected with the parliamentary scene than Vantoux. Yves Beauvalot, one of the great authorities on the subject, has identified in its decoration the statement of a position, an architectural assertion of the claims of the magistrature *vis-à-vis* those of the king.

For there was a long history of resistance to royal commands by the parlement de Dijon. In 1658 the Premier Président Brulart refused to register certain edicts and boldly confronted the young Louis XIV with the words: 'Sire, I kneel only before God who is my master and yours.' He was imprisoned in the fortress of Perpignan. Years later, after his return, he was again confronted by the prince de Condé, governor of Burgundy, with a demand ro register the same edicts. But Brulart was immovable; 'Monseigneur,' he said, 'je vois d'ici les tours de Perpignan.'

The king maintained that he held his crown direct from God and that he was responsible to no human court, which is what Charles I had tried to maintain in England. A law approved by the king became a law, so ran the formula, 'car tel est notre bon plaisir'. On the other side the parliamentarians maintained the supremacy of justice – a law by which even the king was bound. But the prison doors of Perpignan, Pignerolo and the Bastille awaited those who openly opposed the king. The point could only be made by more subtle means, and Jean de Berbisey used the decoration of the Château de Vantoux for the expression of his beliefs.

His family had owned Vantoux for most of the seventeenth century. In 1622 they had been ennobled. 'Duly informed of the great extent of the lands of the said Vantoux, composed of a large village ornamented by a fine château accompanied by several fiefs,' Louis XIII conferred upon its owner 'the title, name, dignity, honour, prerogatives and pre-eminences of a barony'. The 'fine château' was 'moated and furnished with towers and a drawbridge'. In 1673 we know that the obligation of the villagers to provide 'watch and ward' was still in force.

The rebuilding of the château began with the outbuildings which lie to the north of the moat. In particular these contained the chapel and a 'maison du fermier' together with cellars hollowed out of the rock 'très bonnes à garder les vins'. The care bestowed upon the *communs* was typical. 'The parliamentarians', Colombet noted, 'took more trouble over the "bâtiments utiles" than over the "logis de plaisance".' That is hardly true of Vantoux, however, for here the 'logis de plaisance' received a very particular emphasis.

The house bears certain affinities with the Château de Navarre, built near Evreux for the duc de Bouillon in 1702. Navarre was square in plan, with four entrance vestibules opening into a central rotunda – a disposition clearly copied from Marly. Neither the plan nor the façades of Vantoux, however, resemble Marly, for there an elaborate architecture of marble pilasters and bas-reliefs was painted in *trompe-l'oeil* upon the walls; here at Vantoux the architecture is extremely simple and its decoration achieved in three dimensions.

The house stands superbly upon the platform of masonry which marks the site of the feudal fortress. Its main façades, facing east and west, are of seven windows and those to north and south of five.

On the east front the architect has placed his emphasis on the first floor by making the windows slightly taller and increasing their apparent height by means of an attached balustrade beneath them. He has further accentuated the windows of the Grand Salon, or Cabinet d'Assemblée, by bringing them down to floor level behind a real balcony. Above the central window the bust of Apollo is framed by the arching of the lintel; to occupy the same space above the windows to either side the architect has placed a rectangular bas-relief over each. The whole frontispiece breaks forward slightly and is crowned by a pediment. Above the cornice the balustrade stands on a parapet deep enough to contain attic windows. It is an architecture which relies for effect on its proportions and on the fine quality of its execution. Ornament is restricted to those elements of the façade on which the architect wished to place a slight emphasis.

The subject-matter does not at first sight seem remarkable. The bust of Apollo reminds us that Mansart, who was working in Dijon at the time and was in all probability consulted about the design of Vantoux even if he was not actually the architect, had been responsible for the final enlargement of Versailles. In the little bas-reliefs to either side Apollo is seen slaying the serpent Python, representing evil, and pursuing Daphne, who represented purity. The consoles which uphold the balcony over the triple entrance arch show Jupiter with his eagle, Juno with her peacock and Cybele with her lion's skin. It is all very much what one would expect.

But Yves Beauvalot has suggested that in these symbolic figures there is a significance deeper than the mere routine reproduction of classical themes. Apollo was, in particular, the god of justice. Jean de Berbisey, as premier président, embodied the law and tried to establish its position as one to which the king's power itself should be subject. In this presidential house the decorations may be saying something about the position proper to a président. Juno, Jupiter and Cybele could stand for the supremacy of justice over all other matters.

The opposite side, the west front, takes up a different theme – the independence of virtue, symbolized by Diana. 'By means of this decoration, at once coherent and unique,' writes Beauvalot,

it is evident that the Président de Berbisey wished to underline the nobility of his judiciary commission and the salutary role of the parlement. It is not too rash to think that he was trying at the same time to give to this institution a place which the monarchy was never willing to accord it and a right which Louis XIV and his successors would always contest . . . The decorative side of the château increases the already considerable interest of this building and recalls the struggles of the parlement de Bourgogne with Louis XIV, from whom Jean de Berbisey dared to borrow his emblem while giving it a new significance.

The same approach can be made to the decorations of the Cabinet d'Assemblée on the first floor. The overdoors represent Justice, Prudence, Temperance and Strength – the qualities expected by Berbisey of the magistrature.

This room, sometimes known also as the 'Salon Bleu', which has been beautifully and accurately restored by the late comte Xavier de Saint-Seine, is the architectural climax to the reception suite. The principles of progressive decoration have been suggested by Charles-Etienne Brisieux in his book *L'Art de Bâtir*: 'The first rooms of the apartment, beginning with the vestibules, ought to satisfy the eye rather by the nobility of their forms than by the richness of their ornaments, and the skilful architect ought to content the curiosity of the spectators by gradual degrees, so that as they advance through the rooms, so they find them more and more richly decorated.'

The building of the château was completed by 1704, for the parish registers record that on 30 April the eve of the Ascension, 'le Château de Vantoux a été achevé et la bénédiction faite par moi, curé de Messigny'.

Jean de Berbisey had half a century in which to enjoy his creation and died in 1756, having bequeathed the house and property to his successors in the presidency. 'I die the last of my family', he wrote in his will;

> nevertheless, not wishing that its memory should be wholly lost, and wishing even more to give to the company over which I have had the honour to preside for nearly thirty years some tokens of my respect and gratitude; considering also that the revenues attaching to the charge of premier président du parlement de Dijon are not sufficient to uphold the dignity thereof, I give and bequeath and incorporate unto the said charge of the premier président du parlement de Dijon in perpetuity the property and estate and seigneurie of Vantoux, of that of Hauteville de Saucy, together with the woods and dependences with all their appurtenances; my house at Dijon, 16 rue de la Chapelotte and the house adjoining thereunto.

Thus it was to remain until the Revolution. In 1789 the premier président was Bénigne Legouz de Saint-Seine, whose descendants are the present owners of Vantoux.

One of the most distinguished of presidential houses in Dijon was one of the shortest lived, the Château de Montmusard, of which only a part of one of the wings survives, incorporated into the building of the Ecole Saint-Dominique.

The Château de Montmusard

Montmusard – 'le Mont des Muses' – was famous as a garden before the château was built which was, for a short time, to eclipse even the reputation of its garden. As early as 1729, Claude-Philibert Fyot, marquis de la Marche and later premier président du parlement, began to lay out the 50 hectares (123 acres) of land to the east of Dijon which belonged to his family as a pleasure garden, which he was pleased to open to the public.

'C'était les délices de Dijon,' wrote Clément-Janin; 'the Président de la Marche had worked wonders at Montmusard – still waters and gushing fountains, bosquets thick with flowers, enchanted grottoes, bowling greens, labyrinths, pavilions, aviaries, statues – all that the caprice of a man of taste could dream of that was most fantastic and most charming, was united here on this little hillside.' Above all the gardens contained a kiosk, a pavilion in which, Clément-Janin informs us, was 'a very ingenious machine, by means of which the table arrived from the depths of the kitchen, fully laden, to the dining-room. The larks did not therefore fall, ready roasted, into the mouth of Monsieur de la Marche, they came up into it which is the same thing even if it is the opposite.' This example of a *table volante* must be linked with that at the Petit Château at Choisy-le-Roi and the one designed, but never executed, for the Petit Trianon.

Claude-Philibert pulled down the old house and began to build a new one, but in 1757 he made it all over to his son, Jean-Philippe, re-signing his position as premier président in his favour. Jean-Philippe was not content with his father's plans for the new house, of which the foundations had already been laid, and in 1763 he summoned Charles de Wailly, later to be the architect of the Odéon, to Dijon and commis-sioned him to design a Pavillon des Muses. The Abbé Fabarel, grand chantre at the cathedral of Saint-Bénigne, who can be seen in the fore-ground of Lallemand's painting, was put in charge of the operation and was sent to Italy to consult the most famous artists and architects; François Devosges designed the bas-reliefs and undertook the decoration of the salon. In 1769 it was completed.

The plan conceived by de Wailly was as audacious as it was original. Two circular areas, one an open peristyle, the other an enclosed salon, were joined by a vestibule with deep-set niches to fill the spaces created by the circumference of the salon, with which it communicated by means of an oval ante-room. The salon was covered by a dome the base of which was encircled by a whispering gallery. These round or elliptical elements were enclosed between two rectangular wings which contained the apartments.

'Ce monument est un des plus agréables qu'il soit possible de voir', wrote Pierre-Joseph Antoine; 'on voit au premier coup d'oeil que c'est le palais des Muses.' Its fame spread throughout France and even reached Russia, where the Empress Catherine II dreamt of building 'a pavilion in the taste of that of the premier président de Dijon, dedicated to Minerva'. Her project, however, remained a dream.

Jean-Philippe was able to enjoy his creation for only three years, for in 1772 he died, a ruined man. During the Revolution Montmusard was sold and almost totally destroyed. It was knocked down to a man named Antony for 100,000 livres; 'the park wall alone', commented Clément-Janin, 'had cost more than that . . . he could not wait to plough the whole place up.'

Montmusard was something in the nature of a folly – part town house, part country house, and it stands alone. The most significant architecture of the eighteenth century was the result of a movement towards the country by the parliamentary aristocracy of Dijon.

261

Among the most prominent of these were Antoine-Louis Verchère d'Arcelot, Pierre Filsjean (sometimes spelt as it is pronounced, 'Fijan') de Talmay and Jean-Claude-Baptiste Suremain de Flammerens. These were the proprietors respectively of the châteaux of Arcelot, Talmay and Missery, which provide typical examples of how the rich parliamentary families seated themselves in the country.

The Château d'Arcelot

If Montmusard and Vantoux were built with an eye to the giving of large receptions, Arcelot was designed for *la douceur de vivre* on a fairly small scale. The records of the building of Arcelot, contained in the archives, give ample evidence of the extreme care and attention to detail bestowed by Philibert de Verchère and exacted by him of his entrepreneurs.

The site was chosen well and wisely. The road from Dijon runs straight as an arrow aimed at the front door of the château, which stands on a slight eminence and is thus visible a long way off. It is one of the most impressive approaches that could have been contrived. This part of Burgundy is for the most part flat and uninteresting, but the park at Arcelot has enough rise and fall to make an attractive landscape. Behind the château the land slopes down to what is today a lake and rises again to a wooded hillside which forms a pleasing prospect from the house. There is almost a suggestion of Capability Brown about the scene.

It had not always been thus. In the eighteenth century the little stream which now forms the lake was regimented into a long canal; there were formal parterres and intersecting alleys. The earliest plan shows all this but with a gap in the middle where the château proper was to stand. This suggests that the plan dates from just before the building was started in 1761.

In the previous year Verchère had obtained detailed descriptions of a number of trees. They were mostly from the New World: 'la chêne de Virginie; le noyer blanc du Mississippi, un très joli petit arbre; le grand érable de Canada'. To these were added the acacia – 'of all robust trees the one of which the leaf is the most beautiful, the most brilliant and the most agreeable green'.

Now these are not the trees of a *jardin français*; they are not the sort

that can be disciplined into the walls of verdure and square-cut
alleys of Vaux-le-Vicomte and Versailles. Monsieur Plichon, 'Dir-
ecteur Général des Arbres', refers in a letter to 'le nouvel arrangement de votre bosquet'. It is at least possible that Verchère's choice
of trees implies a lay-out, to which an undated plan may well refer,
that was in the very latest fashion for gardens. Somewhat typically,
Verchère had written to Plichon enclosing a large order for trees
and some careful instructions: 'Lose no time to get them to me as
promptly and in as perfect condition as possible . . . one cannot
take too much care in uprooting them and in seeing that they are
not damaged in transit.'

Having settled the new plantations, Verchère now turned his
attention to the building of his château. The plan already
mentioned left blank the space which is occupied by the main
building today; it shows the two smaller-scale wings and capacious
outbuildings.

These wings were the subject of controversy between Philibert de
Verchère and his architect Thomas Dumorey. No architect likes to
be constrained by existing buildings and Dumorey wanted to pull
down the old wings. In May 1761, however, it was decided that 'the
two pavilions of the Château d'Arcelot were built long ago in far
too simple a style . . . but since they contain a large chapel and
several lodgings, it was thought best to conserve them and to marry
them with the new buildings by means of two small staircases'.

The house built was almost as it stands today – a fine example of
the dignity of simplicity and the first appearance of the neo-
classical style in Burgundy. The façade is divided into three
sections, with the central portion breaking slightly forward. It rises
higher than its two attendant pavilions so that its boldly projecting
cornice rides clear of the rather low parapets. Above the cornice the
impressive sweep of the mansard roof forms a striking contrast with
the low-pitched roofs to either side. This feature needed special
attention to the disposition of its timbers and the carpenter had
precise instructions to make this *avant corps* 'in the form of a pavilion
with a mansard roof so as to make the pavilion dominate as a
frontispiece'.

The house was built between 1761 and 1765, during which years
a considerable expenditure was recorded for masonry and
brickwork. The building must have progressed fast for by October
1761 there are already accounts for glazing. In 1765 the centre of

activity shifted to 'les pavillons pour les basses cours'. We can assume that the building of the main block was in all important respects finished by that date.

The decorations also were well in hand if not completed. The marbles for the Grand Salon were being worked in Paris by a 'Monsieur Robert, fils, maître sculpteur et marbrier'. The main item was the fireplace – 'une cheminée de marbre brèche violet' – which cost Verchère 800 livres.

Monsieur Robert was not left without supervision, for Dumorey wrote to a colleague in Paris: 'M. d'Arcelot, qui parle par ma plume, vous prie de jeter de temps en temps un coup d'oeil sur la cheminée que lui fait M. Robert.' He was to ensure that great care was to be taken that it should be executed 'in conformity with the model in clay that I have had made'. The carved decorations were to be 'bien recherchées' but the high quality of craftsmanship must not be at the expense of speed – 'le tout fait dans la moindre délai qu'il sera possible'.

The stuccators working in the salon needed a model and M. Robert was to send it to them as quickly as possible. A Monsieur Chasle was doing the medallion of Minerva, which is still to be seen over the fireplace of the salon; he was to receive the plan of it 'que j'ai copié exactement sur place'.

The same meticulous standards were demanded for the woodwork. It was to be 'en bon bois de chêne' that had been seasoned for at least five years. Before positioning, the pieces chosen were to be carefully inspected for any defect – no sap-wood, no splitting, no 'defectuous knots' nor anything 'qui pourrait déplaire audit seigneur'.

In July 1763 the parquet flooring was being laid. Verchère, vigilant as ever, required that 'tous ces ouvrages seront fait avec le plus grand soin et avec les plus beaux bois'. Between April 1763 and March 1766 he had spent a total of 5,347 livres on the woodwork. The result of all this care and attention was to be one of the finest rooms in any château in Burgundy, the Grand Salon of Arcelot.

The effect is achieved by an alteration of tall panels, imitating the marble of the fireplace, and the bays formed by the doorways and chimneypieces. In each of these bays a large console against the cornice surmounts a bas-relief achieved with the delicacy of a cameo. Over one fireplace is the face of Minerva and over the corresponding one the profile of Louis XV. These medallions are oval and surrounded by palm leaves; those over the doors are rectangular and swagged with laurel. A room such as this owes as much to its furniture and pictures as to its architecture. Here both are wholly appropriate.

In the chapel is a monument erected by Antoine-Louis Verchère d'Arcelot to his wife, who died at the age of twenty, 'après deux ans et demi de l'union la plus tendre'. One feels that Arcelot was built as a place to be loved and lived in, but not without a certain stateliness of style. It has something to say about the art of living.

The Château de Talmay

The building of Talmay by Pierre Filsjean has something to say about the attitude of the new patricians towards the feudal lords into whose shoes they sometimes stepped. At Talmay a tall tower dating from the thirteenth century still stood, crowned with a lofty pyramid roof, on one corner of the moated platform of the château. It stood obliquely, like the towers of Sully. Filsjean was clearly determined to retain this vestige of the feudal castle and his architects were faced with the problem of accommodating the new house with the old tower. No less than eight projects, involving eight architects, exist in the Talmay archives. The solution of the problem was bound to lie either in the use of triangular courtyards or of triangular rooms.

Unfortunately Filsjean's comments on these successive designs have not survived. Presumably he had grounds for rejecting all but the final, successful one. The *projet Lenoir* shows two blocks at right angles to each other with a triangular court linking them to the tower. The larger wing was to contain a 'Salon à l'Italienne'. The *projet Caristie* leaves no court but fills the gaps between house and tower with triangular ante-rooms. The façades were simple and the disposition of the rooms carefully thought out: each bedroom was to be part of a little suite with a *cabinet* and a *garderobe* which contained a bed for a servant.

The *projet Bizot* was far more grandiose, with a heavy mansart roof unrelieved by dormer windows. The *projet Legouz de Gerland* introduces a balustrade with urns and groups of figures on the skyline. Finally, in 1772, comes the design of Daviler which shows the house more or less as built. Daviler was a Parisian somewhat advanced in age and he did not live to see his project realized. It was left to Caristie to carry the work to a conclusion.

It is a very successful design, dignified without being ostentatious and simple without being dull. Two short wings advance on either side of the entrance court and enframe the façade. They have received the most careful treatment by the architect. Two round-arched windows, one above the other, with strongly moulded surrounds, are each slightly recessed in a rectangular frame. The panel thus formed is again slightly recessed between two vertical bands of rusticated masonry the full height of the façade. This feature is repeated on all three sides of the projecting wings with the angles rounded off between them. The shallow relief thus obtained makes a pleasing play of light and shade upon the façade.

These wings enclose an entrance front in which the central section breaks slightly forward. The ground floor of this frontispiece is rusticated and the windows are round-arched, in contrast with those to either side which are rectangular. It is by these subtle notes of variety that the façades are saved from dullness.

A colourful Burgundian roof, with large scrolled dormers and handsome leaden urns at the apex points, crowns the whole building. Behind it looms the rough masonry of the thirteenth-century tower. They form an amazing contrast – the beautiful and comfortable house of Filsjean and the crushingly large tower, some two and a half times its height.

The retention of such a tower was a common feature in châteaux of the French Renaissance whose builders were anxious to identify themselves with their feudal forbears. For feudal rights continued to pass into the hands of the purchasers. Many of the new seigneurs had rights of *haute et basse justice* entailing the right to erect a gallows. One must not imagine that they were in continual use. In March 1760, Louis XV wrote to 'Notre cher et bien aimé François David Bollioud' at the Château de Fontaine-Française granting permission to re-erect the gallows 'pour inspirer la crainte et retenir les licences des crimes'. Richard Gascon, however, the historian of Fontaine-Française, could find no record of their having ever been used, but the old intendant, Louis Magnieux, told him that his uncle, who died in 1832, could still remember three men being hanged – 'but they were foreigners', he commented, 'believed to be of Spanish origin'.

What is more strange is that there appears to have been no

financial advantage in claiming feudal lordship. The principle *Justicia magnum emolumentum est* ('Justice is a great source of revenue') does not seem to have been maintained. Alexandre Mairetet de Minot was probably not alone in finding that 'the income from fines and confiscations does not suffice to pay the wages of my officers of justice'.

These feudal rights were seldom grievous, but they created a sense of inferiority in those who were no longer content to be called 'vassals'. There were rights of *péage* (toll) and the obligation to use the lord's mill, bread oven and wine press. The most unpopular in this region was the *droit de banvin* by which the seigneur could choose the days for the vendanges of his own vineyards and forbid his tenants to work on theirs until they had finished his. The Legouz at Jancigny exchanged this right for the *droit de pêche* on the grounds that fishing 'was only of use to a few idle people'. The Legouz family had a good reputation for liberality and good works.

It looks as if Filsjean was trying to claim, or at least to proclaim, his feudal status at Talmay, but he lived in an age in which feudal rights were beginning to look increasingly obsolete. The villagers of Talmay took him to court over the *banalité du four* which obliged them to bake at the common bread oven. A lawyer named Poinçot espoused their cause. 'The return to liberty is greatly in your interest', he wrote to the inhabitants; 'especially in the present century when the rights of man and of the citizen, whoever he may be, are better known than ever and the will of the majority of the inhabitants assembled represents the general will.' Those words were written in 1786. They are already in the language of the Revolution.

Filsjean, however, was a generous and considerate lord. In 1778 the village of Talmay was all but destroyed by fire. He immediately provided money, clothing, medical aids and bandages and arranged for the sufferers to be released from paying the *taille*; they were also authorized to cut wood for the repair of their houses. But Filsjean was more lawyer than lord. 'I think that in the distribution of the charities', he wrote, 'one should have regard not only to the evaluation of the loss which each has suffered, but also to the extent of this loss in proportion to what each possessed and to what he was unable to save: in fact someone who possessed only 12 livres and has lost them all is in worse case than one who, having 200 livres, has lost only 120.'

The mind of the administrator is revealed also in one of his letters at this time. 'I will see if I can get someone on the cheap [à bon marché] who will establish the plan of the site which each house used to occupy in order to make a new distribution of the land in proportion to what each possessed, so that in rebuilding they are not all on top of one another as they used to be.'

Another parliamentarian who appeared anxious to make his way into the old aristocracy was Jean-Claude-Baptiste Suremain de Flammerens at the Château de Missery.

The Château de Missery

There is a painting at Missery which dates, judging by the style of the coach and the costumes of the figures in the foreground, from the early years of Louis XIV. It portrays the château as it was at that time.

The four towers, set in an ample moat, are clearly those which survive today. On the south side of the quadrangle a long *corps de logis* runs the whole length of the site, breaking forward into a square tower which rises high above the roof. Adjoining the south-east tower is a gatehouse with the usual equipment of a double drawbridge, one for vehicles and one for pedestrians, behind which rises a spire which must have belonged to a chapel. The figure surmounting the spire, however, bears a suspicious resemblance to Cupid. The god of love seems to have replaced the love of God.

But it is in the western range of buildings, the situation occupied by the present château, that the greatest interest lies. It presents to the courtyard two superimposed galleries with wooden supports, not unlike those of the Hospice de Beaune.

To this medieval habitation has been added a vast Renaissance garden. Two elaborate archways, each like the crowning of a gargantuan dormer window, mark the extremities of a balustraded walk along the northern arm of the moat. To the north of this lies an extensive walled garden centring upon a fine fountain surmounted by the figure of a woman who might be Ceres.

Behind the house and garden, the landscape is recognizable in spite of the liberties which the artist has taken. The two hills, with their corona of trees, have been moved further in, so that the coppice known as 'la Buchinelle' appears immediately behind the château and the 'Mont Rond', which in fact is some 4 kilometres to the north, has taken its place and shows vineyards, now long since vanished, on its eastern slope.

In 1653 the estate passed by marriage from the family de la Plume to that of Bernard de Bernard, président of the parliament at Dijon. In 1750 the family was heavily in debt and Missery had to be sold. It was bought by Suremain de Flammerens, who held the position of *conseiller* in the parliament. Seven years later he pulled down all the old buildings except for the four corner towers. As at Talmay, the retention of these towers as signs of the feudal *seigneurie* was significant, for Suremain de Flammerens insisted on the recognition of his rights as *seigneur*. These rights secured his title to nobility.

As at Talmay this led to a confrontation with some of the local inhabitants. They maintained that the new house which he built, being 'in the modern style', was no longer a fortress and therefore afforded no protection to his tenants. On these grounds they rejected their own obligation to repair the moat.

With its simple but dignified eighteenth-century façades and homely brown Burgundian roofs, Missery is a fine example of the provincial Louis XV style. An attempt was made to harmonize the architecture of the towers with that of the new building. The towers, being part of a defensive system, were provided with a minimum of windows and presented large surfaces of bare wall. This discrepancy of style was overcome by the expedient of painting in *trompe-l'oeil* a number of large and regularly spaced windows on the walls of the towers.

This may have been inspired by the similar treatment of the fifteenth-century towers at the Château de Longecourt-en-Plaine, which had been brought *au goût du jour* between 1757 and 1761 by the architect Nicolas Lenoir le Romain for another parliamentarian, Nicolas-Philippe Berbis. The façades at Longecourt were of brick and the simulated windows here were achieved in stucco.

By his preservation of his towers and his seigneurial rights, Suremain de Flammerens nearly lost his own life. He was arrested during the Revolution and imprisoned in the château at Dijon. It was not a propitious time to be trying to step into the shoes of the ancient aristocracy.

It is not possible to generalize about the relationships of the old nobility with the estates from which they drew a large part of their income. Arthur Young was pleased and surprised to find that at the

Château de Liancourt 'the mode of living and pursuits approach much nearer the habits of a great nobleman's house in England than would commonly be conceived' – in other words, the duc de Liancourt was improving the agriculture. Louis Dutens, after a visit to Chanteloup, claimed that 'the duc de Choiseul had given the French nation the first and best example of the happy effects of the nobility paying proper attention to their estates'. But there were many more whose only interest in their land was to make it provide the highest possible income to subsidize their living in Paris or at Versailles.

The result was that the land, more often than not, was bled dry by the owner. 'Great lords', grumbled Arthur Young, 'love too much an environ of forest, boars and huntsmen, instead of marking their residences by the accompaniment of neat and well-cultivated farms, clean cottages and happy peasants.' That would not have been a common sight in France. In 1766 Smollett was in Burgundy.

I saw a peasant ploughing the ground with a jack-ass, a lean cow and a he-goat yoked together. The peasants in France are so wretchedly poor, and so much oppressed by their landlords, that they cannot afford to enclose their grounds, or give a proper respite to their lands by letting them lie fallow, or to stock their farms with a sufficient number of black cattle to produce the necessary manure, without which agriculture can never be carried to any degree of perfection. Husbandry in France will never be generally improved until the farmer is free and independent.

It was to take a revolution to achieve that.

In Burgundy the house of Saulx-Tavanes, at the Château de Lux, pursued a policy of extortion which made it prudent for them to emigrate when the Revolution came. They did return when it was all over, but never re-established the position which they had enjoyed under the *ancien régime*. At Fontaine–Française, only 12 kilometres from Lux, the family of La Tour du Pin were in a much closer and healthier relationship with their tenants; they did not emigrate and were able to maintain their position well into the present century.

The Château de Fontaine-Française

'Fontaine-Française! Le joli nom!' With these words Madame de Chabrillan begins her eulogy:

Fontaine-Française! Charming name! A source from which wells up the thought of our beloved land. At the very heart of Burgundy, here where often the destiny of our history was decided; rich earth where passed our legendary kings, merry vignerons, noble ladies, mighty lords, men of letters and honest men of solid good sense and clear minds whose influence throughout the centuries has preserved our sound traditions. A happy destiny has made this place my home.

In the sixteenth century the château had been part of the vast estates of Claude de Longvy, Cardinal de Givry and bishop of Langres. He was also, as we have seen, responsible for much of the building of Pagny-le-Château and some of his enthusiasm for the architecture of the Renaissance was lent to the redecoration of Fontaine-Française. It passed through his niece to the house of Chabot-Charny and thence, through various alliances, to the great family of La Tour du Pin. In 1748 it formed part of the dowry of Anne-Madeleine-Louise-Charlotte de La Tour du Pin on her marriage to François Bollioud de Saint-Jullien. He held the lucrative post of receveur général of the clergy and was immensely rich. At the time of his marriage his fortune amounted to 1,810,359 livres, 2 sols and 5 deniers. Although a member of the lesser nobility he was considerably beneath the dignity of the La Tour du Pin family and it is said that while Anne-Madeleine was in labour producing their only son, she cried out 'Tant souffrir pour un petit Bollioud!'

In 1754 Saint-Jullien pulled down the old château and commissioned the architect Souhard to design a new one. Although there was here no visible retention of any portion of the former castle, as at Talmay and Missery, some of its walls are incorporated in the present fabric and account for their great thickness.

It is a palatial structure, built on a large scale and with a certain Augustan grandeur which is not diminished by its brown Burgundian roof. The two main façades are in distinctly different styles. On the entrance side, towards the north, the windows are widely spaced, leaving a large area of wall space between them. Those of the upper floor are crowned each with a neat little pediment and each opens on to a little balcony behind a delicate wrought iron grille. The central frontispiece carries an enormous pediment, enriched with armorial sculptures, above which rises a square-based dome, typical of the times, which is the central feature of the house. It is common to both façades and is almost the only feature which they share.

The garden front, which overlooks the lake, is of a heavier build. There are no pediments and no balconies. In the central portion, which breaks slightly forwards, the windows of both storeys are set into the masonry between shallow recessed panels. This panelling gives a moulded relief to the façade which creates a bold shadow projection in the westering sun.

The interior is all that one might expect of a house of that period built with little regard to expense – beautifully carved panelling and overdoors alternating with magnificent tapestries. But it was supremely the pictures which inspired Madame de Chabrillan. 'Looking at the portraits of our ancestors who have lived between these walls, one feels under the influence of their protective and beneficent force.' They surrounded her with a sense of contact with the past – 'comme un musée de belles histoires, celles de la France'.

Here, in the first salon, is the portrait of Françoise-Thérèse de Choiseul-Stainville, princesse de Monaco, and beneath it a chair upholstered in tapestry which she worked herself, only finishing it in the prison of La Force just before she mounted the scaffold. Her husband had emigrated, taking her with him, but they had to leave their two daughters in the care of their grandfather. She returned to France, hoping to be able to rejoin her children, but was promptly arrested and imprisoned. It was felt necessary even in that system, which was the negation of all justice, to produce a trumped-up charge on which the victims could be condemned. The most usual one was 'plotting'. Of this she was convicted and sent to the guillotine.

To gain enough time to write to her children she pretended to be pregnant. With a piece of broken glass she managed to cut off one of her locks to send to her daughters as a memento of 'your unhappy mother, who died loving you and whose only regret at leaving this life is that she can be no further use to you'.

At the same time she wrote to Fouquier-Tinville, enclosing the lock and admitting that her pregnancy was false.

Citoyen, je vous demande, au nom de l'humanité, de faire remettre ce pacquet à mes enfants ... Ayez regard à la demande d'une mère malheureuse qui meurt à l'âge du bonheur et qui laisse des enfants privés de leur seul ressource; qu'au moins ils reçoivent ce dernier témoignage de ma tendresse.

It was no use appealing to the humanity of Fouquier-Tinville, but as a scrupulous bureaucrat he filed the letter in the archives.

It was 9 Thermidor (29 July) 1794. The tumbrils were already on their way to the place of execution. Meanwhile at the Hôtel de Ville all was in turmoil. The enemies of Robespierre had had him arrested and he had been shot in the jaw and taken before the Committee of Public Safety. The next day he was to go to the guillotine himself. The Reign of Terror was over. 'Messengers were sent', writes Madame de Chabrillan, 'to all the prisons to stay the executions. A man on horseback rode after the tumbrils which were already crossing the Faubourg Saint-Antoine. In his haste he fell from his saddle and knocked himself out. He was unconscious for a quarter of an hour. When he arrived at the Barrière du Trone the head of Madame de Monaco had just fallen. She was the last victim of the Terror.'

Her portrait hangs at Fontaine-Française because one of her daughters, Princesse Honorine de Grimaldi, married in 1804 Louis-René-Victor, marquis de La Tour du Pin, who later inherited the château.

Honorine died on 8 May 1879, at the age of ninety-five. The sufferings of her early life had given her a sweetness of character and a depth of religious devotion which made her beloved by all at Fontaine-Française. The Abbé Carra, pronouncing her *oraison funèbre*, dwelt at length on the generosity of her charity – 'Her heart, like her house, was always open to everyone.'

Adjoining Madame de Chabrillan's bedroom is her dressing-room, a small, intimate *entresol* panelled with mirrors. 'Here I am in my kingdom,' she writes, 'where the châtelaines of bygone days appear to me . . . Going back in history I see emerging from the shadows Mme de Saint-Jullien, my mother-in-law. She too inhabited my room.'

There is an oval portrait of the latter showing a face alert, intelligent and suggesting a sense of humour. She was the friend of Voltaire, of Madame de Genlis, Madame de Staël, Madame Récamier and the Chevalier de Boufflers. These were her guests at Fontaine-Française. It is said that the plays of Voltaire were performed in a little theatre contrived within the dome. Here Madame de Staël began writing her *Corinne* and Boufflers his *Libre Arbitre*. Voltaire, who called Anne-Madeleine his 'papillon philosophe', has painted a miniature of her in verse:

L'esprit, l'imagination,
Les grâces, la philosophie,
L'amour du vrai, le goût du bien
Avec un peu de fantaisie.

Assez solide en amitié,
Dans tout le reste un peu legère;
Voilà, je crois, sans vos déplaire
Votre portrait fait à moitié.

But in spite of her recherché literary connections and cultural pursuits, Anne-Madeleine did not lack the common touch. Her memory was still alive in Fontaine-Française in 1891 when Richard Gascon was writing his history of the place. He was born in 1829, only nine years after her death, and he had talked with many who had known her well.

She knew all the inhabitants by name and addressed them all as *tu*. Many old people have talked to me about her, of the pleasure which she took in conversing with them on those subjects in which they were interested, giving some advice here, some alms there. Right up until her death she enjoyed brilliant good health and, in spite of her great age, she held herself upright and alert like a young person.

Madame de Chabrillan, Madame de La Tour du Pin, Madame de Saint-Jullien – all lived at Fontaine-Française and all loved it. All were loved by the local inhabitants. The Revolution did no damage to the château. Madame de Saint-Jullien was placed on the list of émigrés in 1792, but a number of acts signed by her in the presence of the public notary prove that she did not leave. She appealed against her inclusion on the list and her name was duly removed from it.

Fontaine-Française provides an admirable, if all too rare, example of a French château in the twilight of the *ancien régime* serving the purpose for which a house should be built. More typical of the times is the picture of the Château de Lux and the family of Saulx-Tavanes.

The Château de Lux

In the eighteenth century the family of Saulx-Tavanes, which we have already encountered at Sully, was still enjoying a period of considerable prosperity. In 1705, on the death of his elder brother, Henri-Charles became head of the family and comte de Tavanes at the age of nineteen. In 1721 he was appointed commander-in-chief in Burgundy and took up residence in Dijon. Here, together with the intendant, Joly de Fleury, he represented the interest and authority of the king. This was a position not infrequently in conflict with that of the parlement de Dijon. Perhaps in order to enhance the dignity of the royal authority, perhaps to flatter his own sense of importance, perhaps from a mixture of the two which it would be impossible to disentangle, Henri-Charles became a stickler for the minutest points of etiquette and precedence, even going to the length of having six prominent parliamentarians exiled by *lettre de cachet* for refusing to acknowledge his pretensions.

Among the six was the celebrated Premier Président de Brosses who thereafter referred to Saulx-Tavanes as 'that impudent impostor of a little pigmy count'. De Brosses spoke with the rationality of the legal mind: 'To exile six people for the idiotic and miserable vanity of one individual . . . is even more comical than absurd.' Tavanes's uncle, however, was the Chancellor d'Aguesseau, and with such powerful support in the government Henri-Charles could do as he pleased.

In 1786 Charles-François-Casimir de Saulx-Tavanes was made a duke by Louis XVI. The preamble to the letters patent by which the *comté* de Tavanes was raised to a duchy lists among the qualifications of the family

several large and beautiful estates in the duchy of Burgundy . . . Outstanding among these are those of Beaumont and Lux, which are considerable by virtue of their great nobility, the number of their vassals and the importance of the rights attached to them. In the last-mentioned domain there is a magnificent château, perfectly suited to become the seat of a domain of high rank . . . It is a grand and handsome château, flanked by towers and surrounded by a water-filled moat, with extensive and beautiful dependencies.

Lux had been a large fortress with great round towers at the corners, but in the sixteenth century it was transformed by the Malain family into a *maison de plaisance* in Renaissance style. The similarity between its entrance porch and that of Clos de Vougeot has already been noted. In the eighteenth century, between the years

1749 and 1751, considerable *aménagements* to the interior were contrived by the architects Le Jolivet and Caristie from Dijon.

The letters patent are silent as to the Château de Beaumont, usually known as Beaumont-sur-Vingeanne. In the days when Burgundy had been a frontier province, Beaumont had been an important fortress, but in 1636 it was partially destroyed and with the annexation of Franche-Comté in 1678 it lost its *raison d'être*. The Saulx-Tavanes family allowed one of their dependants, the Abbot Claude Jolyot, to build here a charming little Louis XV pavilion.

Jolyot's abbey of Bournet was in the diocese of Angoulême, some 350 miles away. Apart from the presence of an abbot's cross and mitre in the coat of arms in the front pediment one would hardly suppose that this was the house of a churchman. The panelling in the vestibule is decorated with the attributes of the Theatre, Comedy, Music and Love. Beaumont-sur-Vingeanne is a delicate expression of the refined hedonism of eighteenth-century France. It has a lot to tell us about an upper-class clergy floating on a sea of wealth in which the Catholic Church had sunk.

Whether the Saulx-Tavanes ever lived at the Château de Lux it is impossible to state, but Lux was certainly the administrative centre from which their vast Burgundian estates were managed. It was probably intended for the occasional residence of the Saulx-Tavanes family, but the most constant resident was the steward, Jean Duboy.

It was by no means a grand establishment. In 1780 there were only three domestics at Lux – one maid, one gardener and a messenger – but the estate administered totalled some 3,275 hectares (8,100 acres), 2,225 (5,500) in forest and the rest in farmland. It yielded a total income of some 90,000 livres. But the trouble was that by the French law of *partage* the other members of the family had their rights to fixed proportions of the revenues. These accounted for nearly two thirds of the total, leaving the comte de Tavanes only 30,000. It was not enough for a *grand seigneur* to live in the style expected of him in a large house in the rue du Bac with a domestic staff of fifteen. His own children were approaching marriageable age and his two daughters would expect a dowry of 200,000 each. He needed urgently to increase his revenues.

On 31 March 1780, he wrote to Billard, the procureur fiscal at Dijon: 'The quantity of debts and charges imposed upon me by my father requires me to raise 15,000 livres more annually from the land. I have no other choice than to raise the leases and rents.'

But there was another potential source of income in the strict enforcement of the feudal dues appertaining to his lands. For this purpose Charles-François-Casimir appointed, in 1781, Jacques Fénéon, a specialist in feudal dues known as a *feudiste*. He was charged with the task of drawing up a complete set of new *terriers*, or records of feudal dues. A typical example of his methods can be seen in 1786 when the dukedom was created. He claimed the *droit d'indire* which gave him the right to double the feudal dues for that year, which would have produced a further 12,676 livres. It was a right which had not been claimed since 1333. He claimed it again three years later on the occasion of the marriage of one of his daughters.

Not unnaturally this policy of extortion produced a counter-reaction. Robert Forster, who has made the most detailed study of the family archives, draws attention to

the lack of docility on the part of the local villagers, an aggressiveness and legal competence that startled both the duke and his agents. The day had passed when the threat of a law suit by the count was sufficient to bring the peasants to reason . . . They hired lawyers and began to question the legal propriety of the ducal agent and *feudiste*. They exhibited unexpected energy and competence. It is also noteworthy that such legal counsel was available to the villagers. It could not have been high legal fees that encouraged local solicitors to incur certain risks in contesting the rights of a great lord. The reaction of the village community reveals an emerging hostility, first aimed at the agent Fénéon, but shifting in 1789 to the duke himself.

The year 1789, however, passed unnoticed in the duke's accounts. His revenues from Burgundy were much the same as they had been. The impact of the Revolution was slow and piecemeal. In February 1791, Fénéon reported a drop in the price of wood – one of the chief sources of income – 'because all the rich families have left Dijon'. In the following year the *dîme*, the most unpopular of feudal dues, became impossible to collect. The duke was slow to recognize what was happening, but he had the prudence to send the portrait of Louis XVI from his house in Paris to Lux.

At Arc-sur-Tille a man named Pierre Jacquemard was emerging as a revolutionary leader, abetted by the *curé* Terguet. He threatened to 'lead the inhabitants of Arc-sur-Tille to Lux to put the château to the torch'. He never carried out the threat, but he did fire shots at the windows of Arcelot in an attempt to encourage Verchère to emigrate.

In January 1792, the duke died and was succeeded by his son
Charles-Marie-Casimir, who was then twenty-three. In July he
emigrated. By the law passed the previous April the property of
émigrés was liable to confiscation. Fénéon urged him to return to
Burgundy and save the estates, but the new duke had never seen Lux
and showed little interest in his estates; indeed, he made them over to
his much more intelligent and active wife.

In April 1793, the furniture of Lux was put up for sale. There were
931 articles sold, realizing a total of 24,483 livres. Beds and mirrors
fetched the highest prices. There followed a protracted sale of the
lands, leaving only the now empty château and two acres surrounding it unsold. The indefatigable Fénéon set about repurchasing as
much of the land as his very limited funds would allow for his absent
master.

Lux gives the sad impression of a house that was not serving the
purpose for which a house is built – to be lived in. It was the status
symbol of an absentee lord who cared nothing for the place nor for its
people. During all the period of the first duke's ownership not a sou
was spent on improving the land, although such a policy, in the long
run, would have increased the duke's income as well as that of his
tenants. But if he was to keep up appearances in Paris and at
Versailles he needed money in immediate supply. So Lux became a
centre of extortion, for the enrichment of the seigneur could only be
achieved by the impoverishment of his vassals, as they were still
called. The only money spent on the place was to equip it with a
court-house and a prison. The château became the symbol of this
oppression. It is safe to say that nobody loved it and only very few
people ever lived in it.

The duchesse de Saulx-Tavanes, the wife of Charles-Marie-
Casimir, records in her memoirs her impressions of her first return to
France after the Revolution. 'I shuddered when first I set my foot on
that blood-stained soil.' Everywhere, however, she was received
with marks of respect and affection. At Dijon, the président du
département, Monsieur Fantin, paid her his respects. In Paris her
loyal servants were glad to rejoin her.

Later she went to Versailles with the Princesse Hélène de
Beauffremont. 'Nothing had then been changed,' she writes: 'only
the furniture had been removed and for a moment one was struck
with the impression of a temporary absence. I yielded to it; the
scenes of horror fled from my mind and, in the room in which I had

seen the queen for the first time, I recalled the kind attentions with which she had sought to overcome my shyness.'

In due course she went down to Lux. 'We set off for Burgundy. I was delighted to see this province. Demonstrations of affection had preceded our arrival and even the Revolution had not shaken those feelings of which M. de Saulx had constantly received proof. The old ways of thought had still great power.'

Their arrival at Lux was marked by a ceremony which took them by surprise. 'We were met by the *notables* of Lux. An old bodyguard, faithful to feudal tradition, presented themselves on horseback. They rode three times round the entrance court, lowering the points of their sabres as they passed the front door, an old custom of which we were unaware.'

They set about restoring their estate. 'Our enthusiasm for gardens, derived from our experience of foreign countries, and the necessity of repairing the dilapidated house turned our attention to buildings, plantations and agricultural improvement.' For a moment it looked as if the *ancien régime* might be re-established. No doubt there was much about the Revolution that had been counter-productive and a reaction may have resulted. It did not last. The duchesse's memoirs end on a note of disenchantment. 'I had experienced once again the illusion of hope . . . it came to nothing and nothing came in its place . . . hardly any traces remained of all that I had known. Ideas, opinions, customs – all have changed, and, like the Daughters of Jerusalem, I weep in a foreign land for the misfortunes of Zion.'

One of the changes which the duchesse seems to have overlooked in the first flush of her enthusiasm was that at Dijon she had been received by the président du département – not by the premier président du parlement. On 24 February 1790, Burgundy was divided into four départements – the Yonne, the Côte d'Or, the Saône-et-Loire and the Ain. On 1 July in the following year the parlement was abolished. Burgundy had lost its claim to the last vestiges of its independence. 'This sad ending', wrote Elizabeth de Lacuisine, the historian of the parlement, 'together with the principal events which accompanied it, is all that we can in the last place report of a company whose entire existence belonged to the history of this ancient province as to its most glorious memories.'

Bibliography

A. Colombet: *Les Parlementaires Bourgignons à la fin du 18e Siècle*, 1937.

G. Roupnel: *La Ville et la Campagne au 17e Siècle*, 1955.

P. Taisand: *Coutume Générale du Pays et Duché de Bourgogne avec la Commentaire de Monsieur Taisand*, 1698.

C. Sauvageot: *L'Hôtel de Vogüé*, 1863.

Dijon

E. Fyot: *Dijon: Son Passé Evoqué par ses Rues*, 1927.

P. Gras: *Histoire de Dijon*, 1981.

M. Clément-Janin: *Les Vieilles Maisons de Dijon*, 1890.

L. Deshairs. *Dijon: Architecture et Décor aux 17e et 18e Siècles*, 1910.

C. Oursel: 'Comment on Aménageait une Ville aux 17e et 18e Siècles', in *Mémoires de l'Académie de Dijon*, 1919.

A. Cornereau: *Le Palais des Etats de Bourgogne à Dijon*, 1890.

P. Quarré: 'Le Palais des Etats de Bourgogne et son Décor Extérieur', in *Bulletin Monumental*, 1970.

Buffon

L. Bertin and F. Bourdier: *Buffon*, 1952.

B. Rignaud: 'Les Forges de Buffon', in *Mémoires de la Commission des Antiquités du Département de la Côte d'Or*, 1963.

H. de Séchelles: *Voyage à Montbard*, 1815.

Beaune and the Côte d'Or

J. Arlott and C. Fielden: *Burgundy Vines and Wines*, 1978.

M. Arnoux: *Dissertation sur la Situation de Bourgogne*, 1728.

R. Dumay: *Le Vin de Bourgogne*, 1976.

M. Lavalle: *Histoire et Statistique de la Vigne et des Grands Vins de la Côte d'Or*, 1855.

The Château de Vantoux

Y. Beauvalot: 'Le Château de Vantoux et son Décor', in *Mémoires de la Commission des Antiquités de la Côte d'Or*, 1974.

M. Gaumé: *Recherches sur le Château de Vantoux*, 1975.

The Château de Montmusard

Y. Beauvalot: 'Un Château Extraordinaire à Dijon: le Château de Montmusard', in *Cahiers du Vieux Dijon*, 1978.

The Château de Fontaine-Française

Marquise de Chabrillan: *Fontaine-Française et ses Souvenirs*, s.d.

R. Gascon: *Histoire de Fontaine-Française*, 1891.

The Château de Lux

R. Forster: *The House of Saulx-Tavanes*, 1971.

Duchesse de Saulx-Tavanes: *Mémoires*, 1934.

E. de Lacuisine: *Le Parlement de Dijon depuis son Origine jusqu'à sa Chute*, 1857.

INDEX